LADDER
TO THE
MOON

A JOURNEY FROM THE
CONGO TO AMERICA

LADDER
TO THE
MOON

A JOURNEY FROM THE
CONGO TO AMERICA

GEORGES BUDAGU MAKOKO

DEVELOPMENTAL EDITOR: VIVIEN COOPER

gatekeeper press

Columbus, Ohio

Ladder to the Moon A Journey from the Congo to America

Published by Gatekeeper Press
2167 Stringtown Rd, Suite 109
Columbus, OH 43123-2989
www.GatekeeperPress.com

The cover design, interior formatting, typesetting, and editorial work for this book are entirely the product of the author. Gatekeeper Press did not participate in and is not responsible for any aspect of these elements.

ISBN (paperback): 9781662905520

To all advocates for peace and justice around the world,
and to the victims of oppression and injustice,
I dedicate this book.

~ ONE ~

A Kinyamulenge saying:
"Where there is not hatred and division,
the skin of a flea can be slept on by two people."
Translation: Where there is love, everything is possible.

I was born in the southern Kivu province of eastern DR Congo, about three thousand feet above sea level, in the northwest of the high mountains of the Ruzizi plain, in the village of Kahuna. My tribe was spread out over the Uvira, Fizi, and Mwenga zones, in an area called Mulenge. We are the Banyamulenge—"the people living in Mulenge."

We lived in a land of honey and milk. Rivers flowed abundantly through the mountains, and wells sprang up in the surrounding forests and valleys. There was no infrastructure—no roads, cars, trains, or waterways connecting us to the modern world. Our village's enclave position behind the high mountains made it totally inaccessible. To reach the cities near the area, we had to walk for several days.

You might wonder why my tribe would live in a place that was so far removed from the rest of the nation. My ancestors discovered the area while grazing their cattle, and chose to make it their home because it offered privacy and endless paces for their livestock.

Because of our culture, I never had a chance to discuss with my mother or grandmother the circumstances of my birth. I was later stunned to discover that the Congo has the world's highest birth mortality rate, due to the lack of infrastructure, the absence of hospitals and medical clinics, and the presence of poverty and corruption which arose from the bad leadership that has characterized the Congo for years.

In this era of high dependency upon medical technology, it may be hard for you to believe that there is a place where people live without doctors, nurses, or hospitals, but it is true. The women in the villages did not have the resources of women in America. Yet, they helped each other deliver the babies in the village, developing a mutual support system that managed to sustain the community throughout the years. The women were devoted, brave, and distinguished by an exceptional tenacity, enabling them to bring thousands of lives into the world and save many who might have otherwise died in childbirth.

Yes, they had many gifts, talents, and skills, but ultimately, I see the grace of God at work. I am a witness to the power of the Almighty hand that protects us all, regardless of the corner of the world in which we may live. I know that if it were not for God, I would never have survived all that came to pass in the Congo.

There are still millions of people who are living in desperate conditions in Mulenge and around the world. As I traveled the world, experiencing and exploring many cultures, I saw certain people living in miserable conditions while others dwelled in abundance and safety. There were times I found this disparity deeply confusing and disheartening.

But as I have grown and matured, and gained more understanding of the world in which we live, I have come to remember the scripture in Ecclesiastes that says, "There is nothing new under the sun." There has been imbalance and inequity in the world for many generations—and there is little I can do to change it. Accepting this fact has helped to ease my mind and release the anxiety I feel when I think about the past. It also helps me to enjoy the present and strive for the future.

In a song by Congolese musician Reddy Amisi, he sings to God, asking him why some people have missed everything in their entire lives, and others have never missed a thing.

As for me, I ask, what really matters in our lives? Aren't peace, love, and happiness the things we need in this world? These are the things humanity has always sought after, from generation to generation. If our environment does not offer what we need, it is time to move to whatever environment offers a greater degree of the peace and happiness we constantly seek. We were created to live in peace. It is human nature to seek it out.

When we were in the Congo during the worst of the troubles and had no peace, we believed we were in Hell. We thought we might find Heaven somewhere else. But, life doesn't really change. Just as you can find both Heaven and Hell in Africa, the same is true everywhere. Heaven is everywhere and Hell is everywhere; it all depends upon your outlook. This is what I tell my loved ones.

When you are suffering, it all comes down to your perspective and how you embrace your experience. You can say, "I am ruined, finished, a failure." Or, you can say, "This suffering must surely pass. I must fight to change this situation."

There is a saying in French that means, no matter how long the nighttime lasts, eventually the morning will come. During those long, dark nights of the soul, we must believe this: God is never far from our side. Without such faith, the burden becomes too heavy to bear.

~ TWO ~

My village was isolated, a great distance from the cities and the bases of leadership, and we were totally neglected by the Congolese government. They left us behind, paying no attention to our needs for education, employment, or other rights and services. We were treated badly because the Banyamulenge are Tutsis. This fact made us foreigners in their eyes, and that never changed. No matter how many years we lived in the Congo, the government never saw us as Congolese. To them, we were Tutsis from Rwanda.

The government did not treat us well, but nature always treated us smoothly and we totally depended upon it. Through nature and our ancestors, we received the peace of God. Peace was everywhere and happiness was our daily song. In the morning, we awoke to the sounds of roosters crowing and birds chirping in the bushes around the small village. At night, we slept in total darkness, but the scattered sounds of our livestock were like a lullaby, and neighboring animals found their way into our dreams and sleep, harmonious and harmless.

It was serene and restful.

Our village was on a hill, surrounded by forests where a variety of animals dwelled. When I was growing up, I never heard of anyone being harmed by the animals, but it wasn't always that way. Legend has it that my grandparents and great-grandparents fought with elephants, lions, tigers and other ferocious animals. My ancestors won the battle. The animals saw their bravery and resilience and fled—running a thousand kilometers away from the villages, deep into the forests.

There were also tons of smaller animals in the forests, but they were scared of human beings and over time, we became good neighbors. We saw them living and playing. We never bothered them, and they never bothered us.

We lived in a modern-day paradise, and our lifestyle was a reflection of that. The weather shifted beautifully from one season to another, and we never had to worry about it. We had two seasons—the rainy season and the dry season. The rainy season began in November and lasted until the end of April. And, the dry season lasted from May until the end of October.

The village in which I was born was tiny—comprised of only ten houses, but full of inexhaustible grace, love, and true brotherhood. I loved my little village and never had to worry over things that might endanger my life or that of my family. We lived with the natural rhythms of life and were unconcerned with time. We knew it was morning when the sun rose and night came as the sun progressively began to set.

We lived in hamlets, in areas suited to our livestock. People rarely got sick and when they did, the area had its own healing power. Not long ago, our elders were semi-nomads who moved from one place to another, basing their choices as to where to live upon the health of the families and livestock. When poverty and death were associated with a particular location, the head of the household had to provide protection for his family and possessions by changing the place of habitation.

The source of economy was livestock—chicken, goats, sheep, and cows.

As opposed to neighboring tribes that hunted or trapped almost every wild animal in the forest, very few in my community hunted at all. When they did, it was only for recreational purposes. The only animal they hunted was deer. Our ancestors lived almost exclusively on milk and cow meat, and had little interest in trying other food, even if it was beneficial to them. Very few types of food were believed to be clean and suitable for eating.

Our nutrition was almost the same as our ancestors, and depended upon the season. Our diet included potatoes, corn—ground into flour for fufu ("umutsima")—beans, peas, spinach, pumpkin leaves, and cabbage. In the rainy season, potatoes were the main food that we ate with milk. In the dry season, we ate fufu, day and night.

For a beverage, we drank mostly milk and loved it. It was rare to drink water and in most cases, unacceptable. It was considered a sign of poverty in a family. My grandmother often yelled at us, saying, "That water you are drinking will kill you!" At the time, I didn't know if anything was actually wrong with the water, but I knew I hated drinking it. I had no choice but to drink water during the dry season when the cows wandered far from the village, seeking good pasture. At those times, we had less milk. The little bit of milk that was available was reserved for kids and we all fought over it.

To my tribe, the cow was the most highly regarded of all the animals, considered next to man. It was more than an animal—it was a benefactor. We depended on it completely for food—milk, meat, and butter. My ancestors used its horns as water containers, its skin for clothing and mats, and its urine for disinfectant. Cow dung served many purposes. We used it to roughcast houses and to fertilize our crops. Most importantly, cows served as currency for the families, and wedding dowry.

More cows in a family signaled bourgeoisie and power. Those who had no cows, or fewer cows, were poor and miserable. Cows were so central to our way of life that they appeared in the tribal poetry, songs, and dance. They were also the subject of our favorite children's game called "cow game."

When I was seven years old, my father decided to move to a bigger village—Kuwumugeti. My father's reasons for making this move were twofold: he wanted to be closer to school and to church. Kuwumugeti was not far away—only about five kilometers. At the time, we were four kids. There was my sister, Nyanoro, the firstborn; my older brother, Shoshi; me; and my younger sister, Nyarukundo.

I don't believe my mother was involved in the decision to move. In our culture, men carried the responsibility of decision making for the entire family. That did not seem to bother my mother as it might have bothered a wife living in the United States. I never saw any problem between my father and mother in respect to decision making.

My mother trusted my father. We all did. Even if she *had* objected to my father's decision, I'm not sure it would have made any difference. In the village, decisions were made with or without the approval of women—a system that worked perfectly fine.

One of the beauties of the zone we lived in was that land was free of charge, and without restriction as to where you could establish your residency. The area had enough room for everyone. As long as the privacy of the existing people was not violated, and as long as we were decent, kind, and did nothing to conflict with our neighbors, we could choose to live anywhere we wanted to, at any time. Money was never an issue in my village; we could live with or without it. Prior to our move, my father and uncles went to our new village and built houses for the livestock and houses for the families, which were all located very close together.

As a child, I had a naturally curious personality. I was young but smart and I knew many things for my age. I always wanted to discover new things, and I questioned everything that passed in front of me. My mother was the person that I interviewed the most, and I loved her for being patient and answering my questions to the best of her knowledge. I knew that I had to work hard to make my parents proud of me but I didn't mind. I was courageous, diligent, and full of energy.

I was always involved in family activities, wanting to make sure I was learning the skills I would need as I grew up. From the very first day I was told about our move, and throughout the whole process, I was very excited. I loved my small village, but my eagerness to see new things was strong. I was so anxious to get to where we were going, I started counting the nights. In Kinyamulenge (my language), this is called "Kubara ama joro," meaning that I could not wait to see something exciting happening.

All I had ever known was our tiny village. In my thoughts and dreams, I tried to conjure up images of our new home. Mostly, I was focused on our new house, the kids I would meet in our new village, and the school I would eventually attend when I became a student. At last, moving day came. Early in the morning, we jumped up and raced through our regular routines of washing our faces and having our morning meal. I could hardly eat, I was so excited. Then, we wrapped up all our belongings, and prepared to leave.

My father coordinated everything, assigning to each of us a specific task. Father tended to our livestock—cows, goats, and sheep. Mother focused on organizing the household things and placing them into bags, which made them easy to carry. Our belongings were of the typical peasant variety—a wooden container we used for milking cows; dishes; calabashes and clothes; hoes and machetes; and many other instruments we used as tools for living.

As we got ready to begin our journey to the new village, I walked out of the house with my small bag on my back. I was very excited to see our cattle gathered outside. I could see their frustration and anxiety, as they had already foretold the change in their patterns. By that time of day, they would normally be in the field, feeding themselves.

I had lived my life around animals and from an early age, I learned that they have feelings. They are different from human beings but they have many similarities with us. I have seen them when they are cheering, playing, and fighting. I have also seen them crying when they lost their loved ones. Just like we do, animals get angry and agitated when we force them to do things that are uncomfortable. On that day, I witnessed their anxiety and their feelings of uncertainty. The only way they had to express their feelings was by mooing constantly.

Our task was to direct our livestock along the path they needed to follow. Some resisted going forward, but our experience in shepherding made our job easier. We knew exactly how to redirect their attention. We also knew which cow to place at the front of the line—the leader among them (called in Kinyamulenge "kizigenza.") That cow knew the voice of my father, so as my father called her to go forward, she immediately lined up onto the right path. Once she was in place, the rest followed.

As for the sheep, they were sweet and kind and got along well with the cows. They were always very good followers and that day was no exception. The goats on the other hand were noisy, problematic, and generally difficult to manage. They were known in the village for breaking potato fences and trying to feed themselves. Quite often, a family would leave the door to their house open, and return to find that a goat had entered and eaten everything edible, messing up the entire house in the process.

I never had a good relationship with the goats, but I loved goat meat and knew that they were necessary for our wealth. On that particular day, I had even more excuses for hating goats. It was different with the cows and sheep, which I loved even to the point of naming each cow.

The path we traveled to the new village was approximately five feet wide and led us through a huge, dense forest. The path was surrounded by bamboo, trees and natural cords—grasses which crossed each other and were hard to walk through. Sometimes the path narrowed and the flock had to squeeze through, fighting each other for room to pass. Sometimes we came to a fork in the path and we had to tell the herd which direction to follow. At those times, all my father had to say was "left" or "right." The lead cow listened to and understood our instructions, following very well.

We marched through the forest, the sounds of my family's footsteps blending with the rhythmic pounding sounds made by our livestock, as they shook the earth beneath their hooves. This symphony echoed throughout the entire area, scaring the wild animals that lived in the forest. We kept crossing paths with the animals, so they thought they were under attack. Monkeys were jumping on trees and bamboos, and deer and raccoons were running.

Those were only the animals which were up close and obvious. Many others we could not see; we could only hear the crunching of twigs beneath their feet as they fled. To know that there were unseen animals so close by, hidden by the forest, did not frighten us. We were confident they would not hurt us, knowing they still remembered our ancestors who had conquered them.

It was a twenty-five minute journey through the forest, provided the cattle cooperated very well. Our biggest challenge was the fact that people frequently used the same path, some heading in the same direction, others in the opposite direction.

When we encountered people along the way, the attention we received made me feel that we were very special. We had a good number of livestock and we were considered rich in the village. In that moment, I felt like my father was the richest man in the world. In my eyes, our flock looked like a thousand. I was so proud and I could tell that my father was proud, too, and our excitement was strikingly obvious.

Even though it was exciting to meet people along the way, from time to time, they frightened our herd, which we had to keep redirecting. After what felt like several hours, at last we exited the forest. The journey had seemed quite long to me, but the excitement of the whole situation kept me going. It felt so good to know that our journey was almost over.

As we came out into the clearing, our first view made my eyes widen and my feet anxious to keep moving. I was looking at a huge, beautiful village on top of the hill, surrounded by the forest. I had never before seen such a conglomeration of houses. My tiny village of ten houses was far behind us now and only God knew what lay ahead.

~ THREE ~

My mother, father, and sisters went ahead into the village. My mother and sisters had to prepare our new house, setting up our dishes and household belongings. They had to leave my brother and me behind in the valley to watch after the cattle, which instinctively wanted to return to the old village. Things had already changed for our livestock and we could not let them go back.

My father instructed my brother and me to stay with the herd for the rest of the day. As was our routine when we needed milk for the evening or morning, we had to keep the calves separated from their mothers. Otherwise, the calves would keep suckling and there would be no milk for us. Father told us to return to the village when we noticed the sun was about to set.

I could not wait to go into the village to meet the new kids and see our new house. I watched the sun in the sky, longing for evening to come. Finally, around six o'clock, the sun began to set and it was time to walk into the village. My brother and I guided the herd up the hill, directing them towards their new home. The cattle were nervous from all the changes they were experiencing and did not like what we were doing to them.

Along the way, we kept meeting new people in the village. Kids ran around us, shouting out many questions. They were curious to know us and we were interested in them, too. Who were we? Where were we coming from?

People called out to each other in loud voices, so they could be heard above the sounds of the cows and the goats. Darkness

17

was about to fall and people hurried around, finishing up their activities while there was still enough light for working.

As we reached our new home, the skies were darkening above us. We were still busy with the herd, moving swiftly, organizing them. Without light to see by, our tasks were made even more difficult. My father had already built houses for the sheep and goats. Guiding them inside for the first time was very difficult because they had to become habituated to their new home.

We had to separate the cows that we were going to milk, do the milking, and lead the rest out of the village to a good pasture, where they would browse all night long. Afterwards, we finally went into our new house. We were exhausted and almost starving, not having eaten since the morning meal—except raspberries and blackberries we picked as we ran after the cows in the fields.

My mother had prepared a good fufu. Made with a mixture of corn flour and boiled water, it was my favorite food. In order for fufu to turn out well, preparation required physical energy and good visibility. At night, when my mother cooked fufu, I lit a dried bamboo stalk and held it over the casserole dish while she was cooking, so she could see clearly.

While we ate, she kept saying all kinds of good words about how proud she was that, at my young age, I was able to take on so much responsibility during the process of moving. I always wanted to prove that I was capable of doing everything my brother could do. I was just as fine and strong as a big man.

Many people came to our house to welcome us. It was the custom for people in the village to bring food, firewood, or anything that would help newcomers to the village in their process of resettlement. I was excited to see all of our visitors, but I was very tired after our journey and went to bed immediately after eating. I fell asleep filled with curiosity and longing to explore our new village.

When the sun came up the following morning, it brightened a whole new world for me. Before I could go exploring, I still had to follow the usual daily routine of eating breakfast and milking the cows. Afterwards, I had to once again stand watch over our cattle in the field. Until they were completely familiarized with the area, there was the risk that they would turn around and instinctively begin heading back to our old village.

With my mind and body refreshed from sleeping and the sunlight illuminating the new landscape, I could see clearly all the details I had missed the day before. The village was situated on a hill, touching a huge forest in the north and west. In the east was a smaller forest. To the south was the beautiful valley with long, thin, green grasses ("umujinja") that were used for roofing the houses.

The village we had left behind was so tiny and now here we were, living among a hundred or so other families. I gazed downhill into the valley, watching the smoke curl out of all the houses at once, as each family started fires for the morning meal. The houses were the same type as in my old village, constructed in the shape of huts and beautifully arranged. They were made of bamboos and trees threaded with natural cords and roughcast with a mixture of dust, water, and cow-dung ("amase").

The name of our new village, Kuwumugeti, came from trees that were prominent around the village. The Imigeti trees were shaped like umbrellas and had green leaves that turned yellow as they grew and prepared to fall. They colored the village with spectacular beauty.

As I walked downhill towards the field, I was able to get a closer look at the village and I was amazed. Dew covered the ground, where I could see complex and mysterious drawings made by the footsteps of the villagers as they went about their morning routines. Low clouds hung over the forest surrounding the village, like balls of cotton candy sticking to the trees.

The village was quite busy and intense with different activities. Everywhere I looked, people were busy going through their routines and each group of people had tasks to do. I saw women with hoes over their shoulders, going to labor in the potato fields. Other women were coming from harvesting, carrying corn in baskets on their heads.

I could see some men sitting in one place, discussing things. Other men were coming from the forest. They carried machetes in their hands and trees and bamboos on their shoulders, and were busy building strong potato fences to protect against the livestock that could potentially destroy the crops.

Scattered over other hills around the village were cows in different colors and young men and boys shepherding them. There were also sheep and goats. Young ladies were engaged in many activities— collecting firewood in the forest, cleaning the sheds that housed the cows and calves, grinding corn and making flour for fufu. Girls and young boys were running down to the river, fetching water.

As the days passed and my family continued the process of getting re-settled, we became more familiar with the people in the village and I learned more and more about our culture and traditions. It was a tradition that the females in the village did most of the domestic work. They were under immense social pressure. Their daily tasks were set as goals that had to be met by the end of each day. There was no leniency, because unless these tasks were accomplished, daily life did not unfold in an orderly way. It was different for the men—each man was his own boss and no one controlled them. As compared to the women in the village, men were less busy.

Although there were no formal roads, our village was situated near the busiest pathway that led from the surrounding villages into the city of Uvira, which was a distance of one day of walking. In any given week, the pathway was traveled by hundreds of people, including businessmen who attended different marketplaces, hosted on various days of the week, in different villages around the Mulenge area. At those markets in the villages, there was a great deal of trading going on, as businessmen purchased merchandise and transported it home on their heads.

These particular businessmen were mostly from the Bafulero, Bavira, and Bashi tribes that lived in the cities that supplied the villages with cloth, salt, and other sundries the villagers needed. They had to travel for days over mountains with an altitude of three thousand feet, carrying many kilos of merchandise on their heads. They were very tough.

There were Banyamulenge who traveled from their villages into the city to buy different things they needed. But, no Munyamulenge—meaning, a single person from the Banyamulenge tribe—did the kind of business as the businessmen from the Bafulero, Bavira, and Bashi tribes. They relied on livestock to make a living.

Because our village sat in the center between the city and other villages, we often hosted travelers who stopped in the village to rest for the night before continuing on their journey the following day. Watching all these different travelers and businessmen on the path with their merchandise gave me the feeling that my family now lived in the big city. It was very exciting for me and I thrived on it. People in the village were very generous, always feeding the travelers and providing a place to stay, free of charge.

In our new home, my father had crafted small wooden chairs called "itembe," used mostly by visitors, or by my father. My mother, my siblings, and I never bothered sitting on those chairs. We mostly sat in our living room ("mukirambi") on the ground, which we found very comfortable, thanks to special grasses called "ingeregeri." The grasses were thinned, lengthened, and beautifully arranged by my mother—an action known as "gutegura." My mother covered the area on top of the grass with a beautiful handmade mat called "ikirago." It was initially greenish, but later turned black from dirty feet and shoes stepping on it.

~ FOUR ~

In my tribe, we are divided into clans; clans are divided into bigger families; and families are divided into second, third, and fourth degree of family. My clan is called Abasama. My bigger family is called Abahindabandi. Only people of my clan lived in my village; everyone was related somewhere in our lineage. I found it amazing that our whole clan tended to know their exact level of relationship.

My grandfather's name was Budagu Rukesha. Regretfully, he died at a very young age. He was survived by his beautiful wife, Ruzabeti Nyateta, one son, Rwatangabo Samusoni, and one daughter, Sharara. When he passed away, his widow—my grandmother, Ruzabeti—was already well-established in her family-in-law. Even though she was still young, Ruzabeti could not leave her children and find another husband in a different clan. So, her brother-in-law, Rufora, took her as his wife, and she gave birth to my father, Makoko Sefaniya, my two uncles, Gitega Simoni and Mupenda Venasi, and two aunts, Gahorero and Rebeka Nyagishakwe.

In our culture, even though someone died, the children left by him and those who were born afterwards to his widow and her new husband, would still be called his children (the children of the deceased man) and carry on his name. This was a unique way of eternalizing someone after they died.

When we moved into the new village, I was surprised to learn of this strange tradition and to meet my biological grandfather, Rufora. I had a hard time grasping the concept that Rufora was my actual grandfather. I already believed that Budagu was my grand-father. After all, the whole village called us Budagu's grandchil-dren and later on when I started school, I was named after him.

Rufora was a very good man. He had a great sense of humor and was well-respected in the village. I connected with him easily and naturally and I really loved him. At the same time, I felt con-flicted, knowing that Budagu, who passed away long before, was my grandfather and the one I was named after.

My grandmother wanted me to understand the dynamics of our culture, and told the whole story to me. "There is nothing wrong," she explained, "with calling Rufora 'Grandfather,' as long as the traditional concepts are kept and believed." This was made a little easier by the fact that as children, we were expected to call every elder in the village Grandpa or Grandma.

The culture was strongly influential to everyone in the village. We believed in it, and our beliefs were reinforced by the knowl-edge that it had been that way for generations.

One of our most beneficial traditions was the practice of liv-ing nearest to our closest family members. A little further away lived those relatives who were more distant. Our most distant rel-atives lived the furthest distance away. This tradition had its roots in the belief that living closest to your closest family members guaranteed mutual support between relatives. This tradition also secured the privacy and dignity of each family.

People in the village believed that the wickedness of each family should not be exposed to outsiders. This traditional lifestyle was exceptionally protective and set us apart from other tribes in the vicinity, including the Babembe, Bafulero, and Banyindu.

Usually, all the kids up to the age of ten slept in the same house with their parents. Children over ten slept in the neighbor-ing homes of their uncles or grandparents. My younger sister and I slept in our house, my older sister slept in my grandmother's house, and my older brother slept in a house called Campus—a free place set up for young people to enjoy themselves.

Our family life was harmonious, with mutual love and sup-port. Most of the time, my mother cooked, and sometimes my older sister did, too. For cooking and illuminating the house, we used wood and bamboo. Those were our only sources of energy.

At mealtimes, my father ate by himself, my mother and sisters shared one plate of food, and my brother and I shared another. We had no use for utensils—we always ate with our hands. Sometimes my older sister cleaned the dishes right after we finished eating, and sometimes in the morning.

It was the custom in the village for the adults to tell legendary stories ("imigani") to kids. So, at night after supper, many true stories about my ancestors were told to us by my father, mother, or grandmother. I was always fascinated to hear about their past life and how things had changed over time. Some stories were very moving and others were scary but each one had a lesson they wanted to convey to us.

These stories were intended to teach us how to love our parents and elders in the village, how to love one another as brothers, sisters, and family in general, and how to welcome and feed visitors. In my early age, I took these stories very seriously and they had a great impact on my behavior up to now.

Among all these stories, the one that stayed with me and influenced me the most was the story of my great-grandfather. To this day, I have never heard such a story of self-sacrifice anywhere—with the exception of the story of Jesus, who died for all of humanity.

My great-grandfather's name was Ruhindabandi. His father was Mutangachuro. When Mutangachuro was about to die, he gave my great-grandfather his last wish, pleading with Ruhindabandi to always take care of Ntumbira—Mutangachuro's youngest son (and Ruhindabandi's brother), who was still very small when Mutaganchuro passed away.

My great-grandfather, Ruhindabandi, was the second born of his family, but because of his character and influence in the community, his father entrusted him with his chiefdom ("Umutware"). As Ruhindabandi grew older, he transferred the power to his brave younger brother, named Sebasamira.

Things were beautiful and safe in my great-grandfather's village until suddenly, the inconceivable happened. One day

Sebasamira, who was now the chief, walked to a faraway village with his nephew, who was the son of his sister, and a great supporter and protector of his. They were going to pick up clothes that were being distributed by the white people from Europe.

Back then, one of the weapons of protection that men carried in their hands was the spear. At the place where people were picking up clothes, there were many people gathered around the white people, selecting items of clothing. Unfortunately, as they arrived there, a dispute occurred between Sebasamira and his nephew.

They were both focused on one particular cloth, and while they were pushing each other out of the way to get to the cloth, Sebasamira accidentally pushed his nephew too hard—and he fell on Sebasamira's spear and died. Sebasamira had not intended to hurt his nephew, and he certainly had not intended to kill him! He was devastated.

This horrible incident sent shock waves throughout the villages. Unfortunately, tradition required that the family members of the victim had to avenge his death. This custom was spoken of in the Bible as "an eye for an eye, and a tooth for a tooth." In this case, it was to be a man for a man.

After a long discussion in the family of the victim as to who had to be killed in my great-grandfather's family, it became clear that it would be Ntumbira, the youngest of the brothers in my great-grandfather's family—and the very one whom he had promised Mutangachuro he would protect! Ntumbira was targeted to be killed due to the fact that he was around the same age as the nephew of Sebasamira and Ruhindabandi who had died.

My great-grandfather completely rejected the idea that Ntumbira would be the one to be killed. He could never watch his youngest brother being put to death. He loved him very much— so much that he had given him the nickname "Gasirwakadata," meaning "the survivor of my father." Also, his youngest brother was the most handsome among all his brothers. Since his father's passing, Ruhindabandi had treated Ntumbira as his own son.

Ruhindabandi was also aware that, if his youngest brother were to be killed, he would die with many seeds still inside him that would have prospered his entire family. On the other hand, my great-grandfather was finished having children.

After a long discussion between both families, my great-grand-father, Ruhindabandi, decided to die on behalf of Ntumbira. Ruhindabandi was prepared to die, and everyone around the villages marveled over his act of self-sacrifice for his youngest brother.

Before his death, Ruhindabandi had one request—to be speared only one time. He insisted that, if they were to miss in their first attempt to kill him, he would kill them all. My great-grandfather was a mighty warrior and a man of his word, and everyone in the village feared him.

The family that was plotting the revenge got very scared, because they could not think of a man among them who never missed a target. They finally decided to pay someone from the tribe of Barega—a man called Kirindi, who had a great reputation for never missing any of his targets.

Kirindi, followed by a huge crew of the avengers, took my great-grandfather out of the village, and Kirindi aimed his spear at the chest of my great-grandfather, and threw only once.

Ruhindabandi collapsed, dead.

Kirindi, who happened to be an accurate spear-thrower, was not an inherently bad man. But, after this event, he became legendary, and throughout my younger years, whenever my father or grandfather was angry, they would often invoke the name of Kirindi.

This was one of the major cultural differences between my village and America—terrible insults would be exchanged without any real animosity arising thereafter. For example, if my father was very angry with me, he might say, "I wish you would be killed by Kirindi!" Of course, I knew that my father loved me, and did not *really* wish for my death, but it was traditional for people to go to extreme lengths to insult one another when they were upset.

The death of Ruhindabandi was a great tragedy in my family. They were greatly aggrieved, and the entire village turned dark. Many in my great-grandfather's family were frightened to get too close to his body. But, a few courageous men went to make a fire of mourning around my great-grandfather's body while waiting for his official burial. After a few days, Ruhindabandi was buried in dignity as a former chief.

This was an exceptional act of self-sacrifice on the part of Ruhindabandi. If his youngest brother, Ntumbira, had been killed, thousands of people who later came to be born would have never come into existence.

Ever since I first heard this story, it has stayed with me. It never leaves my mind. It reminds me of the Bible scripture at John 3:16 that states: "For God so loved the world that he gave his only begotten son that whosoever believeth in him should not perish but have everlasting life."

This scripture, and the story of my great-grandfather, makes me willing to sacrifice myself for my brothers and sisters. While I do not expect that I will ever be asked to give up my life for them, I nevertheless go to any lengths to ensure their safety, prosperity, and well-being. This is why I continue to work two jobs—so that I can help support my family back home.

Often after supper, my father enjoyed playing "inanga"— the harp—but he did not play for us every night. At those times, I constantly dreamed up ways to change his mind and get him to start playing.

Some evenings when he was tired of sitting on the small chair, he lay down by the edge of the fireplace ("mukirambi") with his back facing the fire. He found this very relaxing. He loved being scratched on his back while he lay there. From time to time, I made a deal with him that I would scratch his back in exchange for him playing the harp for us. In most cases, he immediately fell asleep after I finished scratching his back. Later, when he woke up, he promised that he would play for me the following night. I never liked it when he did that to me, but I had no choice—I had to wait for him to play.

We were Pentecostal Christians and believed in the healing power of music, so Father played Christian songs. This was the time of fellowship as family, and the incredible melody of the harp revived our spirits and souls. Whenever there was music in the house, the night went by smoothly and restfully.

As I write this memoir now, the songs we sang as a family resonate within me. They strengthen my mind and soul and help me to focus on my daily activities, even though I am thousands of miles away from my home.

~ FIVE ~

After we got settled in our new place, I entered a period of my life where I was spoiled, unburdened by the heavy family responsibilities which would later overshadow me. At that time, most of the chores were shared with my older brother and sister. My only individual chores were assisting my father in milking the cows, and helping my mother with a few things when she needed me.

I loved my cousins very much and often played with them and other friends in the village. I was free like a bird—but I had to remember my responsibilities, even though they were small.

Both my days and nights were quite enjoyable. The sun was our only clock. We knew how to predict the time as the sun rose in the morning and grew up to set in the evening. A few people in the villages had watches and we could ask them to tell us the time, but possessing a watch was not popular. We had to guess the time, sometimes by looking at our shadow and watching how it shifted from front to back as the day passed.

I always awoke in the morning feeling hungry. One of the first things I was taught to do was wash my face and mouth before eating anything. This was our tradition and if I did not follow it, I was not allowed to eat. Before sunrise, the mornings were cold, so my mother would already have the fire set up. Before dawn, we sat around the fire as a family.

This was our time to strategize about our daily activities. Father or Mother gave each of us the daily tasks we needed to accomplish, according to our age. As I mentioned, in our culture, daily activities were also determined by gender. There were duties considered solely for the males and others solely for females.

Around seven o'clock every morning, my older brother, my older sister, and I took turnings going with our father to milk the cows at their pasturage ("ikiraro"). When we first moved to our new village, we kept our herd around us. They soon created issues with our neighbors by breaking potato fences, so my father decided to move them about two miles away from the village.

The cows fed all night around their pasturage, roaming in the forest or bushes nearby, and sometimes they were hard to find. The time we returned from milking the cows varied, depending on how soon we were able to find them. Once I came back from milking the cows, it was my time to play in the village with my cousins and the other kids. I loved to play so much that sometimes I even forgot to eat. My mother called me at mealtime—always at the same time every morning and evening.

If I was playing and didn't come when my mother called me to a meal, it was never an issue. She knew I could always eat at the home of my grandmother or any of my uncles and when I got back home, she made sure to check and see if I had already eaten.

The games we played as kids were numerous and changed from time to time. One game I remember very well was the cow game. This was played by cutting branches off the trees and making them into toys that resembled cows. The branches looked pretty to me and since my house was closest to the forest, I was the one constantly cutting branches. I enjoyed playing the cow game with my cousins.

We also played the family game. This was the only game we played with girls. Otherwise, the boys and girls played separately. In this game, the older boys played the part of the fathers, the girls played mothers, and the rest of us played the parts of kids. We all pretended to engage in the various roles and activities of village life. It was very preoccupying, and took up so much of our time that we often forgot to go home at the appointed hour to do our real-life activities. Whenever that happened, we were punished for wasting time playing in the forest.

Girls also had their typical game called "ikidoti," which involved drawing on flat ground ten three-foot squares called classes. The girls would throw a one-inch or two-inch flat piece of wood into each class and jump with one leg, using the other leg to kick the wood out of the class. Then, they would jump again and step on the wood outside the surface. This went on until they had made it through all ten classes.

Two people played the game and the winner had to keep playing until she beat everyone. This was an exhausting game because they jumped with one leg, over and over. It was almost impossible to go three rounds without falling down and when they fell, they had to restart the game, completing the series of classes until there was a winner.

Some of the games we played were not typical Banyamulenge games but were copied from somewhere else, as the community interacted with other tribes and modern society.

I loved playing many different games but I loved soccer most of all. I was a good player, I was fast, and I was adept at making the handmade balls we used. We played during the day and at night when the moon was on. As the sky turned blue and the stars shone, we ran around the village, chasing each other. I always liked to play and do things that made me happy. I was never a lazy boy and whatever I did, I did courageously and with the intention of reaching certain goals.

I did not start attending school until I was almost nine years old. Because we lived in a remote area which was behind the scenes politically, there was no organized, official system in place requiring kids of a certain age to start school. The age at which a child started school was left to the discretion of the parents—and it was based upon the ability of the parents to understand the importance of their children's education.

I had been waiting and crying out to go to school since I was six, but my father would not let me go. He felt that I was too young and it was a waste of money to spend school tuition fees on someone my age. It never made any sense to me because sooner or later, he was going to have to send me to school and pay the tuition fees.

Most of the parents in the village were uneducated, themselves, and many of them shared my father's mindset. Having

never attended school, they did not see the benefit of supporting their children's education. From their perspective, school
was nothing more than a recreational place for kids, and a place
to waste financial resources. My parents never experienced the
importance of education and its direct impact on their lives, so I
can't really blame them for their attitude towards school.

Our area was less influenced by the modern world, where
people who are educated are the ones who lead and have the
power in society. It is also important to point out that because the
Banyamulenge have been discriminated against for many years,
many members of the community who *did* make an exceptional
effort to get higher education could not find jobs, either in government institutions or the private sector. Some spent many years
searching for jobs, only to end up returning to the villages and
living the same lifestyle as those who had never been educated.

This lack of available employment for tribe members who did
have higher education reinforced in people's minds the idea that
pursuing education was a waste of resources and time. It was hard
for them to get a big-picture perspective on the potential for future
change, so they got left behind in the area of self-development.

I was the first generation in my family to go to school. Neither
of my parents went to school and none of my uncles could read,
except my father's younger brother, Mupenda Venasi. Even he did
not formally attend school—but since there was so little schooling
actually available, the informal lessons he received in reading and
alphabet were considered an education, and those who taught him
were thought of as educators.

Another uncle of mine—or, I thought of him as an uncle anyway; he was actually a cousin of my father's—did attend primary
school and was a very good, smart student. He really wanted to
continue his education, and the school principal encouraged his
parents to send him to the nearby city for high school.

His father would have done just about anything to keep him
away from the city. In addition to the attitudes I already mentioned
about schooling being a waste of time and resources, there was the
belief that the cities held the promise of peril. Parents wanted to

protect their children against malaria, which was prevalent in the cities and nonexistent in the village. In parents' minds, kids that went away to school were risking their lives.

The father of my uncle said to the school principal, "I will give you anything you want. Just keep my child out of that process." In the end, my uncle's father bribed the school principal with a cow to keep my uncle away from high school. My uncle was devastated; his opportunity for higher education and a bright future was sold for a cow.

For all the reasons mentioned above, children in the villages did not have the support of their parents for schooling, and so they lost many opportunities for education and better lives. Children of rich parents had an even smaller chance of going to school. If parents were rich, that meant they had a lot of cattle—and if they had a lot of cattle, they trained their children to be shepherds. It was the opposite of developed countries, where the children of wealthy families were the ones given the best opportunities for education.

Parents found all kinds of excuses not to send their children to school. When we were still living in our old village, I desperately wanted to go to school with my older brother and sister and our cousins. Whenever I would plead with my father to send me to school, he would say, "Not yet. You are not grown up enough to go."

There was a common belief in our village that before attending school, a kid must be "grown up." The test of this was to be able to reach your right arm around your head and touch your left ear without getting close to your head. There was also the belief that kids grew up as they slept in the night. So, every morning, I would jump up and start exercising, reaching my right arm around to touch my left ear.

"Look, Papa!" I would cry out. "See! I am grown now!"

"No, son," my father would say, shaking his head. "Your arm is still too close to your head."

This was an excellent excuse because there was no way to challenge it. Parents were the only ones to judge whether or not a kid left enough space between his arm and his head when he tried to touch his ear.

~ SIX ~

The day I had long awaited finally arrived. My father decided I had grown up enough to go to school, the school was near enough to our new village that distance was not an issue, and the school—which could not accept everyone because of space limitations—agreed to accept me.

As I said, I had been anxious to go to school for so long. Yet, when my first day of school came at last, it was the most frightening day I'd ever experienced. I was terrified of everyone—students, teachers, and school principals. I walked down to the school by myself, trying to imagine what would be waiting for me there. All that I knew of school was the dreams in my head and the stories I had heard.

Outside the school compound, I saw a group of teachers standing around, chatting. They said to me in Swahili, "Jina lako nani?"

"Nkumbuyinka Budagu," I responded, giving them my name in Kinyamulenge.

Once I had identified myself, the teacher of the first-grade class told me to follow him, and took me into a classroom measuring approximately seven by fifteen feet. When we got inside the classroom, I saw many children. I didn't notice the number of kids in the class; I only knew that some looked to be around my same age and others looked older. As I entered the class, all eyes were focused on me as if I were falling from the sky.

Some of the students were relatives from my village, but there were others from surrounding villages that I did not know. The students were murmuring like bees in their hive, quietly laughing at me. I could tell that if they hadn't been afraid of the teacher, they would have laughed louder.

To see this whole crowd of kids in the same place was overwhelming. I didn't understand—why were they laughing at me? I had made sure I was clean. My mother had warned me to clean myself before going to school so the other students wouldn't mock me. I had a good shirt and shorts on me. And, I was wearing shoes. Not everyone in class had shoes.

Still, the kids were laughing at me, violating the main rule in the classroom—"Don't make noise."

I knew this rule way before I started school because my brother had forewarned me—but it was impossible for the kids to be quiet. They kept murmuring, looking at me, my clothes, my shoes. I was a stranger to them and they could not keep quiet. It was easy to understand why the first grade was called "fuyo" in Swahili, meaning "the noisy grade."

Benches were made of bamboo and tied with natural cords, and kids sat three to a bench. I took my seat beside someone I knew. On my lap was my small blackboard and chalk.

We learned almost everything—science, math, history, geography. Despite my awful fear, I was intrigued by all the lessons and information provided in the class. But, like every other new student, I felt overwhelmed and distracted by everything that was happening in the class. And, most of the time, I had no idea what the teacher was saying.

Swahili was the language at school and I knew a little bit already, but it was not easy for me to switch from Kinyamulenge and become comfortable speaking Swahili with the teacher and other students.

School began every day at eight-thirty in the morning and finished at one o'clock in the afternoon. At ten o'clock, we had a break called recreation. Break time should have been enjoyable but it was a nightmare because kids started bullying me. Luckily, I had my cousin who was in the third grade there to protect me. Between being overwhelmed in class and being bullied during break time, I almost quit on my first day of school.

Every morning before school, the custom was to line up the students in front of the school and have someone lead everyone in songs called animation. The songs were mostly praising President Mobutu. When the animation songs were finished, we sang the national anthem and prayed. Afterwards, we marched towards the classroom. I enjoyed the ritual and even when I didn't understand the songs, I loved them for their melody. It was the most exciting moment at school.

Before beginning classes, we also had a moment of inspection. We were required to wear a uniform—a white shirt and blue shorts. During inspection, the teachers and the principal checked students to see if they had washed themselves before coming to school. I always tried to remember to wash myself before going to school but whenever I forgot, I would wipe dew from the grass on my legs, so that they would appear clean. This was a common practice among the students whenever they forgot to wash. Whoever wasn't clean was severely punished.

In every class, there was a chief, either appointed by the teacher or chosen by the students. It was the chief's responsibility to keep the students quiet whenever the teacher was not present. The chief was respected and tried to keep the students orderly, but it was almost impossible to maintain silence in the classroom. Kids were never calm in the absence of the teacher, and there were kids who fought with the chief, regardless of his authority. When the teacher returned to the class, he always asked the chief for a list of noise makers. And, the chief always had the list ready.

Being noisy in class was a cause for punishment. The teacher severely punished all the delinquent students. As punishment, we were beaten by a stick made of a piece of wood measuring about four feet long. Sometimes we were hit with a plastic cord on our backs, rear ends, or the back of our legs. Sometimes the teacher took off his own belt and beat us with it. They could use anything that was handy to give us a beating. Afterwards, we swelled up with welts and turned black and blue. Being punished was unpleasant and embarrassing and the bullies took advantage of the situation, using it as an excuse to bully the ones that were punished.

Everyone who misbehaved or neglected to wash themselves was punished, but the girls were not punished equally to the boys. Generally speaking, our teachers were men and generally speaking, boys were most vulnerable to punishment. Girls were believed to be better-behaved, naturally quieter, more respectful, and more likely to listen to authority figures. When girl students were punished, they received fewer strokes and were hit with less pressure. They were believed to be physically weak and some level of protection was always necessary.

In my own family, I never saw my father punish my sisters the same way he punished my brother and me. Maybe my sisters didn't make as many mistakes; I don't know. But, I never saw my father give them a real beating; he slapped them instead. It was a contradictory concept in our culture—females were recognized as weak and in need of protection, and yet they were the ones who did ninety percent of the household duties.

Students were also punished by the teacher whenever they failed a quiz, or failed to respond correctly to a question. The grading scale ranged from zero to ten. A five or above was considered a passing grade and a four or below was a failing grade. Anyone who received a grade between zero and two was beaten. Getting a zero was humiliating, and anyone receiving that grade was mocked by the students. It was shameful.

Our school was restrictive, with all its rules and procedures, and the environment was competitive, with all the students trying to out-do each other. And, because of the beatings, it was also emotionally and physically challenging. Many less resilient kids abandoned school for that reason—sometimes on the very first day. Since most parents did not really value education in the first place, they did not insist that their children return to school.

It was a strange contradiction—the very same parents who did not value education nevertheless had complete respect for the powerful position held by the school teachers and principals. The parents never dared to stand up to them, and they would not have dreamed of challenging the school system to get them to change their abusive practices.

The relationship between students and teachers was not friendly, either at school or after school. Students were scared to death of their teachers, and would never set foot in the same house with them outside of school. In general, students were taught to be respectful to their teachers, their parents, and anyone older than them. The doctrine itself was not bad, but there were many abuses of power and many kids victimized.

After adapting myself to the classroom, I became one of the most influential students and assumed many responsibilities. I had many talents. I was a very fast runner, good in soccer, and unafraid to fight with anyone when I had to. Of course, fighting was prohibited at school and whoever was caught was severely punished. This did not stop the students. They consistently fought, mostly because they could not avoid the older kids who were determined to draw them into fights.

The last hours of the school day were exhausting. By then, I was starting to get hungry and I desperately wanted to go home. Twenty minutes before the close of the school day, we were allowed to sing a pleading song to our teacher, the words of which said, "Beloved teacher, our time is up and we are hungry, please allow us to go home now!"

I was luckier than some students because my home was not too far from school. Many villages did not have their own school, and there were many students that traveled from far distances to reach the school. The government imposed many requirements before they would authorize a primary or high school in a certain village.

On the way home, students would run and play on the beautiful hills and plateau. It was so refreshing to get back home where I could enjoy playing different games without the pressure of school. As I said, I loved playing with my cousins. We had a strong soccer team and no other team in the village could defeat us.

Not only were my cousins good at soccer, but they made me feel very secure. Whenever a village game would turn into a fight, I was able to face my opponent without fear because my cousins were strong and the other teams were afraid of us. Most of the time, we could walk safely through the village, confident that other kids would not dare bully us.

Of course, there were times when I could not avoid being drawn into a fight. Thankfully, my older brother taught me some techniques and strategies I needed on such occasions. I applied what my brother taught me and it worked very well. One basic principle I learned from him was that I should never fight when I was caught up in fear. He taught me that I should either fight fearlessly or avoid the fight.

It was a common practice, both in the village and at school, for the older students to provoke the younger ones into a fight. Older boys took pleasure in watching kids fight, and this was one of the areas where kids were victimized. Not only did the older boys in the village enjoy seeing the kids fight, they loved to tease them. They called kids names that were upsetting. The language they used was negative and offensive, and I took it all very personally. For example, they might say that someone was ugly or had a big nose. It was not the older boys' intention to hurt or abuse the kids, but in this way they did so without realizing it.

Personally, I hated their teasing. It felt like intimidation and harassment to me. It made me nervous about going into the village, and I avoided meeting new people.

I didn't often hear parents in the village telling their kids that they loved them. Even though these parents did not express it openly, I could see that they loved their kids very much. The women especially were very smooth, nice, and compassionate with their kids. Mothers were more verbal than fathers.

My own mother approached me and spoke to me in a very tender way, and called me different sweet names that made me feel happy. One of the names she often called me was Shimirwa—meaning "someone to be praised or thankful to." This is the name I decided to pass on to my own children, because it is my name and I love it so much. The rest of my names are of my father and grandfather—Makoko and Budagu.

Everyone in the village knew me by the nickname Yorogo. It was a nickname given to me by my parents, but people used it to tease me. I hated it. It did not sound good to me. Back then, I did not know anybody else in the community with the same nickname. In the entire Banyamulenge community, there were very few people with the name. I only knew of one young boy with the same name, from the Bafulero tribe.

I was angry and wondered why in the world my parents had given me a nickname that nobody else in my community had. Later, I came to learn that Yorogo was a fisherman with a big fishing company in the city of Uvira. He fished in Lake Ntaganika, and originated from Greece.

~ SEVEN ~

Three years following our move, when I was finally comfortable with our new village and my school, both of my uncles suddenly decided to move again. (They had not moved to our new village on the same day as my family, but they had followed us about a week later.) I was completely shocked by this terrible news. I didn't understand why they had to move again, after finally getting established in the new village.

The older uncle, Rwatangabo, was moving into another zone called Mwenga, in a village called Mugatenga, at a distance of one day walking. His motivation for moving to Mugatenga was that it was more fertile and more suitable for raising cattle. My younger uncle—who had already prospered as a businessman and was richer than any of his brothers—was planning to move into the city of Uvira, also at a distance of one day walking. This uncle had two boys and one girl, but my cousin, Jules, who was closest to my age, was the one with whom I had the strongest bond.

People in the cities lived by commerce or employment. Not everybody in the villages could decide to move into the city because it required more resources. Few Banyamulenge had resettled in the cities of Uvira, Bukavu, Lubumbashi, and Kinshasa— only those who were educated, employed, or involved in conducting business. Those who did live in the city were well-respected by the rest of the community members because they were open to modern civilization and had greater access to information. Their peasant lifestyle was behind them.

Even though my uncles were moving, my father was not going with them. That meant that I was about to be separated from my cousins—my protectors, my confidantes, my teammates, my companions. My uncles were moving them away from me, and that was not something I was going to take easily. My cousins were important in my life and we had built between us a shared confidence and trust.

How could my father and my uncles contemplate removing my cousins from me? Who would even consider separating the inseparable? These were the cousins I played with every day, the cousins I loved, the cousins who were there for me when I needed them.

I could not understand why my father was not interested in moving with his brothers. I believed that as brothers, they should live together forever—and I also believed it was the right thing to do for my cousins and me.

I was devastated, confused, and angry. But, I didn't know whether to be angry with my uncles who made the decision to move, or with my father, who made the decision not to join his family. All I knew for sure was that this was a very depressing event. I felt that when they left, I'd be completely alone in the village, and I had no idea when I would ever see them again. To me, the place they were going to be living seemed like the edge of the earth.

When moving day came, the world I knew came to an end. I cried like never before. Watching them go, I knew my life and my patterns were about to change dramatically. Now, I was going to have to find new friends and learn how to trust them.

Once my cousins were gone, I missed them terribly. Memories of them were at every step of my day, from the time I woke up until the time I went to bed. And, every time I remembered them, I cried like a baby. Part of me wanted to erase their memories so I would hurt less—but how could I remove them from my heart when they were a part of me?

I constantly asked my father if we would ever move. He did not say no but he was vague as to where or when we would go, and I wanted it soon. I was desperate to see my cousins, and live with them again. But, the time for it happening was still far away.

Now that my cousins were gone, I had to rely on my brother. He was older than me, so he wouldn't play with me, and he attended high school, which was in a different location than my school. But, I had no choice except to become more familiar with him because I felt abandoned and alone in my own world.

Missing my cousins made me miserable, and it wasn't long before I began to hate my village. I never ceased asking my father and mother when we could move. I completely refused to recognize the fact that things had changed and life had moved on. I cried—but never allowed myself to be consumed by my grief. I was not completely weakened by the whole situation. I stayed strong and used my loneliness to fuel my hope.

Over time, I began getting used to living without my cousins and I started making new friends. Somehow, I gained the energy necessary to rise above the sadness. I knew I was going to survive and I thanked God. I came to the understanding that no matter how bad the situation seemed to be, there were always ways of surviving.

I found refuge from my emotional pain deep in my soul—but having my older brother on my side is what refreshed my mind. My brother became a rock for me, the foundation of my spiritual and intellectual growth. He became my mentor, teaching me almost everything I needed to survive. And, he inspired my future. He was there when I needed him and supported me in every corner of my life. I grew to love him to death.

~ EIGHT ~

As time advanced and life unfolded, there came another event which would hit me hard emotionally and leave me in a state of social embarrassment: the marriage of my older sister.

Unlike neighboring tribes, our culture prohibited marrying someone from your own clan. So, my sister had to marry someone from a different clan. Since we only lived in the same village as people from our clan, my sister's marriage meant that she would not be staying with me. When she got married, she would live with her husband and his family, and be taken away from my family and me forever.

I loved my sister very much, and it was a blessing for her to get married, but I was terrified to hear that she would one day leave us. Her name, Nyanoro, meant "gold" and that is how I felt when I imagined losing her—like the gold in our family was being stolen from us.

My beloved cousins had already left me, and it was too soon to also face the departure of my sister. But, I had no control over the situation; I had to accept it. My only comfort came from the knowledge that traditionally, the process of getting married took time.

The spirit of genealogy was always strong in my village. Our survival depended on maintaining tight bonds with the family, clan, and community. So, even after generations, everyone knew who they were related to, no matter how removed or how distant that relation. Family records traced our status back for generations, and established the status of my grandfather and great-grandfathers. Our family had a good reputation and we were highly regarded within the community. We were considered to be decent ("infura") and wealthy, thanks to all of our livestock. This made my sister a good marriage prospect.

A young man could never approach a girl directly. Marriages were always arranged between parents. The way it all unfolded was amazing. The father of a young boy and the father of a young girl from a different clan might have a good relationship. The two of them would make an agreement that their children would someday marry. The promise would be in place as the years went by, and then one day, the marriage would finally take place. None of the other neighboring tribes had such a culture of friendship and commitment.

My clan had a reputation for our beautiful girls, and people competed for them, trying to get their parents to agree to a marriage before an arrangement could be made with someone else. My sister was a most beautiful girl, so she was the target of many families who wanted to take her. Fathers traveled from great distances to meet with my father, in an attempt to arrange a marriage between their son and my sister. Their attempts were all in vain.

When my future brother-in-law's father had made an agreement with my father many years earlier, it was based upon their personal relationship. He said something like, "I know you have a beautiful daughter. If she grows up healthy and becomes ready to marry, can you give her to my son?"

My father may have said something along the lines of, "Yes, sure. If the time ever comes, we can work it out."

Now, the time had come. My sister was grown up, and my father felt she could be married.

She was the firstborn in my family, but traditionally, a female could not be regarded as the actual firstborn and could not inherit my father's responsibilities. Our culture treated girls in the family as passengers; we believed that they were born for others. If a boy was the last born among many others, he was still considered the firstborn.

Early marriage depended upon how well a girl excelled in her domestic abilities. From a young age, girls were taught how to do domestic chores such as cooking, fetching water, collecting fire-wood, and cleaning the cows' and calves' sheds. The wealth of the parents also contributed greatly to the desirability of girls as wives. But, there was no aspect more highly honored in a prospective bride than her virginity. Girls were taught how to keep themselves pure, so as not to destroy their lives and reputation.

My sister kept all these values and that put her in a good position to be solicited. Of course, as I said, the solicitors were all too late, as my sister's marriage had been arranged long before.

Even though the groom's family and my family had an understanding between them, they still had to follow the traditional marriage protocol. The first step in this process involved my sister's in-laws coming to see my father for what is called "the introduction."

Although it was called the introduction process, the bride and groom would not actually meet until their wedding day. During the introduction, the arrangement that had been made years earlier was formalized. The process would begin with a very indirect conversation between the father of the bride and the father of the prospective groom.

The father of the groom would never say outright, "I am ready for you to give your daughter to my son in marriage." Instead, he would say something leading, letting my father draw his own conclusions. The conversation might start like this, "I am hungry, and I need you to feed me."

Then my father might say, "Then let me go find some milk and food for you..."

"No, no," the prospective father-in-law might say, "I am not hungry for that kind of food. What I need is this beautiful cow you have..."

"Which cow?" my father might ask.

"The human-being type of cow," the other man would say.

They would go on talking that way, even though it was perfectly obvious to everyone concerned what they were talking about.

The next stage of the marriage ceremony after introduction was engagement—but the engagement occurred between families, not between the groom and bride. The engagement period stretched over many months or years and involved the payment of a down payment towards the dowry, final payment of dowry in full ("gukoshanya"), and lastly, the wedding.

The dowry down payment was usually one cow, given as a sign of commitment that the families were going to engage in the process of dowry negotiations and see the process through to its conclusion. But, there was no guarantee. It was always possible, if the negotiations did not go well and the families were unable to reach an agreement, that the engagement would be broken, and there would be no marriage.

After my sister's prospective in-laws came to ask my father for her hand and the engagement period began, I believed I had nothing to worry about for awhile. I knew the marriage process involved a long-term relationship between the families of the bride and groom, and I figured it would take awhile. But, I was wrong. The traditional rituals and meetings passed quickly and before I knew it, the date was fixed for my sister's wedding.

~ NINE ~

My family began preparing all the belongings necessary for my sister's journey, including new clothes, shoes, lotions, and soaps. There were many things she would need for her new life and according to cultural norms, everything had to be purchased new.

My sister was about to begin an entirely new lifestyle, and it was going to cost us the value of one cow to buy everything she would require. Once my father had purchased everything my sister would need for her married life, he set the specific date that my sister would leave, and then secretly informed everyone in the village—everyone, except my sister!

Everyone in the village was warned not to tell Nyanoro anything about the date of her wedding. This secretive way of handling an upcoming wedding was traditional in my tribe, and was intended to keep the bride from suffering emotionally.

Nyanoro's journey to her new home would require one day of walking, the wedding itself would last one day, and then those who accompanied her would return on the third day. My family, and the people in the village who would accompany my sister, began making preparations to leave.

My sister could see that my father was buying her new things, and she knew that the day of her wedding was approaching—but she never knew the exact date. Girls never participated in any decisions concerning their marriage. They were rarely happy about their upcoming marriage, and many had neither interest nor pleasure in their wedding ceremony. It was a time of separating themselves from their families, and it was very heartbreaking for them and for their family, as well.

Some brides were still young when they married, but because of the healthy diet we followed in our village, they developed their figures at a young age and usually looked mature by the time they reached marrying age. Long before a girl's figure developed, the women in the village counseled her to remain pure and preserve her family's values.

By the time a girl was ready to become a bride, either her aunts, her grandmother, or another female elder in the village would have already spoken to her about marital intimacy. Culturally, it would be considered taboo for the mother to have such a discussion with her daughter. The relationship between a girl and her mother did not involve that type of interaction. Direct relations would never share such information.

My sister was only eighteen years old. At that age, it was emotionally overwhelming to leave her entire family and take her place in a completely new family. As she faced this major transition in her life, the whole village empathized with her. Because they could not openly talk to her and say, "We are sorry you are leaving, and we know this is hard for you," the only way they could offer comfort and support to her was through the expressions on their faces and the special care with which they treated her.

These were the signals to her that her departure was imminent. She knew the culture and understood what was happening perfectly well. She had seen what the other girls in the village had gone through as they were preparing to marry.

From my perspective, it seemed as if the entire village had betrayed my sister. Everyone was informed about what was going to happen to her, and yet no one would tell her—not even her best friends. During this entire process, I felt terrible.

In the Sunday worship service one week before my sister's departure, it was the religious tradition to present her in front of the whole congregation. They had to give their approval and blessings for the new lifestyle that was unfolding for her. She was still in the dark about the date that she was leaving.

I wept, along with my whole family. I could barely contain all the emotions I was feeling as I watched what she was going through. I was heartbroken and angry with my father. I felt like he had betrayed my sister in exchange for some cows (the dowry he was paid by my sister's in-law family).

As was customary, my sister had to leave the church as soon as her presentation was over so she wouldn't hear anyone talking about her departure date. Her best friend was waiting, along with a few other friends, to escort her out of the church. I could see that she was soberly crying.

Once she was gone, the rest of the congregation stayed to openly discuss the arrangements for her journey, and decide who should accompany her. At least fifty people had to be chosen—men, women, girls, and boys. My older brother was the only one from my immediate family who was going to be there.

Culturally, my mother and father were not supposed to attend the wedding. It was too hard on the parents to witness such a sad event. It was not like it is here in America, where the wedding of a daughter is a cause for celebration. For us, it was a time of grieving, for we were saying goodbye to a member of our family.

I was not selected to attend, either. Customarily, young people did not travel long distances. There was also concern that someone so young might not be mature enough to handle themselves at that kind of a ceremony, and might start crying or cause some kind of trouble. There were a limited number of people allowed to attend from our village, and great care was taken to choose the right people.

In my tribe, marriage was always a family affair—never a private matter between bride and groom. The bride was always in the center of the family.

Once the bride and groom were married, the bride would stay away from her family for an entire year. She wouldn't visit unless there was a death in the family. Then, after the year of staying away, she would come for a two-month visit. Then, she would leave, and stay away for another whole year. After that year, she would return for a year-long visit. Her husband had no choice but to accept his wife's year-long absence, as it was part of the culture.

Following that visit, the bride would return to her husband's village, where they would finally be allowed to live in their own private home. Before that, all of their activities as a couple—except sleeping—would take place in the home of their in-laws.

This tradition allowed the brides—who were all fairly young when they got married—to have a period of training. During that time period, their mother-in-law taught them how to be a wife and mother. This was done to ensure that the bride matured enough to sustain a family.

The day of Nyanoro's departure finally arrived—and she was still unaware that she was leaving! It was a nightmare for our whole family. She had to leave early in the morning, because she was traveling a long distance—a full day of walking.

The night before my sister left, I witnessed the nervousness of my father for the first time. We couldn't stand to see my sister moving around us so innocently, having no idea that early the next morning, she would be leaving. My sister often slept in my grandmother's house, and that night, we made sure she slept there. Otherwise, she might have had a sixth sense that she was leaving the following day, because of our expressions and the careful way we were treating her.

It was easy to tell that my sister was miserable, contemplating her upcoming departure, and having no way of knowing for sure when it was coming. It truly broke my heart and even now, when I think of it, the whole tradition seems abusive to me.

Not just anyone would be able to break the news to my sister that the time had come for her to leave. But, the following morning, there came a guy who had a reputation for being strong. He went to my grandmother's house, found my sister, and said, "Get up! This is the day you are leaving."

Her mind had been alert throughout the whole process, and she expected the news at any time. So, when the messenger came to her, she immediately understood what he was talking about, and she started crying.

I was still asleep in my father's house. Suddenly, I heard the cries coming from my grandmother's house, and I realized they had told Nyanoro. The sounds of her weeping resonated through-out the village. It was heartbreaking—like someone had died. The whole family began crying with her. I, too, cried very hard.

In our culture, it was believed that men have to be stron-ger than women, so my father never showed his emotions. That morning, he had left especially early to milk the cows. He could not stand the cries of his daughter. His beautiful, firstborn girl was leaving, and it was not easy for him to see her go.

Women in the village could never wear pants or any of the men's clothes—and women wore a different outfit than girls. When the messenger came to tell my sister that the time had come to go, he also brought women's clothing for her. Girls in the village wore a skirt, polo shirt, and a scarf on their head. They also wore a kilt that draped over their shoulder and hung down to their hips. It was a piece of fabric measuring approximately a meter and a half, and was called "urupande" or "waxi."

The women wore the same outfit but their skirts were always covered with another kilt that was tied at their waist, and draped down around their legs. It was obvious as you entered the village, based upon their outfits, who were the women and who were the girls.

When my sister emerged from my grandmother's house, she had completely transformed into a woman. Because of the way they had dressed her, she no longer seemed like the sister I knew.

As the party chosen to accompany her walked with her through the village and down the hill, Nyanoro was crying, and calling out our names to say goodbye. Women and girls were traditionally believed to be emotional, and it was understandable that they would cry. Men, on the other hand, were not expected to cry unless there was a death in the family. They were expected to be strong. A man who could not hold his emotions was considered weak.

I knew these things, but I could not help myself. That day, I cried loudly, joining my mother, grandmother, younger sister, and aunties. Other boys in the village were laughing at me, but I did not stop. I went and hid myself in my grandmother's house, and cried constantly.

Within about an hour, everyone in the village who had been selected to accompany my sister had gone. They were not expected back for three days. The entire village suffered the loneliness caused by the fact that fifty villagers had left all at once.

In my immediate family, it was like a day of mourning. We were so depressed, we hardly ate or did anything. My father stayed away all day long, shepherding the cows. As for me, I could not distract my mind. I was consumed with thoughts about my sister. All kinds of evil thoughts plagued me. I was tortured by visions of how she might be treated by her in-law family.

In our home, my sister had been spoiled, and could ask for anything she wanted. My mother loved her very much, and never left her to struggle to figure things out on her own. It was depressing to think of how my sister was going to survive in her new family. Who was going to be there for her as she took over all the female activities in her in-law family, as required by tradition? And how would *my* family ever be the same?

After three days, the people who went to accompany my sister were expected to return home. We were anxious to see my brother, Shoshi, and hear the story of my sister's wedding, and we waited late into the night for his return. I did not really look forward to hearing the story, because I knew it would stir my memories and thoughts again, but it was traditional to tell the story of the whole celebration. As we awaited my brother's arrival, I kept wondering how he could return home without my sister, leaving her there all alone. I didn't know how I could possibly live without her in my family.

The news my brother brought to us was news of celebration—in my sister's in-law family, anyway. Just as we were depressed by the absence of my sister, her in-law family was happy like never before. They had gained everything that we had lost. It was so unfair to hear this kind of news, and I just didn't understand how it could be possible.

But, it was true. The gold of our family was gone.

~ TEN ~

Not only did my sister's departure create a feeling of emptiness in our family, it left me in a disastrous situation in my life. Now that Nyanoro was gone, all of her chores were left on the back of my mother *and me.*

By the time that Nyanoro got married, my mother had given birth to a new baby—my younger brother, Sabuwera Patrick, who was about eighteen months old at this point in time. With a baby to care for, my mother could not handle all the family chores by herself. She couldn't count on Shoshi, who was about sixteen years old. A teenage boy of that age was considered a man and could not do anything related to women's work. My mother couldn't count on my younger sister, Nyarukundo, who was still too young to help.

There was no one else to help my mother but me. I was the only one in the middle. I was not yet old enough to be considered a man, so I had to take over my sister's entire portfolio of chores. It didn't matter that I was also a full-time student. I loved my mother and could not let her suffer. I was obligated to help her in every way possible.

The work I took on after my sister got married was female work—chores that a boy in a normal situation would never do. For four years, from the age of ten until I was about fourteen years old, I was forced to do these chores. Few boys in the village did that type of work, and when they saw me doing it, they treated me with contempt. They knew I was not supposed to be doing work meant for girls and women.

I cooked and cleaned, and after we ate, I cleaned the dishes. I fetched water. I went to harvest corn, beans, peas, and potatoes. I had to extract flour from the corn, at any one time pounding approximately a hundred kilos of corn grains with a mortar and pestle.

Prior to doing the extraction work, we had to put the corn in a huge casserole full of water, to soften the dry corn. Once the corn was soft, I had to pound and filter the flour, until all one hundred kilos were finished. It was work that was suitable only for a machine. On the day that was set aside for that work, the sun had to be shining to dry the corn, which had been softening for weeks in water. The corn was then dried on a mat ("umukeka").

Every time my mother and I had to do this work, we spent the entire day outside in the sun and heat. At the end of the process, our hands would be burning and cracked. I hated this ridiculous work for two reasons: It was exhausting—and it was shameful work for a boy. It killed me to be the only boy in a group of women and girls.

The women in the village considered this to be the most exhausting, time-consuming and energy-draining work, and they preferred to do it in groups. That way, they could share some of the instruments needed. Doing that difficult kind of work in a group was also easier on them, psychologically.

I also hated harvesting beans. This task required my mother and me to travel almost thirty kilometers, because our village was not warm enough for growing beans, and they had to be grown elsewhere. The harvesting process involved pounding the dry beans, which were covered in leaves, and breaking them into measures of twenty kilos or so. It took us an entire day to do this work. Again, traditionally, this was work only women should do, but every dry season, I had to do it.

In addition to helping my mother with all the activities Nyanoro used to handle, I had to go with my father to do the milking early in the morning. Shoshi was attending high school far away from home, and he had to leave earlier for school than I did, so he couldn't go with my father. Helping my father with the milking interfered greatly with my school activities, and I was angry with my father almost every morning. My schooling was never a priority to him.

On most mornings, I was so late, I missed the majority of the early classes. My teacher punished me severely for being late on so many occasions. I could never convince my teacher that it was not my fault. And no matter how many times I explained the situation to my father, nothing seemed to change. He was the chief of the family and the one who paid my school tuition. He controlled me on every level of my life.

All through primary school, I was put in a position of trying to satisfy two masters—my father and my teacher. I was obedient to my father and endured the punishments from my teacher. After school, my life was not like the lives of other kids in the village. My schedule was full of family responsibilities, and I never got a chance to play. I was caught up with many household activities that interrupted my mind and interfered with my studies. So, I did not do as well as I would have liked during primary school.

I never understood why my father was so careless concerning my school responsibilities. He knew exactly how severely I was punished every time I was late at school. Yet, he did not make sure I arrived on time. I felt as if he were intentionally setting me up to be in trouble with my teachers. It made my life very difficult.

I was so young to be carrying those heavy responsibilities. The whole situation imposed upon me a lot of anger and frustration, and left me with the constant feeling that I lived in an unpleasant world.

Eventually, I hit a growth spurt and began looking like a man. The older I got, the more humiliating it was to be doing woman's work. At a certain point, I made it clear to my mother that I would not go spend an entire day with the group of women. I was too embarrassed. After that, my mother decided that we could do the work privately, inside a shack, on a separate day from the rest of the women.

My mother could see that it was not good for me to be responsible for female chores. She was always on my side, and would do whatever she could to support me and make me happy. But, other than making the decision to move that hard work indoors, there was not much she could do to save me. She had little influence over my father. In most cases, the best she could offer me was good advice and instruction on how to organize my time.

Even when my mind was preoccupied with my chores, I was thinking about the bigger picture, especially school. When I wasn't being punished at school, I really enjoyed my studies. My favorite classes were also the ones in which I excelled—geography, history, and science. It is hard to explain why those classes were the most attractive to me. Each of those subjects was like a song the teacher would sing. Whenever I heard the song, it moved me deeply and became like a song in my heart.

Only the teachers had books, so there was no way to further my education independently. It was a shame, because I would have been very interested in reading more about my favorite subjects. I loved to learn new things and listened very well. We didn't have any other sources of information, either—no TV, radio, or newspapers. The only sources of information were the teachers, and other grownup individuals in the village. My mother did not know how to read at all, and my father could barely read the Bible.

Our environment was peaceful but totally isolated from the rest of the world. I loved our village—but not as much as I had when I was younger, before I had to take on my sister's responsibilities. I often lay awake at night, wondering how I would ever break free from the difficult life I was now living.

There were only two possibilities that could free me from female work: Either my younger sister had to grow up enough to assume the responsibilities that I was handling, or my older brother had to bring home a wife.

~ ELEVEN ~

Eventually, it came to pass that my older brother, Shoshi, was mature and ready to be married. His marriage was going to be a transformational event in my life. It would change my social consideration in the village and restore the confidence I lost when I had to step into my sister's shoes in the household. I was filled with anticipation for the wedding.

I had become completely exhausted and confused from all the domestic work I had been doing—but even as I was doing it, I knew deep in my heart that one day I would become the man I was made to be. Like any boy in the village, one day I would be free.

From the first time I heard that my father had introduced himself to my future sister-in-law's family, as required by our tradition, I got extremely excited. I did not place a lot of weight on that first introduction, because it routinely took more than a year from the time of the first introduction to the conclusion of the wedding. But, just knowing they had met began to ease my mind and increase my hope significantly. Something I had awaited for so long had finally been announced.

Many of the rituals for the wedding of my brother were the same as when my sister got married—only, this time, we were going to be gaining, rather than losing, a member of our family, and she would be with us forever. This was a joyful event for my entire family. For the honor of adding a brand new person to our family, we would trade a lot of cows.

The wedding celebration was always one of the village's most social gatherings, and every time a wedding was announced, the community anxiously looked forward to the event. Naturally, the family hosting the wedding looked forward to it most of all, and this time, it was my family's firstborn boy that would be bringing joy to the village.

As I said, for me, the excitement was doubled, because I knew how much my brother's wedding would positively impact my life. It was not like my sister's wedding, which caused me to dread the day when she would leave. This time, I looked forward to the event with great anticipation—and because I couldn't wait for it to come, the days passed by at the pace of a snail crawling uphill. Frantic emotions caused me to doubt that the event would ever arrive.

It wasn't easy, but I had to be patient. Every day that I continued to do the female chores I hated so much, I told myself, *You are playing the final game. Soon, it will all be behind you.* I had already waited years to be released. I knew I had only to wait a maximum of one more year—and, if everything went well, perhaps only months.

Four months after the initial introduction came the time for paying the dowry. This was a monumental event, and signified a serious moment between the families of both the bride and the groom. I was greatly encouraged by this development, for it meant that everything was moving more quickly and smoothly than I had anticipated. This was a big step in the process.

My father was about to lose a portion of his wealth—cows—to the bride's family, and not just any cows. Inevitably, the most productive and best-looking cows were targeted by the other family. The exchange was handled like a very important business deal. It was a major moment in the life of my brother. He would be officially receiving his portion of the inheritance from his parents. In our culture, only boys could receive an inheritance. Girls shared with their husbands. It does not sound fair, but it was our culture and we believed in it.

The inheritance a boy received was the starting point from which he—along with his bride—would begin to progressively build the foundation for his personal life. The number of cows to be given depended upon how wealthy the groom's parents were, as well as the willingness of the father to support his son. Some parents were very greedy and would not give enough cows to their sons. This provoked an incendiary situation, as both the family of the groom and the family of the bride fought to ensure and secure the future lives of their children.

On their side, the bride's family fought to ensure that their daughter was delivered into safe hands, economically speaking. In other words, they did everything they could to get as many cows as possible from the groom's father.

In a case like that, it was easy for the groom to see that the goals of his future father-in-law were most closely aligned with his own. The bride's father wanted as many cows as possible for his daughter and son-in-law—and that's what the groom wanted, also. So, even though the groom did not wish to turn against his own father, his father's greed prompted him to partner with his future father-in-law in his efforts to secure as many cows as possible for him and his bride.

This partnering of the groom and father-in-law happened in secret, of course. In the course of the dowry discussions, the family of the bride might not know how many cows the family of the groom really had in their herd. Perhaps the father of the groom had a certain number of cows from his own herd combined with a few donated by friends, but he did not intend to reveal the true number during the discussions.

The bride's father might sense this, and say aloud to the group, "I would like to have some private time with my future son-in-law." Then, the two of them would go to a secret place.

The older man might question the groom, saying, "Is it possible that your father has more cows than he can remember at the moment?"

To which the young man might reply, "Yes, I believe there are five more cows."

For instance, if a groom's parents decided to give a total of twenty cows up front as their son's share of the inheritance, only a portion of those cows would go to the bride and groom. The bride's family would take some of the cows set aside for the young groom and his bride—maybe eight or nine cows out of twenty.

In the eyes of the bride's family, this dowry was intended to be equivalent to the "head" of the bride. In fact, the dowry was called "igitwe," which literally meant "head." Once the dowry had been paid, the remaining eleven or twelve cows would go to the bride and groom as the financial foundation for their lives.

During the dowry negotiations, the goal of the bride's family was to raise the bar higher. That way, the bride's family would have enough cows for them to take home in exchange for their daughter— while still leaving enough cows for their daughter and son-in-law.

As I said, this was very serious business, and both families played to win. During this process, men from both families were there to act as mediators, ensuring that the traditional proceedings unfolded in a way that was fair to both parties.

Everything was at stake during these discussions. There were many instances among the Banyamulenge where the families involved refused to compromise, and as a result, they shattered the marriage possibilities for their children. So, although I tried to patiently await the marriage of my brother, I was constantly anxious about what might happen during the dowry negotiations. To make sure that there would be a good understanding reached between my family and the bride's family, I engaged in intercessory prayer, earnestly asking God to bless the transaction.

Traditionally, the dowry event was hosted by the bride's family, so my father asked the family of the bride to give him a specific day for the dowry celebration. He chose Shoshi and one of Shoshi's best friends, as well as a few other family members, to accompany him to the bride's village. No female members were allowed to participate in the discussion, and I was too young to go.

A goat would be killed to feed the special guests, and the entire celebration would take two days, minimum, provided that everything went well.

The time came for my father, my older brother, Shoshi, and the whole team to leave for the ceremony. I stayed home with my mother, and my younger sister and brother, patiently awaiting the return of Shoshi and the others, and hoping that they brought with them good news. Anything other than good news was going to be a shock for us.

After two days of discussion, an agreement was gracefully reached. My father agreed to give sixteen cows in total—seven as dowry, and nine as my brother's share. For my brother, this was a pretty good start. It was a good share of the wealth.

When I heard this news, I started jumping up and down. This was a victorious event—my prayers had been answered! Thank God, my father had been very decent and easygoing throughout the dowry process. Everything went very quickly and smoothly, unlike similar events I had witnessed in the village—events which involved several days, or even a week, of serious argument before the agreement was reached.

Had I been living under more normal circumstances, instead of shouldering all my sister's female responsibilities, I would have sided with my father, encouraging him to make the most advantageous deal for himself. I was the next to be married, and typically, I would have wanted to make sure he kept enough cows for the time of my own marriage, whenever that might be.

At that time, however, I could not have cared less about the cows. I was interested only in my brother's wedding—which meant a new female under our roof, and ultimately, my freedom. I would have been a fool to do anything to compromise my liberation day. Domestic work had kept me in captivity to the point that I was desperate for the light at the end of the tunnel.

The dowry agreement signaled the coming of the big day. I just had to bide my time. My family was occupied with many preparations. Anxiety blended with anticipation over the arrival of something I had awaited endlessly. The combination blew out the fuses that had been strengthening my patience. The four months that remained before the wedding became to me like two years.

My brother's wedding was going to lift me up to another level of social consideration within the community. I kept wondering— could this actually be real? There were times when I felt like I was in a deep sleep, and my mind was plugged into a wonderful dream. I was afraid I was going to awaken into deep disappointment.

Thankfully, I was not dreaming—the date for the wedding was fixed. The dowry process had concluded in August, and the wedding was set for December. Preparations were underway. The wedding celebration would be very expensive, so the first step was for my father to sell another cow. He would then use the money from the sale to purchase food for the wedding feast, new clothes—first for my brother, the groom, and then for each of us in the household—and various other necessities for the party.

I had never seen so much money moving from one hand to another within my family. All the members of the extended family from both my mother's and father's side were invited, along with the bride's family, and friends from the surrounding villages. That meant that we would be feeding at least five hundred guests over a period of two days.

After my father sold the cow, my mother and I began visiting the markets that were hosted on different days of the week. We were joined by several village women and girls who helped us buy the food and carry it home. The traditional wedding food was fufu—my favorite. Considering how many guests we needed to feed, we had to buy and store ten huge bags of cassava flour and corn, each weighing approximately one hundred kilos.

This was not an easy task for my family to fulfill, but we managed, thanks to the collective action of the entire village, who gave us their heartfelt support. The villagers strongly believed that a wedding was a community celebration, and that each individual had to provide his or her help.

Right up until the wedding day, I worked hard, helping my mother with the preparations. Each marketplace we needed to visit was at a far distance—an average of eight hours walking, round trip. I told my mother I was willing to go even further—up to ten hours, round trip, carrying twenty to twenty-five kilos of flour, just to make sure this event would be as successful as possible. I was so motivated to see the wedding day approaching, I was able to muster exceptional diligence for the tasks at hand.

My mother was always amazed at my inborn strength and courage, but in this instance, she was truly stunned by how hard I worked. I was resilient and energized like never before, because I knew where the road was leading me. Thank God, the wedding preparations took place during off-season at school, so I was able to devote all my time to helping my mother.

While my mother and I—along with the females in the village—were busy going to market to collect all the food, my father and brother were busy building my brother's house. The houses in our village were round in shape, and constructed without the aid of any nails or glue. The men cut bamboos and cords. Then, they forced the bamboos into the ground. There was no foundation—the bamboos sustained the house. Once the bamboos were forced into the ground, they were connected with natural cords, and tied in such a way that they would not come apart.

The roof was also constructed of bamboos. Here's how it was made: once the house was erected, they measured the house, and then went inside to where the center was located. At that center spot, they forced one big bamboo into the ground. They took the other end of that bamboo stalk and split it, so it fanned out into enormous leaves. At the point where it was split and started to fan out, they tied it securely. Then, they began to attach other bamboos to the spreading leaves with natural cords, and in that way, they created a roof.

Once the house was finished, they mixed mud with water and added cow dung to hold the mud together. Then, they used that paste to rough-cast the house. This technique covered the holes between the tied bamboos. To one section at a time they applied the paste, patting it down. After rough-casting, the house was painted with paint created by mixing water and cow dung with naturally pigmented clay found in the area. The roof had an overhang that allowed the rains to flow downward without soaking the sides of the house and washing away the paint. Only when the rains fell sideways did they dilute the paint.

My brother's house was very small in size—perhaps twenty feet by twelve or fifteen feet. It was one large area, which was divided into a tiny bedroom and a living room.

After my brother's house was completed, he had to go to the nearby city of Uvira to buy his wedding clothes—a beautiful suit, a nice shirt and tie, and new shoes. He also had to buy a mattress for his home. My brother was gone for an entire week, and while he was away, I had a smile on my face. I knew that every detail that was coming together was bringing me that much closer to my liberation.

The bride's family was also very busy during this time. They were purchasing the necessities the bride would need for her new life. And, they were experiencing the emotions my family had suffered—the turmoil of losing the beloved daughter in the family. In the same way my sister did when she got married, the bride had to endure the secrecy and discretion of the villagers, who attempted to protect her from the knowledge of the exact day she would be taken away for her wedding to my brother.

Thank God my family was on the other side this time, with joy and happiness awaiting us at the wedding, instead of sorrow.

~ TWELVE ~

It was now two weeks before the wedding. We had finished buying all the food and shopping for clothes. At this time, we were busy with cleaning, roughcasting, and painting the exterior and interior of our houses. We also had to lay new grass in the living room. My older sister came home to help us with wedding preparations, and she had her baby boy with her. Getting a chance to spend time with her again increased our joy.

We weren't the only family preparing our house for the festivities. The entire village was getting ready, because each family in the village was going to host two or three visiting guests, depending on the size of their house.

The night before the wedding was a busy night in our house. The majority of the women in the village had come to our house to help peel beans. There were fifty kilos of beans that needed to be soaked in water and peeled before they could be cooked in a manner designed especially for weddings. Peeling fifty kilos of beans by hands was a very detailed process, and took time and many helping hands. It took the women almost all night long to get the beans ready to cook first thing in the morning.

Three types of food were going to be eaten during the wedding—fufu, beef, and "urukoronge"—a very sweet, popular dish which was made from the peeled, cooked, and mashed beans the women had prepared.

Staying overnight with us were three aunts and three cousins who were married and living in surrounding villages. Their intention was to help my mother that night, sleep over, and then rise early on the wedding day to help with all the work that would need to be done.

Wherever people were gathering and things were happening, the village kids were naturally curious and loved to be around. Feeling the excitement on the eve of the wedding, kids flocked to our house and were playing inside and outside.

The night before the wedding, my brother also had a house full of guests. It was traditional for his friends to be with him the night before his wedding, telling jokes and having fun. A boy's wedding could be a frightening event for him, and having close friends around him helped to calm his nerves. The pre-wedding party for the groom was nothing like an American bachelor party. We are Christians, so there was no alcohol and no girls. There was a slight possibility that someone might sneak alcohol into the party but there was no chance of girls being there. It was simply not the way things were done.

Traditionally, about two weeks before the wedding, the groom would stop doing most of his normal work—anything involving machetes or other tools that could cause injury. The only work the groom would do during those weeks was the easy, less risky work. He had to avoid doing anything that could bring on a disaster and prevent the wedding from happening. The entire village looked upon him as special during that time, and prayed daily for him to be protected and healthy all the way through to the day of his wedding.

At last it came—the day different from all others! It was a Thursday, and the day arrived bright and pleasing. In the morning, I heard the strong voice of my father, calling my name.

I had spent the previous night in a different house, along with two of the three cousins who were staying with us. (The third cousin was older, and stayed in a different house.) These were the same cousins for whom I had grieved so deeply when they moved away years earlier. We had missed each other terribly, and were thrilled to see each other and finally have a chance to get reacquainted.

Despite our exhaustion, we stayed up half the night, talking about everything that had happened since we parted. As we talked, we completely forgot that we had to get up especially early the next morning. We had to travel to a distant pasture village to bring home the calf that would be killed for the feast.

At the time my father's voice came to us, sounding as far away as the call of an animal in a distant field, we had only been asleep for two hours, so we were still snoring deeply. My father wanted to know why in the world we were still sleeping at that hour! Hadn't he warned us the night before that we needed to get up earlier than usual?

We sat up, startled. Then we rushed out of bed, and quickly began washing our faces. Then we went back to my house and found my mother making fufu for us. All of my aunts and female cousins were busy with different activities in and out of the house. It was already six-thirty in the morning, and we were behind schedule, so we ate in a hurry.

The task that had been assigned to us for the big day was a challenging one. We were going to travel at least seven hours, round-trip, on foot. Our instructions were to return with the calf *no later than one o'clock.* When we returned, the calf would be slaughtered. By two o'clock, they needed to start cooking it.

Everything about our assignment was going to be challenging. We had to travel to the field and select one calf out of hundreds to bring home. Capturing the calf would require a very complicated maneuver. The calf had been raised in an area unsolicited by many people, so they were completely unfamiliar with humans. The cattle had become almost savage.

Because we had gotten a late start, we had to run as fast as antelopes in order to make it to the pasture, capture the calf, and bring it home on time. My cousins and I ran with unbelievable speed that day, making it there in approximately an hour and a half, instead of three hours! I don't know where we found the stamina to run so fast. I had never run so fast before—and I haven't since.

Out of breath and dripping with sweat, we reached our destination—an enormous valley surrounded by a forest. We had to meet with a shepherd who was going to show us the calf to be taken. He worked for a friend of my father's who was rich, had lots of cows, and had agreed to give a calf which had been fattened, and was suitable for eating. In exchange, he would receive a cow from my father, which was bigger, but less suitable for the wedding feast.

Upon our arrival, we found beautiful cows in many different colors. Some were sleeping deeply and others were slowly feeding. They were taking their time eating because they lived in their own place, with an abundance of grass. They were all healthy and fattened.

All the cows were afraid of people. Only rarely did visitors come to see them or feed them salt. For those cows to see four or five people at the same time was a very frightening situation. When they saw us, they became alert. We were completely strange to them.

How could we capture a calf when the cows were already spooked by our presence?

We had two options. One option was to catch the calf, tie a cord around one of its legs—or separate cords around two of its legs—and make a leash that could be used to lead it to the path we were going to take. This option would require a lot of energy and maneuvering. We would have to run behind it until we caught it. Once we caught it, we would have to struggle with it before it reached the point of surrender, and followed our orientation. Calves are faster than anything you can imagine, especially the young ones. With this option, we knew that we might wind up in a situation where we had to run for hours before the calf got tired and slowed down enough for us to catch it.

The second option was to run behind it, and keep directing it until it got used to the direction we were going.

Neither of these options would be easy, but we had to pick one or the other. We had no choice but to get the calf home by one o'clock in the afternoon. After discussing it, we all agreed that we would use the first option. It was the harder of the two, but once we caught the calf, it was the fastest, surest way to get the calf home.

We had to be careful because there was a danger that the calf might run into the closest opening of the forest before we ever caught it. This would be disastrous, requiring us to search for hours, with no guarantee that we'd be able to find it or capture it. I had faith that we could complete our task. One of my cousins was a very strong guy, and more experienced than the rest of us, and I trusted him. The shepherd was also there to help us.

After the decision was made, we ran into the forest and cut the strongest cords we could find. We returned and were trying to approach the calf. When the cows saw this, most of them stood and started backing up toward the forest. We had in front of us thousands of big eyes focused on us. They surely realized that something strange was transpiring. We kept approaching our target, and as we did, the cows kept retreating at a fast pace. They were scared to death.

For our first attempt, we decided to target a calf in the middle of at least twenty cows. We had to pick a calf in the middle of a group of cows, so we could hide behind the other cows and have the element of surprise on our side. Otherwise, the calf could see us coming and run away. The plan was to rapidly rush towards it, and trap it with cords.

Few people knew how to accomplish this on the first try. Many unskilled people could not even accomplish it on the tenth try. My cousin was well-trained in this practice, and we were all relying on his technical skills. He made a first try, and a second and third. No success.

So, we regrouped and decided to use the second method—run after the calf until it exhausted itself. As we started running after the calf, the entire valley became alert. All the cows realized that we had attacked them. Some started fleeing into the nearby forest, and others ran as far from us as possible.

We kept following them. They screamed, cried, and ran every which way. They could not understand what we were trying to accomplish. It was amazing to see hundreds of cows on high alert, running tirelessly through the valley, trying to save themselves.

After an hour, we successfully caught the calf! We were all seriously exhausted and sweating. We tied cords around both legs—like leashes—and led it back home with us. We would be arriving home around one-thirty—about half an hour late. If we had not gotten off to a late start that morning, we probably would have been on time.

My cousins and I started to feel concerned that my father would ask us why we took so long—but it could have been worse. We could have failed to capture the calf and returned empty-handed. We were very proud that we would be coming home with the calf.

As we got closer to the village, we could see that the movement of the villagers had intensified. We could see women who had just come from fetching water at the river, carrying gallons home on their heads. Others were coming from the forest, where they had been collecting firewood. All wedding preparations had intensified, but our late arrival delayed many activities.

Our house was the focal point, and all activity was concentrated there. People moved to and from our house, crossing each other as they went. As they often did when they noticed great activity someplace, the village kids had gathered around our house, playing and watching all the happenings with great curiosity.

My father's house was a big house, with two bedrooms, a living room, a room for my new sister-in-law, and a kitchen area. All supplies were being stored at our house—everything that would be used during the wedding ceremony. Certain things were stored outside our house—hundreds of gallon containers and casseroles filled with water, as well as wood for fires. From our house, the supplies would be distributed to whoever would be using them. You will recall that there were a hundred kilos of flour already being stored at our house.

The entire village had been waiting and watching to see if we were bringing the calf to kill. As everyone saw us coming with the calf, they became very excited, jumping up and down. The men were waiting with machetes and knives to kill the calf. They had decided that if we were delayed another half hour, they would kill another calf, and then replace it with the calf we were bringing home.

The calf was completely exhausted from the journey. So, we knew it would not take a lot of maneuvering to tire it out before killing it, as it would have under normal conditions. The poor calf had already accepted its destiny and was ready to give up. I felt so sad to see it dying of exhaustion, and only God knows what it was thinking about us and the whole situation.

I hated to watch anything being killed, whether it was a cow, a goat, or a chicken—but especially a cow. Because we loved and cherished cows, killing them was almost a contradiction of the love we had for them.

After killing the calf, they started cooking. Three men were appointed to cook just the beef. It was the only time in the village that you would see men cooking and managing the distributions of the beef meat. Because it was a wedding, they had to make sure that the portions were evenly distributed, so they did not run out of meat before the end of the wedding. Due to their natural generosity, women were considered less effective in the distribution of the meat.

Now that my cousins and I were home, I was tired but free from other responsibilities for the rest of the wedding day. So, we stayed there, watching and enjoying everything that was happening. Everyone in my closest family was there, and they were arriving from different places. Some of them were relatives I hadn't seen in many years, and some of them I was meeting for the first time. So many things combined to bring me inexplicable joy that day—being surrounded by all the family members I had missed so much, and being introduced to others I'd never met before.

In our tradition, as you know, when a woman marries, she leaves her village and joins the village of her husband. Since my mother had left her village to marry my father, she had been separated from her relatives. Some of the uncles and cousins on my mother's side who were invited to the wedding were relatives I'd be meeting for the first time. It was a real family gathering, which warmed the hearts of everyone in my family. But, it was just the beginning of our joy.

There were two categories of people in attendance at the wedding—the residents of the village and the guests. All of them had to be there on time. Around four o'clock in the afternoon, guests from the surrounding villages began arriving. Progressively, the women in our village were cooking and feeding them as they arrived.

Among the guests were guests of our side of the family, including friends and relatives who didn't live with us in the village. There were also special guests of all—those who were coming with the bride. Our culture dictated that they were to be the last ones arriving in the village, and fed in a special way that surpassed what all the other guests were receiving. This was because they were bringing a special gift that we were all curious to see, and so we had to treat them very well.

It was the custom that guests must be served first, and then the residents of the village. When the special guests arrived, we were all going to focus on accommodating them, and making sure they had the comfort they deserved during the wedding. Certain men and women were appointed to be in charge of knowing how many guests had arrived, which houses in the village they were staying in, what they wanted to eat, when they were ready to be served, who was cooking for them, and who was serving the food to them. These people had such amazing organizational skills, they held the whole process together, and kept it going easily.

According to our culture, some people were not allowed to share food or eat together. For instance, kids could not eat with adults. Women could not eat alongside men, or share the same plates. Uncles on the maternal side of the family could not share food with their nephews. Even between groups of people who could technically sit and eat together, whether or not they were allowed to share food was determined by their level of family relationship.

There were so many crossed relationship lines preventing the sharing of food—and beds—it made the whole process of hosting wedding guests very complicated to manage. In light of that, you would think that these men and women in charge of the guests had written plans for moving the wedding ceremony forward, but they did it off the top of their heads, and everything went perfectly.

~ THIRTEEN ~

The bride—along with the group of special guests accompanying her—was expected to arrive around six o'clock in the evening. All the guests of my family, and the residents of the village, had finished eating. Now, the only thing that remained was to welcome the bride and the special guests as they arrived. They were not all coming from the same village, or even from the same direction. They were meeting in a central spot, and then coming as a group.

At five o'clock, we started to see their group progressively forming at the top of the hill overlooking our village. The first ones to arrive at the meeting place sat waiting for the others. We were filled with curiosity. We couldn't wait to see them walking into the village so we could welcome them. Around six o'clock, the group had grown significantly, and at last they were ready. They began to come down the hill and march into the village toward our house.

As we watched them coming down the hill, the joy I had anticipated for so many years filled my heart. It was no longer a dream but a reality that engaged not only me, but the entire village. For everyone in the village, laughter and tenderness were the expressions of the moment. Never before had I seen my family capture the attention of the whole village.

As the bride and her guests approached, the entire village mobilized to welcome them. We all wanted to show them our love and gratitude for their faithfulness in fulfilling the promise they made.

They kept coming downhill towards our houses, moving very slowly. It was the tradition. We were all lined up in a huge group, made up mostly of young individuals. We had drums and tambourines, and we were ready to sing for them. When they got within a hundred feet of us or so, we started singing a song in Swahili that was commonly sung at weddings, *"Ninheri kuona wandugu njiyani pakwenda mbiguni..."* Translated, "It is a joy to see brothers and sisters in the journey to Heaven."

When they were within fifty feet of us, they started singing a different song. At twenty feet, we stopped singing our song, caught up with them, and together, we all joyfully sang, ending the song at the same time.

One person on our side raised his voice and welcomed them. Afterwards, we all shouted, clapping our hands, and beating our drums and tambourines. After our official welcome, we went to them, and collected their bags and traditional walking sticks. Men and women could not stay in the same house. We prepared two houses that were close together to make communication between the men and the women easier. As we walked them to the houses that were prepared for them, we walked around them and continued singing.

We were all curious to see the bride, but we couldn't even see her feet. She was surrounded by the rest of the group, hiding in the middle. She and the two girls beside her were completely covered by a wide fabric piece that was draped over their heads, and hung down to their waists. The three of them walked along with their heads bowed, unable to see anything but the footsteps of the women ahead of them, which they followed.

The head coverings were meant to express that a special gift would be unwrapped the next day and presented to all of us publicly. I felt that this traditional concept reflected something special and I loved it. I have been told that, over time, this tradition has changed.

As we began to get our special guests settled, it was growing dark outside and then it started raining. This was believed to be a sign of blessings, especially at the time of a wedding ceremony. It was as if Heaven had just confirmed with the entire community the extraordinary happiness and blessings that would result from true love, and the union of the new couple.

The entire village was busy preparing food for them. Darkness crept into the village. As we had no electricity in the village, we had to use petroleum lamps for light. Normally, we built wood fires, but on this special occasion, with so many activities happening that night, and so many people walking around with their arms filled with supplies, they needed lamps to light their way. Still, many others had to find their way without lamps, because we did not have enough for everyone.

It was fascinating to watch from a distance, as people with lamps moved around the village in complete darkness. They looked like stars falling from the sky, circling and criss-crossing each other on their way down. There were also people from neighboring villages, coming to participate in the night's celebration, and we could see their lamps swinging, as they came down from the hills surrounding our village. These were very unusual sights for us, and very exciting.

It took us approximately three hours from the time the guests arrived to prepare the food and serve everyone. There were approximately eighty people, not counting babies.

After everyone finished eating, it was time to go to the night-time church service. The drum sounded, signaling that it was time to prepare to go. The second sounding of the drum meant it was time to start heading down to church. The third sound meant that the service was beginning. Many people were already in the church, but others kept coming. Once again, the bride's guests would be the last to enter the church.

Because the bride and groom traditionally do not see each other the night before the wedding, the bride, herself, would not attend the night services—only the groom.

The church service included a special welcome to the guests, and joyful singing. The sermon focused on the biblical meaning of a wedding here in the world, compared to the second coming of Jesus, where he is going to be the bridegroom and the church his bride. The preacher talked about the differences in the earthly and heavenly celebrations, and described how in Heaven, there would be shouting and singing, with all possible musical instruments, in the presence of the angels, twenty-four elders, and four creatures singing, "Holy, holy is the one that sits on the throne…"

That climate of enthusiasm reigned in the church service of that night, and would continue through the night and the next day. The church service lasted for three hours, and by the time we got out, it was midnight, and yet the party was just getting started.

The following ceremonies were most traditional, and all the young people in the surrounding villages came to take part in them. Even if some people were not officially invited, they came to participate in the nighttime party, enjoying the time of singing and celebration, and then leaving very early in the morning. We all knew each other, anyway, and we loved to see as many people as possible come join us for this celebration of happiness.

The nighttime celebration was most spectacular, and no one wanted to miss it. Of course, anyone who was tired could go to bed—especially the bride and her guests, some of whom had traveled long distances. There were people in charge of making sure that all the guests found decent places to sleep throughout the village. They were placed in one house initially, but the house had only two bedrooms. The better places to sleep were reserved for the men in the village. The women and children all slept in the one small house we had prepared for them. It was amazing to see the way they all fit in there on mats on the ground—approximately forty-five adults and a few children!

As for the bride (and a few others) she found a beautiful bed, and rested peacefully.

Everyone who was tired went to bed. Then, throughout the rest of the night, the wedding celebration progressed in three places, lasting until five or six o'clock in the morning. In my father's house were women, including my mother, my grandmother, all my aunts on both sides, and several adult women from the villages.

Sitting on the mats in the living room, they made butter from the milk with calabashes. The milk had been conserved, and kept in huge quantities specifically for this event. Some of the milk was kept for the wedding tradition that involved turning the milk into butter. And the rest of the milk was set aside for drinking by the many wedding guests. Because we lived in a mild climate, and we did not treat our milk with any chemicals, milk could be left sitting for a week and never spoil. Instead, the milk became concentrated, like butter.

Milk was turned into butter by a process of shaking the milk in the calabashes until it produced butter. The milk that didn't turn to butter became watery, and that was filtered out, until all that remained was the butter. Although the process of turning milk into butter was a wedding tradition, the butter wasn't actually consumed during the wedding celebrations. It was set aside for later use. It was a symbolic act, meant to wish the new family an abundance of cows and milk.

The women kept singing while they were shaking the milk. The blending of their melody with the sound of the shaken calabashes produced an incredible musical rhythm that stroked our emotions. People very much enjoyed watching this celebration.

Many of the songs praised God for his protection during the time of raising my brother. Shoshi was born in a difficult time of war, a time before my birth. (I was born five years later, and in between, another boy was born, who died suddenly. My mother never told me the cause of his death. There were also many of our family members lost one Sunday when a church where they were praying was burned down by rebels.)

During those war times, there was not enough food or milk for kids, so my brother suffered from malnutrition. Later on, my mother went without food and tried to find whatever she could to feed my brother and keep him alive. My mother suffered so much at that time, people suggested that maybe she should just let my brother die. Eventually, they moved from that particular place to another location where they found people who helped by sharing their food and milk.

As the women sang and shook the calabashes, my mother and grandmother were remembering those times. If my mother had given up on my brother's life, this joyous time of his wedding would never have come to pass. She was resilient, and determined to hold on until the time of deliverance finally came.

As the women sang and expressed their gratitude towards God, some cried and others laughed. But, everyone knew very well that, without the protection of God, it would have been impossible to raise my brother up to that point.

This celebration had started late—around two o'clock in the morning—because the women were busy wrapping up the activities of that night. Knowing they would be tired the next day, they were preparing in advance some things they would need early in the morning. It had been almost two days since they started working hard, but happiness had fueled their energy and kept them going. I could see that they were going stronger every minute, and there was no doubt in my mind that they would keep on going up to the conclusion of the wedding.

Another celebration was taking place in the area surrounding our house, where the bride and the other female guests were housed. This celebration was for the younger generation. I was among many boys and girls that had gathered there right after the church service, with drums and tambourines. We were singing, dancing, and playing for the bride, as a way of welcoming her. It was spectacular to see all of us boys and girls singing in a group. The bride's female guests who were not already sleeping watched us through windows.

The third celebration was taking place in my uncle's house, where some of the adult men had gathered, and were drinking alcohol called "akanyanga" and "umumera." The majority of the people in the village were Christians and very conservative, and therefore believed that drinking alcohol is a sin and should not be allowed in a Christian wedding ceremony. There were others who were not Christians, and did drink alcohol, as well as Christians who drank where the church elders could not see them, because they did not fully adhere to the belief that they needed to abstain from alcohol.

So, my uncle, who was not saved (in the Christian sense of that word), was joined by the group that believed in the old way of celebrating a wedding—by drinking and dancing the traditional dance, while reciting poetry and praise about the historical and victorious moments of their lives.

This celebration was very interesting in its way, especially the dance and poetry aspects of it. There was a storytelling competition among the men, and it was amazing to hear them speaking, word by word, continuously for an hour. Some men were able to use such poetic language to brag about their accomplishments during a difficult time. Here, we learned how they fought with lions and tigers, and conquered and survived many other enemies. It was interesting to see how the women's celebration mostly involved praising God, while the men focused on their power, and their ability to protect their families and livestock in a time of war.

Having all these festivities going on at one time was challenging for us young people. We wanted to be everywhere at the same time, and kept switching from one celebration to another. I, personally, did not want to miss any of these events. The young people's gathering outside the bride's place had finally ceased around four o'clock in the morning. At that time, we merged into the other two celebrations, which continued going strong, and became even more interesting, as the night finally gave way to morning.

~ FOURTEEN ~

By six o'clock in the morning, we were all exhausted, and most of us had lost our voices due to singing all night long. We finally went to bed, knowing we would get a maximum of two hours sleep before starting the morning activities. There was much to do before the wedding, which would take place at one o'clock in the afternoon. When we woke up a couple of hours later, we immediately had to start getting ready to feed the guests. The bride's guests would be fed first and everyone else thereafter.

When my sister and aunts woke up, they were completely exhausted, and had lost their voices. They could barely speak.

We ate a meal of beef and fufu, and started getting ready for the church service. This was the greatest and most crucial moment of all the wedding. We were curious and excited to see the bride and groom revealed to us. As everyone began heading down to the church in their wedding clothes, the sounds of the drumbeat matched our footsteps on the ground.

Tradition called for the guests of my family, a few women from the bride's side, and all grown men to proceed into the church and begin the service. My brother was still dressing, and preparing to meet his bride at the home where she was staying and walk her to the church service.

He was going to be meeting his bride for the first time and, for many people, that was frightening. You see, in my culture, boys who are not yet of marrying age live their lives completely protected from the sight of a woman's body. Unlike women in

America, the females in our village dressed with great modesty, taking care to cover themselves from head to toe. So, a young man preparing to meet his bride would be thinking of their wedding intimacies, and be filled with overwhelming emotions.

Many grooms became terribly nervous—and I had even seen young men in a similar situation collapse in front of people. So, since the beginning of the wedding festivities, my brother's team of best friends and advisors had stayed by his side, to provide comfort and ensure that he was not nervous over the whole situation.

When Shoshi was ready, he came out of his house looking like a brand new person. He was a changed man—more elegant and handsome than ever before. I had been waiting with a group of my friends and other kids to see my brother coming out. I missed him because I hadn't seen him at all since the wedding festivities started. I was anxious to see him dressed up.

As my brother walked towards the house that the bride was in, we all walked around him, watching him as if he were someone we had never seen before. When we got to the house where the bride had been staying, we all stood quietly in front of the house, waiting for the bride to come out and meet her groom. All of our eyes were focused on the door that was open in front of us. There was complete silence. All we could hear was the occasional cough among ourselves or coming from inside the house.

The bride group was nearly finished dressing the bride. There was a photographer with a tiny camera, and he was attracting our attention as he took pictures. All of us kids were watching with great amazement. For many, it was our first time seeing that technology.

Finally, one by one, the whole group of girls and young women started coming out of the house. They were all beautifully dressed in the traditional outfit. They exited slowly, until there was only the bride and her maid of honor left in the house. It was traditional for the bride to delay her appearance a little bit. This stirred the anticipation of those of us waiting outside her house, as well as those inside the church who were waiting for the bride and groom to come walking in.

For another ten minutes, the rest of the group stood with our eyes focused on the door, waiting for the bride to emerge. We had heard about her, and people said that she was beautiful. The silence seemed to stretch on forever, as we waited and exchanged glances with each other. We did not speak, but there were low whisperings among the group. We were all familiar with our customs, and we knew that this was exactly the way it was supposed to be.

At last, she came out. My brother and his best man advanced toward her. Then, my brother took her hand and he crossed their fingers.

Finally, the silence was broken into songs and loud shouts, and the whole group immediately started singing. Together, we all walked down to the church, singing. As we walked down towards the church, we couldn't take our eyes off the bride and groom. They looked elegant and lovely, and the enthusiasm that arose from the music made the whole situation spectacular.

As always, my brother was calmly observing. I could not tell if he was nervous or not because he is not an emotional person. He is a brave and smart guy, and was known for his good conduct in the village. People liked him a lot.

Seeing this entire ceremonial event for my family, I almost burst from the joy in my heart. The sensational feeling I experienced all that day was beyond anything I could have anticipated.

As the bride and groom made their way towards the church, we continued to serenade them with song after song and loud shouts of joy. They frequently stopped and listened to us, as they walked slowly along. I had participated in wedding ceremonies before but this one was unique. It was easily the most moving scene I had ever experienced—perhaps because it was my own brother.

The church service had already been underway for an hour or so, with the congregation singing as they awaited the bride and groom. When we arrived at the front door of the church, the whole congregation stood up and joined us in the song that we were singing. After the singing, the preacher spoke. Then, the bride and groom took their vows. Afterwards, the family stood and made speeches, thanking God for his goodness and mighty protection.

It was their cultural obligation to say something to express their happiness and emotions.

As I sat there listening to all kinds of stories of my family—some of which were very sad—I was uncomfortable and filled with all kinds of emotions. I had the nervousness that comes from hearing family members speak in public. I was on edge, worried that they might not be able to speak well, and afraid that people might mock them.

My father was the first one to speak. I had heard him speak in public before, so I had no concerns. I knew that he was well spoken and eloquent. Both he and my mother would be talking about many of the same issues that the women sang about during their pre-wedding celebration.

My father talked about my brother's birth during the time of war in the 1960s, when there was no food, all the livestock were taken by the rebel movement, and my brother suffered from malnutrition because of the lack of milk—the primary food for kids. When Shoshi got sores all over his body, my father had prayed that my brother would be able to grow up healthy and get married. He now thanked God, saying it was God's grace that allowed my brother to survive.

When my father had finished his speech, my mother got up. She was crying as she began speaking. The story of my brother was very close to her heart. She was the one who paid the price of raising him. In our culture, men were not as involved as women in the raising of the kids.

As she spoke, I had trouble containing myself. As I've said already, men were not supposed to cry, and it was considered shameful and wicked for a man to be emotional. I tried as hard as I could to hold back my emotions in public, but it was difficult not to cry as I listened to my mother saying how hard it was for her to raise my brother.

She now spoke publicly about the same events the women had mentioned in their ceremony the night before. She detailed the whole situation—talking about how, at one point, some family members were telling her she should just let my brother die, because there was no hope for him to live. She talked about how she kept her faith and prayed to God, looking for any way possible to keep Shoshi alive. She concluded her speech by thanking God, who had protected my brother, and led him to the point where his marriage had caused thousands of people from around the villages to come together. Her conclusion made almost all my family members cry.

Following my mother's speech were speeches given by my grandmother, my aunts, uncles, and cousins. At the end of the three-hour service, there was an announcement instructing us to allow the bride and groom to leave the church before everyone else. We all stood in the church and waited for the bride and groom to depart. As they exited, everyone followed them, singing and shouting.

After we exited the church, some of the guests began making their way home. It was getting late, and they had to walk for a long distance to get to their villages. The bride's guests had to accompany the bride until she entered my father's house. As we got to the front of our house, there was a man standing in front of the door, refusing to let the bride inside the door.

Before the bride could enter the home of her father-in-law, there was a custom that had to be observed. My father had to promise to give a cow to the bride's family whenever one of his daughters was married. He had to choose a daughter—one of my sisters—and say, "If this girl is married, one of the dowry cows will be given to the bride's family."

My father showed them Nyamberwa, my youngest sister (born after my younger brother, Sabuwera Patrick), but the bride's family wanted the gift of the cow to be based upon the wedding of the older of my two unmarried younger sisters—Nyarukundo. That way, they would be receiving the cow sooner. A discussion followed, lasting for about twenty minutes. They finally agreed upon Nyarukundo. It was amazing to see the way that all these details were respected in our culture.

Once the discussion was concluded, the maid of honor immediately separated my brother from his bride. Up until that moment, they were still holding hands. She covered the bride with a lace garment, and walked her into our house to an area called "mumbere." This was a place in the corner of our house that was hidden and darkened, with a small window. Up until this point, it had been used as a storage area. Now it was designated specifically for the bride, so she would have a private space during the process of getting familiar with her new family. She would stay in that space for two weeks.

As the bride and the maid of honor entered, they were followed by the rest of the women and girls in the group. Everybody was soberly crying. During the service, the bride had been softly crying, but now she was sobbing more loudly. Hundreds of people were standing outside—guests of my family, all the men from the bride's side, and residents of the village. People who knew each other were greeting each other and talking. They were discussing the news of the day, but over their conversation, you could hear the cries of the bride and all of her female guests. The sound was loud and heartbreaking.

All of the pre-wedding celebrations were filled with music and laughter. But, the wedding day, itself, was a very sad occasion for many in the bride group, as they prepared to leave the bride alone in a strange new village, with her new husband and family. The bride group was now experiencing the same emotions my family experienced when Nyanoro got married and we had to say goodbye to her.

Typically, those in the bride group—saddened over being separated from the bride—were the only ones crying. But, many women in my family were crying, too, because they could relate to the situation. They, too, had experienced the same adjustment, and they personally knew how it felt. As we were standing outside, I saw Nyanoro and a few of my cousins with tears in their eyes. Then, I looked around and noticed that my mother and my aunts were empathizing with the bride, and also beginning to cry.

From outside, we could hear the bride weeping inside the house. She was calling the names of her friends, and asking them how they could leave her alone in that strange environment. She was crying out, asking how she could survive without her friends and family. Her voice strongly resonated among the crowd and saddened us all. Suddenly, the atmosphere in the village had completely shifted. For two days, loud, happy, joyous sounds had filled the air. Now, the pounding rhythm of the drums and tambourines had completely faded, and sorrow prevailed.

~ FIFTEEN ~

Within half an hour or so, I saw a man from the bride group walk into our house and over to the area where the bride and the rest of the females in the group were gathered, weeping and hugging each other. He started telling the women to get out—it was time for them to leave and go home. At the sound of the man's voice, the women's cries intensified throughout the house. They knew that the time had come for them to leave the bride.

As the women clung to each other, crying, the man had to force them out of the house—physically pushing them, one by one, to the front door, until the very last one was out. This man had to be the strongest man, emotionally and physically. He had to stand in the middle of all the distraught women, and separate the bride from her group. Who could possibly undertake such a heartbreaking task?

As the poor young women and girls exited the house, they had completely changed. Their beauty—which had brightened the marriage celebration—had been swallowed by sadness, and their faces and clothes were soaked with tears.

After all the women and girls were out of the house except for the maid of honor, it was time for all the men from the bride group to start going inside, one by one, to say their goodbyes to the bride. Tradition required them to go inside, but some of the men who were not as emotionally strong had difficulty going in, because they were afraid they would fall into the trap of crying.

As the men started coming out, many were choked up and could hardly speak. The whole bride group was out of the house now, except for the maid of honor, who was still inside, trying to take advantage of every minute that she could spend with her best friend. She and the bride were almost inseparable, and they were crying bitterly.

The same man had to do his last hard piece of work, taking the maid of honor away from the bride. When she finally came out, she was wailing, and her face was swollen. Once she had joined the group, it was time for them to leave. They had a long distance to travel—approximately six hours of walking. They were rushing as we accompanied them down the hill.

Once they had gone, it started getting dark, and the whole village slipped into complete silence. All the singing, dancing, shouting, and hallowed voices faded away, and we fell back into the routine of the village. Of course, special moments cannot last forever.

Everyone was exhausted that night. My sister and some of my aunts had lost their voices, and still had laryngitis. As for the bride, she now found herself apart from everything and everyone familiar. She was in our house, along with Nyarukundo, Nyanoro, and cousins who were like sisters to us. They all took care of the bride, and tried to help her adjust to her new life and family. They loved and comforted her, but that first day was still hard.

As for my brother, he was sitting in his new house with me and a few of his friends. As we ate our evening meal, I noticed that he was a new person, even quieter and more timid than usual. He may have been frightened by the next steps he was going to take in his life. He may also have been apprehensive about how he was going to meet with his new bride for the very first time, alone in their house.

The tradition of uniting the bride and groom was very complicated, and had never been easy in my tribe. The process was very different from what it has become since integrating traditions from other cultures. For shy and timid individuals, it could take days before any intimacy relationship between bride and groom was begun. Because of her fears, the bride would often make entering into the intimacy relationship purposely complicated. She might say, "I'm not going to lie down on that bed with you!" Then, the groom might reply, "We have to do this!"

It wasn't uncommon for the bride to delay the first moment of marital intimacy for hours and hours. She might remove each garment of her wedding clothes at an excruciatingly slow pace, hoping to buy herself some time. Their shyness was understandable. Before marrying, every bride and groom lived their entire lives as single people—and, almost without exception, each bride and groom was a virgin. It was hard to suddenly break those routines, and begin to live as husband and wife.

For the most part, the husbands—who generally also felt shy about the marital relationship they would be experiencing for the first time—were patient with their brides. There were even occasions when the in-law family of the bride would see the bride so distressed at the thought of the wedding night, they might say to the groom, "Let her stay with us tonight. She can come to you tomorrow night." In that way, some brides delayed the inevitable—but just for twenty-four hours.

For some, the transition into the marital intimacy relationship required the assistance of other people. Friends of the groom sometimes had to intervene. In those instances, the groom's friends would wait until the morning after an unsuccessful first night together, and then have a talk with the groom.

Unlike other cultures, our village did not use any form of birth control. We depended on God's will and timing in this regard, as in all things.

On the wedding night of my brother, some of his friends, along with other young people, stood outside and listened for what was happening in my brother's house. I paid no attention to what was happening that night. I was exhausted and slept at a friend's house. I did not want to know anything related to my brother's first experience with his bride, so I did not ask my brother for details, but I'm sure he survived.

For two weeks, my sister-in-law stayed in her area, hiding. At night, she would go sleep in my brother's house. Every morning, she would wake up before anybody else, go back into her room in my father's house, and stay there all day. My sisters and my mother could enter her room, and bring her food or anything else she might require. But no males were allowed to go into the bride's area.

My sisters were there with her, teaching her the traditions ("gutsinda"). They taught her names she would need to memorize. Once she memorized them, she could never say them directly. She would have to find synonyms for these names or words. This was a way for the bride to show respect to my father, my mother, my close uncles and aunts, and other adults she would be expected to honor. Familiarizing herself with all these names and words was a very difficult task.

This custom was similar to the American custom of having children put Mr., Miss, or Mrs. in front of the name of one of their teachers or another adult. For instance, my father's name is Makoko. My sister-in-law was not supposed to call him by his name. It would have been disrespectful. In fact, she could not say any word or name that even *sounded* like my father's name. In my language, the chicken is called Inkoko—which sounded like Makoko. So, she called the chicken Intoraguzi, from the vocabulary women created in order to comply with the traditions.

During those two weeks, she was busy practicing this new language. Every night, there was a huge group of young women who came to teach her that language. At the end of those two weeks, my father called her out of her room and told her to go out into the community. From that day forward, she was officially out of hiding, and could start meeting new people. But, she was very shy, and sometimes avoided meeting new people.

Even after the two-week period had ended, my brother and his bride rarely saw each other, except at night. It wasn't like it is here in America, where a husband and wife might find themselves with leisure time and spend it together. In my village, even during leisure time, the men went with the men, and the women stayed with the women.

During the day, my brother was busy with his personal activities, and my sister-in-law spent her time doing chores with my sister. Overall, she spent more time in my father's house than in her house with my brother. It was the tradition, and we were used to it, but it sounds strange now that I am writing about it.

I was amazed by the way she quickly adapted herself to all of these new things. Seeing the way she was crying on the day of her wedding, I was concerned that she would never laugh again, or enjoy anything in our house. I thought she was going to be the most miserable person in the world. But, things had taken a positive turn, and she was laughing, smiling, talking, and getting involved in our family activities. I was excited to see her happy again.

All of us in my family treated her very nicely, because she was ours now. It felt good and natural to see her happy, loving my brother and our entire family. She was a beautiful and hard-working woman, worthy to be the wife of a brother I admired on every level of life.

I was also thrilled for myself. All the female chores I had been doing since my sister's marriage had been lifted from my back. My sister-in-law was now carrying that burden entirely on herself. My pain, hard work, and suffering were over at last.

~ SIXTEEN ~

After my brother's wedding, everything started settling down on my side. I had waited endlessly, and a new life began unfolding. I drew a great sigh of relief. The pressure of my household responsibilities had drifted away.

There were things I had always desperately wished to do, but had never had a chance. Or, if I did them at all, I did them in a hurry, filled with fear that they might completely mess up my tight schedule. That situation was now a thing of the past. Now, I could look back and say, "What days there have been! They were not easy."

Suddenly, everything was available to me, and I had plenty of time to do whatever I wanted. I came to believe I had finally made it to the top of the high mountain that I had been climbing for many years. So many times while I was in the deep valley, exhausted, I would lift up my eyes to the top of the steep mountain, saying, "If only I can get there, I will be happy for the rest of my life."

Hope was never an issue for me during those times of hard work. I felt deep in my soul that I was strong and would overcome. But, in that period of endless waiting, time was my great enemy, and I had to summon unprecedented patience.

I had few responsibilities now, related only to taking care of our livestock. I felt I had the best responsibilities I could have, and was grateful to be doing work meant for boys and men. And, at last, I had time to play with my friends. After being discharged from the domestic work that had held me back for so long, I also had sufficient time for education, and I became fully engaged in my studies, and eager to learn new things.

My brother and I had become best friends, and he became a great resource for me. Even though he was married, he still had to finish his last years of high school. I was able to learn many things from him that even my own teachers didn't know, because they had graduated only from the fourth grade of high school ("deux quatre"). Shoshi was more highly educated than teachers qualified to teach only primary school.

Thanks to Shoshi becoming my mentor at that time, I matured and grew in intellectual insight. Things I learned from my brother helped me to develop cognitively, and were very inspiring. I had changed tremendously at school. When I acquired new and important information, I thought about it deeply, and cherished it. I enjoyed engaging with friends and teachers in concept analysis, and sometimes I even challenged my teachers.

I was growing up—both physically and intellectually—and striving to become a stronger man in the village. In a few years, I could also get married if I wanted to. It was common, culturally, for young boys in the village to get married at earlier ages—starting at fifteen. It all depended on how wealthy the boy's family was, and how desperately the mother needed help in her domestic work. As I've already described, in most cases, women in the village were overwhelmed by their domestic chores.

Around this time, my brother was going into the city frequently, and started introducing me to a whole new world that existed outside of my village. Wherever I went, visions of that new world resonated in my mind. I began to experience a greater desire to explore the unknown. I kept gaining more understanding of the concept of life outside our villages, and the knowledge I gained made me a smarter boy. I started to compare our life with lifestyles in places I had heard of but never seen.

As Shoshi filled my head and heart with information about how things worked in the city, he was inspiring me to want greater things for my future. I also had many friends who were moving to the city to go to school. Since my village was far away from the cities, the educational system was not as good as it was in the cities. I began to feel like my village, with its limited academic opportunities, could no longer offer what I needed. Things were becoming boring to me, because my pleasure center had expanded to include many options.

My desire to move into the city, where I could benefit from the best education, continued to increase significantly. I had just completed my primary school, and I started bugging my father to let me move into the city. I had heard so much about it, but I'd never been there before, and I was desperately curious to see it. I had never laid eyes on a car or a road, or many of the interesting things I'd heard about.

Even though I had not yet experienced the things the city offered, I believed in their value, and they began to take a more prominent place in my life. There was no way I could stop myself from thinking about them.

When our ancestors searched for an area in which to live, they did so mostly with our livestock in mind. It was thought that connection with the urban areas meant exposure to robbery, corruption, and many other cultural influences too scary for them to embrace. They only looked at the downside of the cities. They did not see that the opportunity to receive the best education was the upside to living in the city. This was very important—crucial, in fact, for future generations.

I wasn't the only one seeking greater educational opportunities. For many years, the younger generation in my tribe had scattered around the cities in the region. Many went to live in faraway places, in completely strange and hostile environments, for the sake of a better education at an earlier age. They were tired of paying the price for their parents' ideology, and risked their lives in order to gain knowledge.

I know many stories regarding the suffering of brave students who left home and had to endure being hosted by other tribes who didn't like them very much. My story is also about the pursuit of education.

It was very hard for me to convince my father that I needed to move in order to pursue a better education. He could not understand where I had gotten the idea that I needed to leave the comfort of home, where I was surrounded by family members, to go wandering in the cities. He wanted me to attend one of the high schools in a nearby village.

He told me, "There is a school near our village, and there is no need at all for you to go further away."

I tried to explain to him that the school he was referring to did not have enough qualified teachers, sufficient books, or other school equipment and resources important for my education.

He seemed to agree with me—but then he came up with a second reason why I should stay closer to home.

He said, "Listen, my son. Your brother has just started his first year of university, and it is going to be too expensive to support both of you in the city. The cost of living is higher. Don't you get this? It is appropriate for you to wait a few more years until your brother is finished with his education. Then you will be free to go."

I tried to explain to him that my brother had his own wealth, and as a married person, his wealth was separate from ours, so he should pay for his own education! My brother was capable of supporting himself.

My father came up with a third reason—the most convincing of all. "If you move into the city where the climate is different, you will be exposed to malaria and other diseases. I could lose you, my son!"

Of course, something could happen to me if I moved to the city! But, I already had cousins there, and the danger did not seem great.

It appeared to me that all these reasons were merely excuses for him to deny my request because of financial concerns. I would not let the subject rest. I pushed harder and harder, showing him how important my education was—not only for me, but for my entire family. I said, "Who knows what the future holds? If I am educated, I have opportunities to help provide for the family."

My father was not being a rude father—not at all. He was just expressing his views based upon his beliefs. It was common for parents in the village to think that way.

There was one thing in my favor during my attempts to convince my father—the fact that a great number of students who had just finished primary school were moving into the cities to pursue their education.

I prayed for my father to understand me. My mother also interceded on my behalf. It was not the first time; she had been my advocate in many instances in my life. Finally, my father approved my request. This meant that he now had to sell a cow to get the money necessary for me to start my new life in the city. This was very hard on him emotionally. He did not want to part with one of his cows.

I would also be receiving a little help from one of my uncles in the city. He was going to let me stay with him to help cut down on my expenses.

~ SEVENTEEN ~

As I was getting ready to leave, I fell into endless waves of thought, and the anxiety that comes with change. It was the greatest adventure I'd ever embarked upon, and I started getting seriously nervous. I was not yet gone, but I was already missing my village.

To suppress the nervousness that kept attacking my mind, I had to find a way to legitimize the decision I had made. So, I intentionally summoned from deep in my mind all bad memories I had of my village. As I got closer to the time when I would shift to an unknown place on the other side of the region, I had to continue to recall bad memories of my village. Otherwise, I would not have been able to bring myself to leave.

I had mixed feelings, with happiness and sadness constantly interchanging in my mind. But more than anything else, fear prevailed in me.

On the one hand, I was sad because I was leaving behind a culture and a lifestyle that had been very important to me. It had formed my personality and shaped that time of my life. I was also frightened because I had already mastered life in the village, but the road ahead of me was unknown. Deep in my soul, I was aware that the new life I was anticipating was likely to be totally different, and probably shocking.

As I looked around at the incontestable beauty of my village, I couldn't help but wonder exactly what I was trying to accomplish by leaving it behind.

On the other hand, I was very inquisitive about everything in the city, the new world that was set before me to explore, and all the experiences awaiting me. I thought about all the interesting things that existed out there—things I had heard about but never seen.

The awareness that the education in the city was greater than anything surrounding me gave me the courage to press on, hoping that life would treat me well when I got where I was going. I tried to stay focused on the good education awaiting me. This was my way of continuing to suppress the fear and guilt that was constantly coming at me, and causing me to ask myself, "What if things go wrong?"

I decided upon a strategy—reminding myself of all the positive aspects of moving into the city, and all the negative things I had encountered in my village. Whenever I tried to balance the benefits of the new place against the pain of leaving my village, I came to the conclusion that the upside of moving was greater than the upside of staying. I became willing to face anything that might come my way, and I made a commitment to do whatever I needed to do to make my mission possible.

The negative memory of my village that came to mind most often was crucial to my decision. It was an event that was hard to comprehend, even to this day. This incident confused me greatly, and was very disturbing. It is hard for me to believe that these occurrences still exist in my tribe. In many ways, they have destroyed the fundamental basis of our culture.

I am deeply saddened that the devil found a way to confuse my tribe. Many people are living in that captivity, and there is little hope of turning back to the roots that made our society great.

Talking about my tribe, the Banyamulenge—which I love very much—and trying to describe the main characteristics of my people in a sentence, I would say, "It is a brave community with an incredible history of sustaining itself with powerful mutual support, which is the fundamental basis of the decency ("ubupfura") of its people; and love of one another is the culture that ties them all together."

There are many historical facts that substantiate this characterization of my people. My tribe has undergone a great deal of suffering through the Great Lakes region of central Africa, and elsewhere in the world. There are many factors that have contributed to the suffering. The ones that are external they have no control over, but others have been generated by themselves due to the inability to manage their internal conflict. This has played a big role in destroying trust and brotherly love.

These days, things have changed back home. What used to be the core values of the Banyamulenge as a community are now considered old-fashioned, and have been replaced by a new culture with which people are struggling to cope. Allow me to describe one important aspect of our culture with which our community struggled for many years, and which contributed greatly to the internal conflict in the Banyamulenge. But, first, a little background.

When my tribe was introduced to Christianity, it was done differently than in other communities around the world. The salvation from God, brought into the world through Jesus Christ, and translated into the gospel or good news, was spread into all corners of the world—first by the apostles, and thereafter by missionaries who went into different communities, preaching about the good news. But, we lived in an area that was not accessible by the roads; the place was completely isolated from the cities where the first missionaries landed in Africa.

My tribe had heard about the gospel, and some members of the community decided to go into the surrounding cities to get more information. They got saved and baptized first, and then came back home with salvation in their hands—the Holy Bible. It was a message they couldn't read or understand, but they brought it home anyway, with the faith that they would one day be able to read it.

I came to learn from my parents that, in the 1960s, there was a great revival that swept through the whole Mulenge area in a miraculous way. A huge number of the Banyamulenge became Christians. This became an historical event, and it was common to hear someone say of a tribe member, "Igihe chu bubyutse" ("He was born in the time of Revival"). (Certain events, such as births, were not recorded by date, but by what was happening in the community at the time.)

The Revival continued for decades. People prayed day and night, and many signs and wonders occurred around the villages of Mulenge. Various illnesses were healed. Many people who had never gone to school, were completely illiterate, and could not read, suddenly started having dreams of being able to read. As they woke up in the morning, they discovered they were able to read the Bible. People were speaking in tongues, and I was told that the grandfather of one of my friends actually flew from one hill to another while he was full of the Holy Spirit. Many more miraculous stories were told.

My village was known for having prophets. I have heard them, myself, foretelling events that were about to come. Thereafter, things happened exactly the way they predicted. I also personally witnessed people writing spiritual scriptures that were totally unreadable, but which were interpreted by people full of the Holy Spirit. I saw people who were possessed by demons find release and healing when they were prayed over.

I believed that the spiritual gifts in the Banyamulenge community were rarely seen in other communities. I can name many more miraculous signs that left our village with no doubt of the existence of God through the Holy Spirit. It was from that well of salvation that I drew my first faith in Jesus Christ. Although, I confess, it fluctuated over the years, it has never left my soul. Since I was a little kid, I believed in God, through Jesus Christ, in an amazing way. I still do. I have seen His mighty hand on many occasions.

I began to pray at an early age, and developed a personal relationship with God that became very intimate. On many occasions, my friends and I spent several days and nights far from the village, in the deep forest, fasting and praying. We had no fear whatsoever; we were happy, praying and singing, and the joy of the presence of the Holy Spirit filled our hearts. I had dreams of things to come, and they happened exactly the way I foresaw them in my dreams.

I wasn't the only one. Signs and wonders were manifested all over the villages of Mulenge. In fact, so many spiritual gifts were given to men and women in the villages, I came to strongly believe that it was the time of the second coming of Jesus. The scriptures of the prophet Joel, in verse 2:28, read, "In the last days I will pour out my spirit on all people. Your sons and daughters will prophesy, your old men will dream dreams, your young men will see visions." This environment abounded in the villages.

We all grew deeper in spirit, and the love of one another was the greatest gift of all. People spent a great deal of time in prayers and worship. Our villages were harmonized by the fear of the Lord, which comes from God's word, and the obedience of his commandments. Christianity emerged throughout our culture, was embraced, and became a perfect fit.

One of the heavenly gifts that manifested among our tribe was the gift of discernment—specifically the discernment to recognize which individuals in the villages were witches. The problem was that there was no way to verify whether or not someone truly had the gift of discernment. They might say that a certain person was a witch, but, in most cases, there was no way to prove whether or not it was true.

Witches were believed to be evil individuals, who, because of their jealous and hateful hearts, constantly looked for opportunities to cause disastrous events. These included terrible sicknesses for human beings and cattle, and even death.

Witches lived a secret life that was invisible to the rest of people in the villages, and it was impossible to tell who they were among the community. They lived in a completely hidden world, and operated in mysterious dark places unknown by the rest of individuals in the villages. They were invisible enemies—and this scared many people. The only time they appeared was through catastrophic events. The only way of fighting against them was by praying for God's protection, constantly asking to be covered by the blood of Jesus.

Because those who supposedly had the gift of discernment would point out people in the villages and call them witches, I was seriously frightened of people from the other tribes around the area, especially when I was a kid. Many of us believed that the witches were constantly causing thunder and lightening to strike the villages, killing people and cattle.

Any event or occurrence with unclear origins was thought to be caused by witches. It was a little bit controversial because, on the one hand, we believed in a powerful God that was watching over us, and yet we were still terrified by the thought that there were witches around us.

When self-proclaimed prophets in the villages claimed that they had received this special gift from God that allowed them to know all the witches in the vicinity, people started suspecting each other and finger pointing. Some people believed in what the prophets were saying and others didn't, and this brought great mistrust and conflict between people in the churches and the villages.

You will recall that people in the same clan and family lived together in the village, and so the conflict broke out between brothers and sisters, and parents and children. It was a hard situation in the villages. Imagine being told that your aunt or uncle was the one who killed your son or daughter, or caused you to contract a troubling disease that is probably going to kill you!

People were completely paranoid, fearing that their neighbors were responsible for their sufferings and bad luck. Some people were even accused of sacrificing their own kids in exchange for witch power.

The situation was beyond the control of the elders and pastors of the churches who, throughout the years, had always been able to manage conflicts arising in the villages.

~ EIGHTEEN ~

A great migration began to happen. Members of the community started moving into different places where they could find refuge and peace of mind by living alone or with the group of people they really trusted.

This was a chaotic situation, and it was the beginning of a division that took place in my community. Since that time, it has increased significantly. It reminds me of the Bible verse, Luke 11:17, when Jesus said that "Any kingdom divided against itself will be ruined, and a house divided against itself will fall."

This situation destroyed my faith completely for a time. I started doubting my faith and thinking that the testimonies I had heard from people were merely performances. It began to seem to me that they were praying and going to church for show, rather than from faith. Hypocrisy seemed to be their way of conducting themselves, and I felt that they were practicing a hollow religion.

I questioned how the presence of the Holy Spirit could bring confusion and conflict among us, instead of the peace and love for one another that had characterized our villages. At that time, I was innocent and naïve, and could not believe that within our own village, we could find a witch. I could not understand what was making people accuse their own relatives of such evil.

I thought people were paranoid and inventing trouble where there was none. It was not until later that I came to learn that there were some witches in our villages.

Out of my confusion, I became rebellious against what had been my strong belief in God and his son, Jesus Christ. I started praying only in times of trouble and difficulty—actually, I wouldn't even call it praying, but rather talking to myself.

It was in this climate, where everyone was suspicious about the presence of witches, that one of the most horrible experiences of my entire life occurred. This experience was so terrible, it confirmed for me that I'd made the right decision to leave my village, and it helped to ease my guilt.

It happened one particular day when I was not far from home. It had been cold earlier in the morning and I looked up to see a sky that was growing dark. A huge cloud was quickly moving from east to west.

I said to myself, "It is going to rain seriously today."

The cattle were thirsty, and were rushing down the hill to the river. I knew they would drink from the river and then cross over to the far banks, to one of their favorite pastures.

I kept thinking, *I can't let them graze there! If it rains, I will not be able to find a place to run for shelter. I must protect myself against the rain. I should stay close to the house today. I know there is going to be heavy rain, and I don't want to get wet.*

I had gone only a short distance with the cattle when I began to see the sky turning quickly to complete darkness. It was only eight o'clock in the morning but it looked like it was six-thirty at night. I made up my mind to stay near the houses of a neighboring village.

I knew my father would be upset with me if he saw me around there, because I was supposed to take the cows far from the village—but I didn't care. I didn't want to get wet, and I knew the rainfall would be terrible that day. I waited down in the valley for awhile, waiting to see if the weather looked like it would change. As I watched the day unfold, it became clear that nothing was going to change.

There were very few people that day traveling the path that led to the fields where they would usually do their farming. They had already predicted that it was going to rain and didn't bother stepping out of their warm, dry houses. They stayed home, no doubt planning to wait until the rain was over before going outside.

I was the only one out grazing cattle. I asked myself, *What am I doing here, nearly alone?* Seeing that none of the other shepherds had come out began to make me frightened. It looked awfully dark and windy.

As I turned the corner of the small hill that had been shadowing me, I could see off in the distance Ruheshi—the mountain to the east from which the rain always came. The rain was coming! A strange feeling of urgency and agitation overtook me.

"Oh, God, this is serious!" I exclaimed. The sounds of the rain were so loud, and the wind was so violent, trees were falling down all around me. There was no way I could reach my home in time, so I started quickly directing the cows toward the north, where there were houses of other tribes that I could use for shelter if the rain got too bad.

"Mahoro, we-e-e-e" came the strong voice of a man echoing from the top of the hill. His son was watching over goats and sheep down in the valley, and the man was urging him to get out while he could. ("Wee" is a word used to get someone's attention.)

"Boom! Boom!" The strikes of lightning interrupted the man's voice and alerted the whole area. The goats suddenly started screaming loudly, and running through the valley towards home.

I ran as fast as my legs would carry me, up to the hill where the houses were. "Oh, God, help me out!" I was saying, as huge drops of rain hit the ground hard, smashing the dry dust onto the ground.

"Boom!" came another strike of lightning, with a flash that nearly blinded my eyes. I was halfway to the houses.

"Mahoro, weee!" I heard the loud voice of the man again, stressing to his son the importance of getting out of the valley.

I could see Mahoro. He was dragging his feet behind the sheep as he busily tried to direct them. The sheep did not seem to be responding. Sheep never care about getting wet. Goats are always sensitive to rain, and had fled long before.

I ran as fast as I could, but the rain had made it down to the ground. I nearly ran out of breath from running, but thank God, I made it into a house. I was completely soaked and water dripped from all over my body.

Every other minute, I could hear the loud booms of thunder, as the water accumulation on the ground grew faster and faster, up to one foot high.

I had found an old man in the house, and he was kind to me. We did not talk much, but he smiled at me, and kept adding wood to the fire so I could get warm and dry.

"Where did you leave the cattle?" he asked me.

As I opened my mouth to respond, a straight flash of lightning swept through and brightened the whole house, interrupting me. A huge crash of thunder followed with a loud boom. The lightning knocked us to the ground, where we lay, unconscious. When I regained consciousness a few moments later, I was shaking badly. I checked my body to see if I was alright and still had all my organs.

We heard the loud voice of a lady crying. She was saying in the local dialect, "God! God!"

We immediately knew that something was wrong. We rushed out of the house, the old man and I following the sound of the woman's cries. In between houses down in the village, we found a man lying on the ground, dead. He had been killed by the same strike of lightning that had forced the old man and me to the ground. The poor man had apparently been running to protect himself, but did not make it into whatever house he was approaching for shelter.

We were all shocked—but I had known something terrible was going to happen that day. I'd had a terrible feeling right from the beginning of the storm.

The cries of the people in the village echoed throughout the area, and people from neighboring villages began arriving to see what had happened. Soon, the entire village was filled with mourners. A few minutes after everyone arrived, the rain stopped completely, and we started putting everything together for the funeral.

It was customary to bury a person immediately, so we couldn't even wait one day. It was believed that a dead person would start to stink if there was a delay in the burial. We set out to find some wood and make a coffin. It was cold and dark, and the whole ground was draining water deep into the ground where he lay. We had to bury him in the same clothes he was wearing, and they were soaking wet from the rain. We wrapped him in a sheet and, around six-thirty in the evening, the man was put in the ground.

We all wept and wept, but despite our cries, we could not save him. The tragedy had already fallen. I kept praying in my heart, "If heaven is there and warm, may this man find the comfort that he deserves."

We found out later that the man was from a distant village. He had been traveling, but never made it home to see his family. Since we could not locate or identify his family members, no one in the man's family participated in the funeral.

That day in my life was one I will never forget. When I went home that night, I could find no rest.

Suspicions ran rampant, and there were rumors that the lightning that killed the man was brought on by a witch who was jealous because the man was rich. I was scared by the thought that there were witches in the village, and I truly believed they could be terrible and hateful. I could not stop wondering, *Who would do such a thing?*

I thought to myself, *They can take away whoever they want, whenever they want to!*

That tragedy—which was rumored to be caused by a witch— caused me to hate my village more than I ever had before. That day, I decided that, if I could ever find a safe place to live, I would go. It was that experience that enabled me to leave my village to further my education without any guilt.

I now felt better about my departure. I was ready to go.

~ NINETEEN ~

The time had come for me to leave for school. I would be leaving on Thursday.

There was a marketplace on the way into the city, and thousands of people traveled that road, including businessmen and women, as well as other travelers.

I got ready to go. I packed my belongings in a small bag that my brother had given me when he left to go to university.

My parents followed me out of the village. The rest of the family was busy with their daily activities. A few other boys around my same age in the village were traveling with me, and I would meet up with them on the path.

As we walked out of the village, my mother kept reminding me that I had to be careful in everything I would be doing. She trusted me, and I knew it, but she wanted to make sure that I fully understood what to do in my new life. I was becoming a man, but I was still her child, and she worried about how I would survive. She knew it would be easy to get caught up with bad elements in the city and lose all my good values, and she stressed to me the importance of continuing in the good habits and behavior she and my father had taught me.

It was the first time in my life I was leaving my family behind, and going on my own to an unknown place. I would not let myself cry, because I felt that it would have shown a lack of personal confidence. Leaving was something I wanted for myself, and I needed to remain strong.

As we exited between the houses in the village, my mother hugged me tight, and my father handed me the money. I left, pressing forward to meet my friends who were ahead of me. It was not exciting at that time at all. I was choked up as my parents waved goodbye to me. I rushed into the valley, anxious to catch up with my friends and the other passengers. In order to subdue my fears and anxiety, I focused all my attention on where I was heading, and tried not to look back.

I kept my mind fixed on positive thoughts about where I was going, and what my new life would be like. All the excitement that I had before was gone, and my mind was filled with fear and sadness. I was troubled by all kinds of negative thoughts, and questions of "What if…?" But, I had no other choice at that time but to keep going.

When I met my friends along the way, they were joking and laughing loudly, and this reignited my courage and restored my confidence. Once again, I felt good about my decision to leave the village, and I started enjoying the journey. As we went along, we kept meeting other students from nearby villages. Some we knew and others we didn't.

We all shared the journey, traveling for four hours together, until we got to the marketplace. There we found many people who had brought all kinds of merchandise from the city. We bought some sugar canes and bananas to eat, and sat down to rest while we ate. Then we took off again. We had at least seven hours left on our journey through mountains, valleys, and forests.

By this point in our journey, there were twenty or thirty of us, with various destinations. Most of us in the group had never been in the city before, and others had been there one or two times. We all shared in common the fact that we were *villagois*. My cousins and I would be staying together for the entire journey.

My friends started making jokes about people they knew from the village that went into the city for the first time, and the experiences they had there. I was with some good jokers that day, and the jokes were very funny. This made the journey less tiring. Here is one of the anecdotes that made me laugh so hard, I started crying:

"A man went into the city for the first time in his life, and as he was walking in front of a house with a big glass window, he saw his reflection. He was a tall guy, but since he had never looked at himself in the mirror before, he had no idea what he looked like. When he saw himself, he became terribly frightened, thinking that it was his older brother that he left at home, hundreds of miles away. He could not grasp what was going on. He screamed in a loud voice, asking 'What are you doing here, Mushojo?'

"His friend, who was distracted a little bit, turned to see who he was talking to—but, looking around, he saw nobody. He asked, 'Who are you talking to?'

"The tall man replied, 'Don't you see Mushojo?'

"'What do you mean?' asked his friend, confused.

"'Look, look! There he is!' insisted the man, pointing at his own image in the glass.

"That's when his friend realized what was happening. He told the man, 'But that is you!'

"The tall man didn't believe his friend. So his friend said, 'Move your arms and legs around, and you'll see that it is your own reflection you're seeing!'

"When the man started moving his arms and legs, he finally realized that he was watching himself. He felt ridiculous…and his friend couldn't stop laughing."

We were laughing our heads off as we listened to this story, but deep within ourselves, we knew that there were many things in the city that were going to be perplexing to us. We also knew that each of us, individually, would end up with his *own* story to tell.

We reached a huge, dense forest. This was the first time in my life I had to pass through such a deep, cold forest. We walked for two hours, wrapped in warm jackets to protect against the chill. As we exited, I could not believe my eyes. We were standing at the top of a chain of high mountains. Never in my whole life had I seen mountains like this up close. Until that moment, I had seen only hills. These mountains were higher than the highest mountain visible from my village.

On my left and right were an accumulation of green mountains that gradually sloped down to an unlimited view. I couldn't see their ending. They seemed to be touching the sky far from where we stood. Before me was a wide plain covered with fog. Looking above the fog, I could see a blue plain that I could not comprehend. There was a huge city with white houses that appeared to be very tiny as I viewed them from a long distance.

The climate had changed dramatically. It felt to me like it was around 29 degrees Celsius. We all took off our jackets, and sat for awhile on some big rocks, while we absorbed the incredible beauty in front of us. During the dry season in my village, the hottest it could be was about 25 degrees Celsius, and I was not used to that type of climate.

So many questions started arising in my mind as I contemplated the view before me. My first question: "What is this huge, blue plain with tiny black stuff in it?"

One of my friends laughed loudly at me and said, "I am not going to tell you. You have to guess."

I said, "But there is no way I could guess correctly!"

At this time, a huge cloud was moving towards us from the valley, and completely blocking our sight. We had to walk carefully along the rocky mountain as we descended. It was very tiring physically, as if we were climbing down a ladder. From time to time, we lost sight of the valley, then regained it as we progressed down from one mountain to another.

I bombarded my friends with endless questions. I was fascinated by the view, and very inquisitive. I wanted to know what in the world God had put in place. As we approached the next mountain, and the scene came into better focus, I became confused because the huge blue plain I was seeing covered the entire valley. My friend had not yet explained to me what I was looking at.

Finally, he began to speak, saying that the huge city sitting above the enormous blue plain was Bujumbura, the capitol of

Burundi. We were heading to the city of Uvira, but I knew about Bujumbura from geography class in school.

I said, amazed, "Oh, my God! You're kidding me!"

It was incredible to feel like I was already connecting to the international world even though we were only a few kilometers outside of my tiny village. Until then, I had only dreamed of the world beyond our nation.

I asked my friend, "But you still haven't told me—what is that huge, blue plain?"

He said, "It is Lake Tanganyika!"

I looked at him in disbelief. "What?" I said. "Are you telling me that the whole blue plain is full of water?" This surpassed all of my beliefs. What in the world had God created?

We could not yet see the whole city of Uvira, because part of the city was hidden by the mountains we were descending. It was getting to be late in the evening, so we were hurrying. From time to time, we would get a glimpse of a tiny portion of the city. The rest of it was obscured by cloud cover, which cleared as we got closer.

We walked deeper down the mountains, our bodies sweltering from hurrying in the heat. Our clothes were soaked through with sweat. But, nothing could detract from the beauty of the scene before us. The mountains were covered with tiny, squared farms of casaba, mango, bananas, canes, and other vegetation that did not grow in my village. I noticed that I could barely hear what anyone was saying. My ears were clogging up.

I asked my friends, "Are you losing your hearing, too?" I was unfamiliar with the phenomenon of hearing being affected by changes in altitude.

They all said yes. One of the experienced ones told us that it was normal, but he couldn't explain why.

By the time we reached the last stretch of mountain, the clouds had evaporated and we could clearly see the city of Uvira. It was amazing to stand on the mountaintop that overlooked the entire city, and gaze out at the beautiful city. The roofs of most of the houses were white metal, which gave them a uniform appearance. In my village, all the houses were made of organic material, so this was a new sight for me.

I also saw cars whizzing past on the roads below. I had never before seen such a thing, except in pictures. To my eyes, the cars looked like pigs running fast. I was so taken with the whole scene, I was anxious to reach the ground level and get a closer look. From where we were standing on the mountaintop, we estimated that it would take us no more than an hour to reach ground level. In actuality, it took us seven hours.

As we rushed to reach the city below us, the sun sat above us on the mountaintop. I could see the sun sliding to the last mountaintop we had stood upon as we had exited the forest earlier in the day. The sun seemed positioned at the same level as my village, and I wondered if night had begun to fall in my village, too. I looked behind me and thought about the quietness of my village. I missed it already—but I had reached my new world.

I could hear loud music playing everywhere, as well as the voices of people walking along the road, and the sounds of cars, motorcycles, and bicycles. Everyone seemed to be moving so fast, and honking their horns at people around the roads. All around me was the scattering of voices like crickets. Kids in the street selling kerosene were shouting to potential buyers, who shouted back in response when they were interested in buying.

I had been walking all day, I had lost my hearing, and I was exhausted. I was also hot, sweaty, and thirsty like never before. The combination of these things consumed all of my energy.

~ TWENTY ~

The city looked huge to me—bright and shining. In truth, probably only thirty percent of the homes in the city had electricity, but I had just come from a place where we relied only upon fires for light and warmth, so the sight was overwhelming. My clothes spoke of the wood fires of my village, and strangely, now that I was away from my village, I noticed for the first time the smell of smoke on my clothes.

There was a river called Karyamabenge which drained from the higher mountains and deposited into Lake Tanganyika. It was the first one that we crossed as we entered into the city.

We all took a deep bath in the river. First we changed out of our bad-smelling clothes, which we had to wash in the river before we could wear them again. It was refreshing, diving into the water, and I stayed in it for while. I did not want to leave the warm water—which was such a luxury in comparison to the cold-water showers of my village.

After taking a bath, we set off again, heading towards my uncle's house. He didn't know the exact day we would be arriving, but it didn't matter. In my culture, you knew that whenever you showed up, you would be welcome.

Everyone who passed by us could tell that we were coming from the village. We looked different, and were curious about everything happening around us, so it was easy to tell that we were not from around there. Along with our backpacks, we still carried our sticks. I had never walked in my village without a staff in my hand.

In contrast, the people we encountered along the road were all dressed up, and walked elegantly, their hands free. We saw boys and girls walking, talking, laughing together, and holding hands. This was very strange for us because at home, girls and boys would never hold hands and walk together publicly. The young kids who saw us started calling us, "Rwandais, Rwandais!" ("Rwandan, Rwandan.") It was very hateful and rude. It was meant to be insulting.

This sort of taunting wasn't new—and it didn't start the day I landed in the city. I had not experienced this prejudice before, but its roots were historical and political.

When we finally got to my uncle's house, we knocked on the gate. We said, "Hodi!" ("Hello!") and waited until they responded "Karibu!" ("Welcome!") This was our cultural routine before entering someone's gate.

They welcomed us, took our bags and sticks, and gave us the chairs. There were six of us guests that night. My aunt and uncle were home with the two youngest of their five kids—my cousins. This was my first reunion with my cousin, Jules, whose departure from my village long before had caused me such heartache.

There were a total of fourteen people in a house with three bedrooms. On special occasions, it was not uncommon for three people to sleep on one bed. We had learned how to live like a family. When we had little, we shared little. When we had much, we shared much. There is a saying in Kinyamulenge which goes, "Where there is not hatred and division, the skin of a flea can be slept on by two people." In other words, "Where there is love, everything is possible."

Later that night, the rest of my cousins came home. We ate together, and they started asking us for news from the village. It was hot in the house, and we had to sit outside as we finished eating. We talked about everything, and as we talked, I continually drank water.

While I was still living with my family in my village, my uncle had come from the city to visit on several occasions, but I had gone a few years without seeing my cousins. It was especially good to be reunited with Jules. For me, it was an intense and heartwarming reunion. But, he was not alone when he returned home, and his friends who were with him were all well-dressed and clean. I didn't experience a full connection with him, and I got the impression that he was not as excited to see me as I was to see him.

We were now speaking different languages—literally! He had become fluent in Swahili, and I was still speaking Kinyamulenge. He didn't want to go backwards and speak Kinyamulenge. I didn't pay too much attention to the change in him. He was my close friend when we were in the village, so he still had my deep affection and respect. I suspected that his changed attitude came from his reluctance to have his entourage see him relating to me completely.

That night, I went to bed very tired. As I fell asleep, I was looking forward to going out in the morning. The first thing I wanted to see was the lake, and my cousin agreed to take me. After I saw the lake, I would contemplate the whole city.

My village appeared to me in a dream. I was looking after the cows in the field, and telling my friend that I would be leaving the following day for the city. As I lay dreaming, I had no idea that I was already in the city. When I awoke, I couldn't immediately place myself. It took me a few seconds to realize where I was, and when I did, my mind again filled with curiosity. I couldn't wait to wake up and go out.

My cousin was already awake. I told him that it was time to go and see the lake. It was already hot, which I found unusual. In my village, it was always cold in the morning, and then as the day grew, it would get hot.

I wanted to take a shower before we left the house because I had been sweating all night long, but my curiosity got the better of me, and I suggested we go swim in the lake instead. It was the largest body of water I had ever seen, and I couldn't wait to see it up close.

My uncle's house was only five minutes away from the lake. Four of us set off on our adventure together—my cousin, the two friends I had been traveling with, and me. (The others who were traveling with us were older, and stayed behind at the house.) We had to cross a couple of streets to get to the lake. I just wanted to be there, already—and finally, we were there. As we got closer and closer, I could see the whole lake. On the left, the lake touched the shore, with houses dotting the shore to a distance of three kilometers from where we stood.

In the front, I could see Bujumbura City, which looked to be about eighty kilometers away. To the right, I could see the whole coast and the extension of the city that surrounded the lake. That was the only place they had built houses; the rest of the area was comprised of the high chains of mountains that we descended the night before. The city covered the entire expanse between the lake and the high mountains. The distance between the mountains and the lake was about three kilometers wide, and lengthened further than the eye could see.

My cousin dove into the water, and was already swimming at a distance of a hundred meters when he called me to join him. I took off my clothes and walked toward him, feeling as if I were in a dream. I progressively moved deeper toward him, the water rising as high as my chest. I got scared because I had never learned to swim. I started backing up toward the shore. I didn't know that it was deeper that way, too—and I let out an exclamation of amazement.

My cousin laughed, saying to me, "You have no idea how deep it is! It is deeper than you will ever imagine!"

There were hundreds of people at the lake—both males and females. Some were swimming; others were fetching water and washing their clothes. Not far from us, there were fishermen cleaning their nets in the boats where they had been fishing all night long. They had also started a fire and were cooking and eating fufu and fish. There was a lot of activity at the lake; in fact, it seemed as though the activities of the entire city were concentrated there.

I sat in the water, worshipping God's creation as I smoothed the water with my hand, pushed it with my palm, and created waves around me. It was warm and clear, and I could see all the way through to the sand and small rocks, which sat on the lake bottom and felt very smooth as I touched them with my feet. I felt so refreshed in the water. It was a unique and heartfelt feeling that surpassed anything I had ever experienced.

From time to time, I picked up a rock and threw it into the deep water. In my village, we had hundreds of rivers and wells that flowed in every corner of the hills and forest, but this lake was huge by comparison, and beyond anything I had ever imagined. I loved the warmth and movement of it. I felt like I could live at that lake and enjoy it for the rest of my life. I truly thought I had found a place to live forever.

We had been at the lake for about an hour, enjoying every single moment of our time, with no intention of leaving that place any time soon. Suddenly, we saw five young men around our age coming towards us. At first, I did not pay any particular attention to them. They seemed to me to be regular individuals, approaching the lake like anybody else who had come there to do their personal activities.

Before I knew it, they were standing close to us, looking at us with a very disrespectful expression. We were the only ones there from my tribe; the rest were from other tribes that lived in the city—Bafulero, Bavira, Babembe, Bashi, and others. We were outsiders.

Their look caught my attention, and I started asking myself why they were there, and what they were trying to accomplish. I had been taught never to trust city people, but I worried little because there were so many people around us. I assumed that they were there to enjoy the beauty that the lake had to offer, just like everybody else.

After awhile they started yelling at us in Lingala—the official language used in the Congo by the military or by anyone trying to intimidate you. (It was also the mother language of certain tribes in the Congo.) They shouted, "Ba Rwandais bozosala nini awa?" Translated, this meant, "You Rwandans—what are you doing here?"

I immediately started paying particular attention to their movements, and wondering what was going on. I could not grasp the whole situation. Why had they targeted us? Why were they being so rude?

We were all in the water wearing only underwear. These troublemakers were standing on the shore where we had left our clothes and other belongings. As they yelled at us, no one said a word. We all looked at my cousin. Since he was familiar with the area, we figured he would know if what was happening was a normal occurrence in the city. My cousin had been swimming at a distance, but when he saw the strangers and heard what they were shouting at us, he immediately swam back to us. He knew that these guys were going to bully us, and he rushed to help.

After calling us Rwandan, the strangers seized all of our clothing and belongings, leaving us in the water, wearing only our underwear. The adult people around us were just watching. Nobody said a word.

I could not believe what I was seeing. I wanted to defend myself, and I stood up in the water. As I walked towards the shore where they were standing, I began asking them why they were doing this to us.

My cousin called to me, saying, "Please don't go to them! Wait for me!" He knew that I was going to get aggressive and demand that they return our belongings to us. And he knew that if I did that, they were going to beat me badly.

I asked him in my language, "Who are these guys? And, why are they doing this to us? I have never seen such a thing before!"

My cousin was insistent, saying, "Please don't go to them! I am going to talk to them, and try to negotiate with them. I will explain the whole situation to you later."

When my cousin came up with the idea of negotiating with these guys, it really bothered me. I didn't understand why we had to negotiate with them. My mind started spinning with all kinds of thoughts of how we could defend ourselves, and save ourselves from that ridiculous situation with the least possible humiliation.

My first thought was, *I am going to fight these guys, no matter what!* I was used to fighting with kids of my age in my village.

I realized this time was different because normally, we fought with sticks, and that day, we had nothing in our hands. But, that didn't stop me from wanting to defend myself. I didn't see what was to be gained by failing to fight these bullies. After all, how could it get any more humiliating than standing half-naked on the shore, surrounded by hundreds of unknown people who were mocking us?

My cousin had warned us to stay quiet and leave the situation in his hands. So, I did as he asked. My friends and I watched him as he started to negotiate with the bullies.

Finally, my cousin came down to us and whispered, "Listen guys, you have to give these guys some money. I completely understand your frustration and anger, but with all due respect—you have to do this. Otherwise, they will beat us, take all our clothes and money, and leave us to walk back home, half naked!"

I was angry and asked him why we shouldn't be willing to fight with these guys who were, after all, around our age.

My cousin explained, "If we try to fight these guys, we will make the situation worse than it is now. It is not only about these guys. Look around us at the whole group of people. Look at their expressions. Everyone will turn against us and stone us to death. Believe me, I know what I am talking about. I am telling you this from my personal experience. They don't like us here!"

What my cousin was saying made sense to me, because I could see for myself that everyone around us was watching and laughing out loud. The whole scene was entertaining for them, and they seemed to enjoy it. They did not try to stop or punish the bullies. Not only did the adults who were present at that time not try to stop the guys from bullying us, they were stirring them up, and encouraging them to continue their abusive and hateful actions against us. Even the adult women around us did not say a word in our defense!

I was furious with the whole scene, and the conspiracy that was perpetrated against us. It was the most humiliating experience of my life, and impossible for me to process.

My cousin continued, saying, "See? Everyone is against us and we have no choice but to give them what they want. Then we can return home safely. I will explain this more as we get home."

At this point, I asked myself, *Should we just accept the fact that we can't defend ourselves?*

~ TWENTY-ONE ~

What do you do when you are certain that everyone around you hates you? Do you hate yourself, or kill yourself, and give those who are bullying you the utmost satisfaction for their heinous actions? Do you fight vigorously against everyone, knowing you will probably be the first victim of the fight, because you cannot win over thousands of enemies? Or, do you humbly accept defeat, and walk into the humiliation and anger of being incapable of helping yourself?

We trusted my cousin and gave him the money. He gave it to the bullies, who took the money, and threw our clothes onto the sand.

We immediately picked them up, put them on, and began to walk towards home. It was too dangerous to stop and rest. We had barely survived. Our time for enjoyment and exploration of the new world had come to a crashing halt. There was nothing left for us there.

As we began to walk away, the people who were watching kept laughing at us. It made me and my friends feel inferior, and terribly embarrassed and nervous. We were so confused by the whole situation that we could barely talk to each other as we walked home. But, my cousin was just fine, as if nothing had happened. I could not understand his attitude in regard to what we were experiencing.

I didn't ask him at the time, deciding to wait until we got home. My mind was still absorbing the whole situation, and grappling with many questions. I was consumed by anger. I was so disappointed and miserable, and I couldn't stop thinking about why the whole city was against us. I was just getting to know the city, and I had already fallen in love with its beauty. But, now I felt hopeless and discouraged.

When we first set out for the lake, our hearts were full of excitement and our minds were clear. I had thought nothing of crossing two streets to get to the lake. But that now seemed like a lifetime ago, and as we approached those streets on our way home, I was frightened. The whole city had turned against us, and I believed that everywhere we went, we would be treated in the same way. I could not conceive of those hateful bullies being isolated in one particular place.

As we walked up the first street, I was on high alert. But, looking around, I realized that things were as normal as they could be. There were hundreds of people crossing each other, busy with their daily activities. I found the same situation when we reached the second street. I could not believe it.

We finally got home and sat down under a mango tree. My uncle was not home; only my aunt and my younger cousins, who were happily playing with other kids. From time to time, my aunt tried to engage us in conversation, but we were all taken away with our thoughts as we tried to process the incident.

What a curious situation we found ourselves in. Just a short while before, a hundred meters away, we were undergoing the most horrific experience of our lives. Yet, at home, things were as normal as they could be.

We were all embarrassed by the humiliation we had experienced, and did not want to talk about it. I kept thinking how we had failed miserably, and had not even tried to defend ourselves. I began to feel a little bit angry with my cousin for being so protective that he would not let us defend ourselves. I thought he had become a fearful boy. We had been so close when we all lived together in the village, and back then, he was a fighter boy. How could he accept that type of humiliation and embarrassment, admitting defeat without even putting up a fight?

In my village, I had enjoyed fighting to show that I was a tough guy—but everyone in our village was a relative, and whenever we fought, we knew fully well that our lives were not in danger. We were no longer in my village, where we were trained to fight with sticks, and carried them all the time to defend ourselves against whatever might come against us—animals or humans.

At the lake, we were four boys, almost naked, with nothing that could be used as weapons to fight the bullies. There were no bushes around the lake where we could have run and cut sticks to use for fighting. Around the lake there was only sand and rock.

I began to wonder if my cousin might have been right, considering that it was impossible for us four to fight everyone around us. I imagined us trying to fight those guys, and the entire community rising up against us and stoning us to death. I suddenly realized that my cousin had made the right decision—and we had survived. Unfortunately, knowing this did nothing to help cool me down. I was still frustrated.

When my aunt asked us, "What happened at the lake?" we were all quiet. After a long silence, she realized that something had gone terribly wrong. She asked my cousin, "Did you meet some bad boys at the lake?"

He responded quietly, "Yes," and immediately changed the subject. We had been seriously embarrassed and frustrated, and he knew we did not want to talk about it again.

My aunt shook her head with disappointment at the bullies, and said, "You will have to get used to that type of bully in this city. Otherwise, you will never go anywhere. You also have to be careful in choosing where to go."

She was letting me know that, by coming to the city to pursue my education, I had to accept the realities of the city, including the bullies. Had I been unable to accept reality, I might have decided to go home to my village, and that would have been the end of my education. It was also important for me to accept reality, so that I didn't let fear keep me inside the house all the time.

When my aunt spoke, I started understanding my cousin's tolerant attitude, and I thought, *Oh, so this is why my cousin was so relaxed!* He didn't think too hard on the situation because that was just the reality. No one had control over it. No one would ever be able to change it, so they had to live with it.

I got very scared, wondering how I would survive, now that I was staying in the city to study. I knew myself—I hated it whenever anyone tried to disrespect me. I could fight for days to gain the respect of someone who tried to disrespect me. And, what had happened to us was beyond what I knew to be disrespect. It was hateful, rude, and humiliating.

One of my friends among the four of us was a very comical guy. He started making jokes out of the experience. He described in great detail how each of us had reacted when we were under attack.

I did not like to hear my friend making jokes. I had taken the situation very personally, and I was still feeling like we could have made the outcome more favorable by fighting the bullies.

I kept urging him to stop joking—until he mentioned something about one of my friends in our group, who became very frightened when he saw the guys coming to him, and rushed into deeper water, not remembering that he did not know how to swim. Suddenly, he realized he was sinking, and he came back to shore, resigned. He was shaking badly, scared of both the water and the bullies.

I couldn't help but laugh, thinking about how in times of trouble, we don't think correctly.

The jokes my friend was making helped relieve some of the pressure, and I was finally able to relax. It also allowed my cousin to open up to us more, educating us clearly about the experience we had just suffered. He shared with us how he had learned to survive in that city in the four years since he had left our village.

"Listen, guys," my cousin began, "I am going to be honest with you, as brothers and as friends. If there is one thing you need to understand better than anything else regarding what you have experienced today, it is this—you need to know that people here don't like us!"

He was referring to the other tribes in the city. They had no respect whatsoever for anyone from our tribe, regardless of the age or status of the person.

He continued, "You all know very well that we are the minority here in this city. They call us Tutsi, Rwandan. For them, calling someone a Tutsi is the most insulting thing they can say. You will hear people from all ages—kids, as well as grown-ups— calling you Rwandan, everywhere you go. When you go to school, to the marketplace, in the streets, you will be lucky if no one pays attention to how you look or how you are walking. They will be mocking you, and calling you all kind of names. You cannot try to fight with everyone who will be calling you Tutsi or Rwandan in a way that is humiliating. They have found thousands of ways of provoking or mocking us!"

My cousin went on to say, "We all know the history of our tribe. Although our ancestors came from Rwanda a long time ago, and have been here long enough to acquire citizenship, being accepted is still only a dream. We will probably never be accepted by the other tribes here in this city. They will consider us foreigners forever. Nothing we do can change their minds."

My cousin was trying to educate us, and to share with us, to the best of his knowledge, the facts of life about the city that he had learned to live in. After his explanation, I got the picture of the conflict between my tribe—the Banyamulenge—and the rest of the tribes in the city. Up to that point in time, we had known little about the conflict, because we were still too young to understand the whole concept behind the conflict, or the reason things had gotten so far out of control.

In conclusion, he advised us that the only way to survive in the city was to make peace with everyone, and pay little attention to the bullying and contempt from the other tribes. He said, "Please walk away from any confrontational situation and avoid being victims."

He shared how stressful it had initially been for him to make peace with the way our tribe was treated in the city. "Many times," he said, "I was walking with my father around the city when I got bullied by kids of my age. I was completely embarrassed in front of my father. He couldn't say or do anything, either, and the more we tried to correct the situation, the more we ended up worsening it instead."

He continued to explain that he once thought, as all children do, that his father was the most powerful person alive. "I trusted him in every aspect of my life. But, since we moved here, I began to realize that, in certain situations that would arise, he could not save me—or himself! Since then, I have learned to cope with the current situation and make peace with myself and others. This has helped me tremendously in coping with the stress that comes with the bullying that is always done against us. We have no power that we can use to change the whole world around us."

He continued, saying, "This is how I view the situation—and having this perspective has allowed me to make very few mistakes. I am at peace with this reality, without feeling the constant need to fight back. It will do no good, anyway. Nothing is going to change any time soon."

After my cousin educated us, everything became clearer to me, and I started to understand why those guys had treated us that way. But, I still had questions. My first question after he had finished telling us the whole story was, "How do you go around the city? Or, do you stay home all the time?"

He said, "I know this situation is disappointing to you guys, but once you get used to city life, it will be less stressful. That much I know for sure. They mostly target people who are fresh from the villages. They can tell who is new to the city by the way they look, the way they walk, and how they speak Swahili. Once you learn good Swahili, and you know how to dress and walk like a city guy, you will see that the pressure will go down. You will still experience discrimination because of your face, but there is not much you can do to change that."

As he finished this statement, I understood exactly what he meant, and I thought, *Well, if that is the case, then eventually we should be fine. It is only a matter of time.*

He added one more important element. "Make friends from the other tribes. The more you make friends with them, the less likely the bullies will be to bother you, because your friends will protect you."

From that day on, I got the whole concept of integrating myself into the city, and began to conduct myself accordingly.

~ TWENTY-TWO ~

The city was very beautiful. The sun shone all the time. It was hot, sweltering even, but it was beautiful. I was fascinated by places, houses, food—almost everything about the way people lived.

The city had many schools, whereas at home, we had only one school that served about thirty villages. My new school was very different from the previous school that I had known. There were hundreds of students in one school, and in my class, we were fifty.

The students in each class were divided into A and B students; the A's went to school in the morning from 8:00 a.m. until 12:30 p.m., and the B's attended school from 12:30 p.m. until 5:00 p.m. This was done because there were not enough locations for all the students to study in one shift. The class was completely full. We sat three to each wooden bench with a drawer for each student.

All students wore a uniform consisting of blue pants and a white shirt. Everyone's body and uniform were clean all the time. In my village, it had been impossible to shower every day. For one thing, it was just too cold. And secondly, the spring that served as our water source was half an hour away. So, when we needed to clean ourselves or our clothes, we went into the river.

In contrast, the city was very hot—almost 95 degrees Fahrenheit—and people sweated all the time. So, they took as many showers as they needed to in order to cool themselves down. And, whenever we needed to wash our clothes, we could wash them in a plastic bassinet because water was plentiful.

The city was not huge; in fact, compared with the big cities in America, it was small. There was one main road, which was paved. There were smaller, unpaved streets, which ran like arteries off the main road. Those streets had houses on either side. Further down the road was a commercial district with shops and stores.

In the afternoons after school, the road and streets were full of blue-and-white uniformed students, crossing paths with each other. It was easy to tell who was walking home and who was heading to school. All you had to do was watch which ones were rushing so as not to be late, and which ones were taking their time.

Just as I had noticed upon first entering the city, I routinely saw girls and boys walking together, chatting, laughing, and holding hands—behaviors you would never see in my village. Car horns blared loudly, as drivers tried to avoid running down students. Music played at a high volume along the streets. The city was alive with a myriad of activities and sounds happening simultaneously, many of which were foreign to my experience.

The city of Uvira was situated on the coast of Lake Tanganyika. The lake connected Uvira with Burundi, Tanzania, and Zambia. Uvira was a big port with plenty of maritime traffic. This strategic placement made the city fertile for business activities. There were only a few functional public sectors, like schools, the courthouse, and the city offices. Most people were involved in private enterprise.

It is safe to say that the majority of the citizens were small-business owners and entrepreneurs, many of whom had emerged from the informal sector, and become bigger business individuals in the city. Many had started at a very low scale of business, selling goods, sweets, or sugar, and then growing to become larger corporations, importing goods from China, Hong Kong, and Dubai.

One of my father's friends, whom I'd known since I was a child, used to hand-carry salt from Uvira, and sell it in my village. When I was about ten years old, he moved to the city, got a car, opened a huge store, and began selling tons of salt to Tanzania.

The city was rapidly expanding at the time of my move. There were houses being built every day, everywhere around the area.

There were so many things that intrigued me in the city, and every day, I discovered something new. The lifestyle was totally different than what I had been used to up until that point in time, but I became very good at coping with my new environment, and grew stronger as the days went by.

One thing in particular greatly impacted my thoughts during that time, and it stays with me even after so many years—the need for money. This had never before been an issue for me. When I lived in my village, I only touched money a few times a year—when school opened in September, and from time to time when I had to buy something. Otherwise, I never even thought about money.

Being without money was never bothersome to the people in the village. But, in the city, the need for money was the greatest need of all. The anthem was money, money, money, and it followed us every step of the way. With it, you could get almost everything, and without it, you were poor and miserable, and not given any consideration. This was not the case in my village.

Another element I suddenly had to deal with—which was also related to money—was the need for nice, stylish clothes, or "sape." Every individual in the city was concerned with their appearance. The way they looked when they went out in the street and in all public places was crucial. People struggled to keep the balance between money and sape.

It was strange to be introduced to the city culture, where people adored having nice clothes. Certain people faced a dilemma when they had to choose between eating and having nice clothes to wear so they would look good when they went out in public. Some people believed that, as long as you looked nice, it was of no consequence whether or not you had food at home. What was visible to people was considered most important. Once someone had nice clothes, they adopted a certain way of walking elegantly.

At first, I could not imagine striving to look good all the time, but I had no idea what the future would bring. At the time, I still had the mindset of a villager accustomed to wearing one pair of pants, one shirt, one jacket, and one pair of shoes for months, as long as they were kept clean.

In my village, I never had to worry about what other people might say about me, because nobody was paying particular attention to what people were wearing. I am not saying that it was ridiculous to dress up in the village, but generally speaking, people paid little attention to their wardrobe.

It was different in the city. Above and beyond everything else, people believed in looking sharp. The younger generation especially loved to look good all the time. Looking good was one of the primary tools they used in their dating lives. Girls loved young men who were well dressed, and this inspired everyone to polish their style.

After awhile, I, too, fell into the trap of loving nice clothes, and it became very personal. I loved to dress up, and most of the money I had went towards the purchase of nice clothes. It was not easy to have enough money to look sharp all the time and stay on top of the current style trend. Following the rhythm of constantly changing style trends was all but impossible for someone like me. My desire to acquire the new style was like an endless thirst that could never be quenched.

After a couple of years in the city, I became acclimated. Somehow, I found a way to interact with people, and I made plenty of friends, with no regard to the tribes from which they came. When I first moved to the city, I knew Swahili, but I spoke it with the flavor of my native Kinyamulenge dialect, and so I spoke with an accent. But, after awhile, I spoke very good Swahili without the accent. I also did very well at school.

I would live in the city of Uvira for six of my eight high school years. (High school took eight years for me to complete due to the fact that during some years, teachers stopped teaching because they were not being paid.) During that time, I would visit my village three times a year for vacation. I came to know almost every corner of the city, and as time went by, I came to realize that the city was not as big as it appeared to me when I first moved there.

As I got used to the lifestyle, and learned the do's and don'ts, my life became less stressful. But, I did continue to struggle with the hateful bullying done to my people. This hegemonic discrimination against us from the other tribes was without cause—but it had deep roots in the whole community. This was something I failed to fully understand, no matter how much time went by.

There were people from the tribes of southern Kivu who did not believe we had the same rights as everybody else in the region. Most of them considered us foreigners. In their eyes, this made us inferior and of less value than the rest of the tribes of the region.

Since day one in the city, when I was subjected to the worst public humiliation and bullying of my life, I became very inquisitive about the tribalism issue in our region, and more specifically, about the discrimination against my tribe.

I asked myself, my friends, and adults of my tribe why the discrimination had such deep roots in the community. I had experienced and witnessed so many instances that proved to me beyond a shadow of a doubt that something, somewhere down the line, had gone terribly wrong in this regard, and was going to be very difficult to remedy.

I would see even very small children from other tribes running around an adult from my tribe, insulting them, and calling them all kinds of names. I wondered if these kids were sent by their parents. I figured this was a possibility because, under normal circumstances, kids were obligated to be respectful to anyone older than them. Every time I saw such a thing, I became furious, but there was not much I could do to change the situation.

At night, I would see one particular young boy in my neighborhood repeatedly taking stones, and for no good reason, throwing them over the roof of my uncle's house. He was the son of a soldier who was a neighbor of ours. There was no way of stopping the boy. One day, he even found me, and took away a wonderful leather belt I had bought for myself. Perhaps because his father was in the military, the boy felt he could abuse us with impunity.

This boy was one of many. Some of these young boys were familiar to us by name, and lived right next to us. But, when we went to tell their parents, the parents did nothing to stop them. And, in Uvira, there were no police that we could call to report abusive acts against us.

I had a few very good friends from other tribes. As we got to know each other better, they began to openly share with me prejudices against my tribe they had encountered along the way.

As I grew up, I came to understand that the discrimination against us was based in a political agenda, initiated and orchestrated by a group of regional politicians, motivated by selfishness and political gain. They wanted to make sure that my tribe would never be accepted by the rest of the tribes in the country.

Their politics were successfully promoted and accepted by many throughout the region. People strongly believed that we were not as valuable as the others in the region, and the situation continued to deteriorate over time. There were regional political events that worsened the discrimination against the Banyamulenge and other Tutsis in Eastern Kivu.

I never got the chance to live in other regions of the country to find out how my people might have been viewed in those other locations, but I heard from other people that discrimination against us was less prevalent than it was in Southern Kivu province.

~ TWENTY-THREE ~

Life does not unfold in a straight line, but by a consecutive series of events that affect us negatively or positively. There are mountains and valleys that rise up before us. No matter how we try to resist, most of the time, we are forced to go through the valleys and over the hills—there is no way around it. All we can do is continue to forge ahead in our journey. For, as the saying goes, "Tough times don't last. Tough people do!"

By 1990, I was doing my third year of high school in Uvira, and life in the city was just fine. In the morning, the city's surface was smooth and bright from the column of sun that rose over Lake Tanganyika, and trailed over the distant mountains surrounding Bujumbura.

I had to walk two hours, round-trip, to and from school. I happened to be one of those who constantly walked home from school around noon. This was never easy because by noon, I had to walk beneath a sun so blinding, I could see only that which was right in front of me. There were days when the midday sun was so hot, I thought it would melt my brain.

I wasn't the only one who suffered in the noonday heat. The sun's heat was so severe that few vehicles were on the road at that hour, and people completely avoided walking along the streets. No fresh breezes blew at that time of day, and those who bravely walked along the streets sweated profusely.

As the sun grew stronger and heated the ground, people found refuge, refreshment, and a bit of fresh air under the trees around their houses, and many people could be seen napping there. Others were inside their homes, resting and waiting for the sun to cool down. Then, they would be free to move about the streets, and enjoy the last piece of the day before the sun set on the mountains overlooking the city. This was a typical day in Uvira.

My cousins always made it home an hour or so before me, as my school was further away than theirs. I had a habit of showering immediately when I got home from school. Then I would have my lunch, and join my uncle and cousins, who would already be taking a nap under a huge mango tree around our house. We would be fatigued from walking in the hot sun, and in need of a rest. It was too hot in the house to rest.

As the day grew up, some fresh breezes would start to blow from Lake Tanganyika. This relaxed us and helped us to sleep very well. We also had a radio onsite which belonged to my uncle. I loved listening to a Burundian station which broadcast beautiful music. One of my favorite radio programs was *Disque a la Carte*— "music on demand"—featuring mostly country music, with which I had fallen in love when I got to the city. In the villages where I used to live, only a few people had a radio. The only place I could hear music in public was in the marketplace.

While we enjoyed our afternoon nap, drifting in and out of sleep, we listened to music. In between the music, we would hear an occasional news headline.

On October 1st, 1990 at 2:00 p.m., I arrived home from school, showered, had my lunch, and joined my uncle and cousins beneath the mango tree. I was exhausted from walking home in the blistering afternoon sun. On this particular day, before we all fell asleep, I heard Elton John singing, "You Gotta Love Someone." This was a song I listened to over and over. I could not get enough of it. Every time I heard it, the melody vibrated in my heart.

As I was carried away on the strains of Elton John's exotic song, I suddenly heard a voice interrupt the music with this news headline:

> "A civil war between the Hutu government in
> Rwanda and the Tutsi rebel movement known
> as the R.P.F. has broken out in Rwanda!"

A group of Tutsis were driven out of Rwanda into exile when the first conflict in Rwanda arose in 1959. Now they had risen up to defend themselves when the latent discrimination escalated into the conflict that would historically become known as The Rwandan Genocide. They called themselves the Rwandese Patriotic Front ("R.P.F.").

The broadcaster went on to say that the R.P.F. had attacked from the northern border with Uganda, where they had lived in exile for more than thirty years. They had the support of the Ugandan government, led by President Yoweri Museveni.

When I heard this news of war in Rwanda, I had nothing on my mind beyond my mild annoyance over the interruption of my music. *What a long headline,* I thought to myself. *And why should I care about Rwanda?*

I could not wait for the news break to be over so I could hear the last piece of my song. The music was so serene, and I knew it would lull me back to sleep. I was in that dimension between consciousness and sleep, and craving more music to help ease my journey into a deeper nap. My body was dragging me down into a deep and smooth sleep, and my mind was too lazy to consider the ramifications of what I had just heard.

My uncle had been paying attention to the news from the other side of the mat, where he was enjoying his own hap. I heard him exclaiming in my language, "Yampaye Inka!" This was a traditional expression of surprise.

He made no further comment, and within moments, we had all fallen asleep.

War was breaking out every day around the world, so I didn't give this particular news much thought. How could I have had the faintest awareness that this news marked the beginning of a conflict that would culminate in a terrible genocide in Rwanda, and thereafter spread in a disastrous way throughout the whole region?

There seemed to be a considerable distance between Rwanda and Uvira, and I could not imagine how any conflict happening there would impact me or my friends and family. But, I was totally wrong. The war progressed in Rwanda and became unpredictably severe. This caused a drastic change in our situation as Tutsis, and as Banyamulenge in particular. The entire Great Lakes region of Central Africa—Congo, Rwanda, and Burundi—was forever changed by the conflict.

When the R.P.F. attacked Rwanda, things became seriously frightening for all Tutsis in the region. The Hutus that lived in Rwanda began raising awareness that, "Tutsis are attacking Rwanda, and coming to reestablish the monarchy." So, people became hyper-aware of anyone who was Tutsi. They hated us before. Now, they hated us even more.

Although the R.P.F. had attacked the Hutu government from Uganda (the northern part of Rwanda), Tutsis *everywhere* were targeted. Other non-Tutsi tribes were influenced by the anti-Tutsi propaganda, and believed the Hutu government when they said, "All Tutsis are bad." From the day it first began, this war created an ethnic division among the population in the region.

This is a memoir rather than an historical account of the conflict, but I would like to give my readers some background to help them understand the context of the conflict in which I lived, how it started, and how it shifted over time, causing me to keep moving from one place to another.

In Rwanda and Burundi, there are three tribes—the Tutsi, Hutu, and Abatwa, with Hutu making up the majority, Tutsi making up the minority, and Abatwa or pigmy tribe comprising only a minute percentage of the population. All the tribes speak the same language. In the Congo, on the other hand, there are more than two-hundred-fifty ethnic groups, and they all speak different dialects or languages.

Certain areas of Eastern Congo—particularly northern and southern Kivu—border Rwanda and Burundi. The population there was aware of the long-term conflict between Tutsis and Hutus in Rwanda and Burundi.

When the war broke out, there were two groups fighting. One was the Hutu government in Rwanda; the other group was comprised of Tutsi rebels known as the Rwandese Patriot Front (R.P.F.). For decades, they had been discriminated against and forced to live in exile outside of Rwanda. After so long in exile, they decided to return to Rwanda, and use force against the Hutu regime that had staged a coup and stolen power from the Tutsi monarchy thirty years earlier.

It is believed that, before the separation of Africa in 1885, the various tribes in Eastern Congo lived freely across the borders. This may explain why, when looking at the non-Tutsi tribes that lived in both northern and southern Kivu, you could hardly distinguish them from Hutus of Rwanda and Burundi. This is one of the reasons why these tribes of northern and southern Kivu empathized a lot more with Hutus than Tutsis—because they strongly believed they were somehow related.

On several occasions, I had discussions with my friends from other tribes, and they always told me that Hutus are their brothers. Because they looked so similar, millions of Rwandan Hutus who immigrated to northern Kivu were assimilated into the culture without having an issue with the Congolese people. They were welcomed more than Tutsis.

There has been much confusion as to how Tutsis are differentiated in the Congo. First there is my tribe, the Banyamulenge—Tutsis who originally came from Rwanda, Burundi, and Tanzania hundreds of years ago. They established themselves on the plateau of Mulenge, in Eastern Congo, in southern Kivu. The exact time of their arrival, and cause of their migration, is not well known by scholars. What we do know for sure is that they were in the Congo before 1885, when Africa got separated. They speak Kinyamulenge, which is very similar to Kinyarwanda (spoken in Rwanda) and Kirundi (spoken in Burundi).

The second group is Banyejomba—Tutsis who lived in a place called Jomba in northern Kivu. These Tutsis lived in that area long before Africa got separated. After the separation, they found themselves in a situation where they knew they were Rwandan, but found themselves to be in an area now designated as the Congo. They spoke Kinyarwanda, and with a few differences, their culture was closest to the Rwandan culture.

The third group is the Rwandan Tutsis, who moved into the Congo when the conflict broke out between Hutus and Tutsis—in 1959, 1973, and thereafter. At that time, many fled Rwanda, seeking safe haven in neighboring countries like the Congo, Uganda, Tanzania, and Burundi. There are, of course, Tutsis who never left Rwanda, most of whom were killed in the 1994 genocide.

I will be talking about Tutsis in general, and sometimes the Banyamulenge in particular, as my tribe. The longstanding political propaganda in the Congo has confused people by stating that all Tutsis immigrated to the Congo in 1959. Tutsis have been made to appear as aliens for generations, and this has been the root of the great conflict in the Congo. The Congolese have tried to make believe there was no such thing as Congolese Tutsis.

When the war started in Rwanda, the population in both northern and southern Kivu was more emotionally involved in the conflict than any other tribes in the Congo. As I said, this was due to their deep empathy with the Hutus. They immediately began bullying and harassing Tutsis who lived in the Congo.

From the moment I was first lying under the mango tree, heard the news of the war in Rwanda, and mistakenly dismissed it as everyday news, the media never ceased talking about it. The days that followed darkened and became more intense for all Tutsis living in the Congo.

Among the Congolese population, the discussion of the war in Rwanda became like a sports game, with two teams playing in the stadium, and everyone finding it impossible to be neutral. The spectators divided into two groups—but because of its popularity, one group had the right to loudly cheer its team, while the other team had to watch the game quietly, with its fingers crossed, hoping deep in its heart to see its team winning.

The other tribes in the Congo were shouting, and saying they supported Hutus in Rwanda and the Rwandan government. We, as Tutsis living in the Congo, were afraid to say anything that might compromise our safety. Since the Congolese population fanatically supported Hutus, and hated and discriminated against Tutsis, all we could do as Tutsis in the Congo was remain quiet, and pray hard for safety and survival while the conflict was moving from one place to another.

If the other tribes realized we were Tutsis, and heard us saying that we were supporting the rebels, they would have killed us. Raising our voices would have meant endangering our lives. The Congolese knew that Tutsis who lived in the Congo were innocents, but they persecuted them anyway. It was like the proverb in French: "Qui veut noyer son Chien l'aquise de la rage," which literally means that if someone wants to kill his dog, he will accuse it of being rabid. Any occasion was an opportunity for the other tribes to afflict Tutsis.

Sadly, even now, as I am writing this memoir, the situation hasn't changed.

A few weeks after the attack of the R.P.F. movement, we heard that the Congolese government was among the first to send military support to the Rwandan government. The unshakable President Mobutu, who considered himself as the king of the region, didn't hesitate to get involved. At that point in time, it made sense to me that the Congolese government would behave like a good neighbor towards Rwanda, helping in times of trouble.

We all thought it was the end of the R.P.F. movement. It was hard to believe that a small armed group of Tutsis could engage a great coalition of different countries.

When the news mentioned the intervention of the Congolese army, the whole Congolese population—both men and women—bragged about how much stronger their army was, and how it was going to destroy the Tutsi rebel movement, never to be heard from again.

By this time, the whole region was paying close attention. Many countries were engaged in the conflict, and the war became quickly regionalized. The Tutsis' predicament had everyone on high alert. We were targeted every time we walked down the street, and we were the subject of repeated bullying and mocking.

A million times I have asked God, "Why are we treated this way? What have we done wrong to deserve such great tribulation?"

Even small kids from other tribes found out that Tutsis had lost respect in the community, and started abusing them. They did this with the certainty that their parents would never punish them—and they were right. Very few parents said a word when they saw their children running around adult Tutsis, insulting them.

This situation was proof of how bad things had become in our society. The basic traditional values that once gave elders power over all the children had dissolved.

The hatred against Tutsis brought us all kinds of evil. We were called snakes, cockroaches—you name it. It was humiliating to be a Tutsi in that city.

I was angry, and at times, I became rebellious. Whenever I determined it was not dangerous to do so, I would turn on those kids from other tribes that were running after me, insulting me and calling me names. I would quietly run up behind one of them and deal a serious blow, immediately running away so as not to be seen. I had to be careful that no one was watching me; had I been caught, I would have been stoned to death.

A few weeks after the intervention of the Congolese Army, the fighting became more intense in Rwanda. Showing greater strength than the coalition had expected, the rebel forces kept pushing the Rwandan Army closer to the capital city. We also heard that General Mayele, one of the general commanders of the Congolese Army, was captured by the rebels. The news spread throughout the whole region, and was very humiliating for the Congolese Army, which viewed itself as quite powerful.

We found ourselves in the midst of a terrible regional conflict, over which we had no control. The situation was made even more intolerable because we could not see how—or when—it was going to end. Hatred towards us was cultivated and nurtured in every corner of the region. As the hatred towards Tutsis in the Congo grew bitter, Tutsis were confused. We did not know what to do or where to go for our safety.

The Banyamulenge were, at first, reluctant to show any signs of support for the rebel movement, lest we face retaliation from the Congolese government. As the rancor and discrimination towards us continued, the Banyamulenge became completely exhausted. We continually prayed for a safe place to live—but that place was still as far away as the moon.

~ TWENTY-FOUR ~

For years, we lived like second-class citizens. In every aspect of our lives, our activities became limited. We were denied access to public areas, and caged mostly in our houses. When we did go out, we had to carefully watch our footsteps to make sure that we walked soundlessly, avoiding tripping over anything that might alert our opponents to our presence. If they realized that we were around, they would stand and chase us. We were like deer, swiftly escaping to save our lives.

What a miserable life we led, and what pain we endured over the years, as we lived with the constant sorrow of a rejected tribe. We lived without hope that we would ever escape the painful mistreatment. Only God knew when it would come to an end. Only time itself would tell.

As time went by and the war in Rwanda continued, the rebel movement experienced a great challenge. They could not advance as they had planned, and consequently adopted the guerilla warfare strategy of hit-and-run. The echoes of the war in the region started fading away. The Rwandan government proclaimed victory over the rebels.

Millions of Tutsis who had hoped to find a safe place once the Tutsi movement won the war saw their hope evaporate into the mist. Heaven had rejected their request at that time, and many years of waiting, suffering, and discrimination awaited us.

Radio Rwanda broadcast the news that Tutsis rebels had been crushed, and survivors had fled into the national park of Akagera, where they were wandering with no place to go. Listeners to the broadcast were told that if they saw any of the surviving rebels, they should kill them. Otherwise, they might return.

On the other side, the Congolese had already forgotten about the whole news of war. They were emotional and quick to react—but quick to forget, moving on to the next thing that was available to discuss or argue about.

Few Tutsis understood the realities of the rebel movement. It came to our attention that the R.P.F. did not have sufficient military equipment or soldiers to engage the Rwandan government, which had become stronger with the support of many countries. So, they decided to withdraw into the forest, where they began to reorganize themselves. We also heard that they had lost their chief commander, General Fred Rwigema. Many believed that the mighty warrior was killed by his closest friends. This story caused great disappointment within the Tutsi community.

We couldn't understand what the rebels were thinking—to attack Rwanda prematurely, with no plan for long-term fighting. Their miscalculation had left us in a confusing and disastrous situation.

With the help of Uganda, the rebels started to reorganize, and appointed a new leadership team led by General Paul Kagame. It was yet to be seen whether the R.P.F., under the direction of Kagame, could once again shine a lantern in the darkness for Tutsis around the world.

The war in Rwanda had never actually stopped, as many people believed. The victory declared by the Hutu Rwandan government had been nothing more than a wish—and political propaganda. The rebels kept attacking at slow paces, and trying to build bases. They were gaining momentum from the support of millions of Tutsis scattered around the world. Many Tutsis worldwide had known nothing about the R.P.F. movement until members of the R.P.F. visited different cities, explaining their mission. This support would prove to be the rebels' greatest resource, and it was impossible to win without it.

A year after the war began in Rwanda, clear information regarding the rebel movement began trickling down to mainstream Rwandan Tutsis. It was the rebels' vision to liberate Tutsis who had been persecuted in Rwanda and other parts of the region. Their mission was to reunite Tutsis who had spread throughout the entire region, wandering in the wilderness for many years like sheep without a shepherd.

The R.P.F.'s radio station, Umuhabura, "a voice that calls from the high mountain," never ceased disseminating information about the movement. This brought a clear picture of who the rebels were, and what they were trying to accomplish. This was the sweetest message I had ever heard.

When this station first started broadcasting, we had to go to the high hills and mountains in order to pick up the signal. As we listened to the message, we had to hide. Otherwise, we would have faced great punishment.

Meanwhile, there were campaigners who traveled around the region in Rwandan diasporas, spreading a message that helped millions of Tutsis believe in the R.P.F. cause. This was their message:

"Tutsis have lost their values, respect, and human dignity. Their culture has dissipated into other nations, because they try to erase the traces of who they are, due to the loss of their nation. Tutsis have been ashamed of who they are, and how God has created them. But, now they have decided to fight, to restore their dignity as human beings, and to bring all Rwandans back to their mother land, the land of milk and honey."

As soon as we heard this message, we were ready to get involved. We did not think twice. The message of Tutsi salvation reached even the least village of Mulenge, and the younger generations, who had been deprived of many opportunities, had good reason for joining the movement. A network of mobilization took young Tutsis from around the world into Uganda to be trained and join the army.

Like a fire which is set on dry land, and catches like a flash of light, the movement grew bigger and bigger, until it became a blazing fire that consumed the region. It was unstoppable. This was accomplished in the Congo with total discretion. We did not want the government to know about it; that would have worsened the Tutsis' situation.

Amatorero groups—"clubs"—started in every city in the Congo. Young people kept flowing into the movement and fund-raising throughout the region grew.

One of my most memorable Amatorero events took place in Uvira on May 11th, 1992—the anniversary of the death of Bob Marley, the king of reggae music. We decided to combine a fund-raising event for the R.P.F. movement with a celebration com-memorating the death of Bob Marley.

We spent months preparing for it. Young Banyamulenge were recruited to join the army. All members of the club prepared snacks to be sold at the event, including meatballs, Sambusa, African donuts, and peanuts.

The most beautiful Rwandese girls from Bujumbura were encouraged to come support us in making this event memorable. We knew that, even though most Congolese hated Tutsis, they des-perately loved Tutsi girls, who were believed to be the most beauti-ful girls in the region. Musicians sang about them all the time.

Our goal was to make sure that every invitee was accommo-dated in a special way, so they would spend money. Everything was organized strategically to accomplish that end. Thanks to our discretion, hundreds of Congolese would participate in this event, without ever knowing that their funds were going towards support for the movement.

On the night of May 11th, 1992, hundreds of Congolese attended the event. The turnout was incredible. Some wondered why we cared so much for Bob Marley that we would organize such a spectacular event for him. They wondered, was he a Tutsi?

It never occurred to anyone that the money being raised that night, through the sale of food and drinks, was going to fund the R.P.F. movement. They were too busy enjoying every aspect of that wonderful evening. They ate, drank, and danced with beauti-ful girls—mostly to songs by Bob Marley and Lucky Doube.

The following morning, many young Banyamulenge were leaving for Uganda to join the army. I was in charge of finding the identity cards and immigration papers they needed to cross the Burundian border. Most of them had come from the villages of Mulenge, and had never had to use any official document before. I knew many of them. They were my cousins and childhood friends.

We had taken them to a place that was very quiet, and given them a brief introduction to the movement. We talked about the vision and the mission of the movement.

The night of the event, after we drank many beers, and danced to reggae music written about suffering, freedom, and liberty, I cried, along with one of my cousins who would be leaving the next day. We joined in a circle of friends, and started dancing to a Lucky Doube: "Wherever you go, remember me, and in whatever you do, remember me…" The words to this song struck us all down, and we cried again and again.

We also had many best friends who had already left to join the movement. We all felt that the cause of Tutsis was legitimate and worthy of sacrifice, and we remembered our friends as we sang.

Around 4:00 a.m., the party became noisier, and those who were drunk started fighting. We concluded the event, and everyone headed home. My cousins who were leaving for the army later that day were lodging at a distant location. I walked with them until we got to the huge red gate of the house, and then it was time to separate. I hugged each one of them as I said goodbye, and together, we soberly cried.

After the gate had closed and they all went inside, I stood outside the compound and waited. When I could hear the pounding of their feet on the stairs of the porch, I turned around and stumbled home. I was a little bit drunk, unsure of where I was going, and filled with an emptiness stronger than anything I had ever felt before. I missed them already.

There were many I would never see again after that day. They would die on the battlefield. When I got home that night, a deep sadness enveloped my heart. For weeks, I could barely eat, and found no pleasure in anything.

It is hard to explain what kept me in Uvira after many of my friends and relatives had joined the army. Every day since I joined the R.P.F. club, I woke up thinking, *Maybe tomorrow, I will leave and join the army.* There were many reasons I never left. For one thing, the club needed people to stay and do the work on the ground which supported the frontline of the movement.

I also learned that you cannot fight against your destiny. No matter how hard you try, you will never win. We are here now because of what our creator, God, meant us to be. The desires and motivations that lead each individual to his or her destiny grow greater every day, but the ones that attempt to divert us from our destiny die over time.

~ TWENTY-FIVE ~

The R.P.F. movement grew bigger every day, and the situation in Rwanda changed every night. We were careful, watching every movement in the region. We understood that every movement was interconnected, and any attempts to separate them would be a mistake.

Under the mediation of Julius Nyerere, the former president of Tanzania, negotiations between the Rwandan Government and the R.P.F. rebel movement began in 1993. The talks centered around the issue of sharing power between the rebels and the Hutu government. It was a huge achievement for the rebel movement to have their causes heard by the international community.

The majority of Hutus, on the other hand, were not at all happy with negotiations. In fact, they were furious, thinking that President Habyarimana was about to give away the power that they had held for years.

There is a saying in my language: "Ukuboko gufashe ingoma kuratemwa ntabwo kurekura," meaning, "The hand that holds the power will never release it, unless you cut it off."

While people were focused on the negotiation process in Rwanda, a new political development was unfolding in neighboring Burundi. This turned out to be a nightmare for Tutsis in the region. In 1993, President Buyoya of Burundi launched a democratic process, which allowed multiple political parties to operate for the first time in Burundi. That same year, elections were organized. Surprisingly, a Hutu candidate named Melchior Ndadaye won the elections, which sent shock waves throughout Burundi and the entire region. This was beyond everyone's expectations and comprehension.

In Africa, whenever there were elections, we expected the current president to win—whether by legitimate means or because he stole the election. This was called "fixing the election." In this case, Buyoya did not fix the election; he humbly accepted the outcome, and handed over the power Tutsis had held since the creation of Burundi.

Hutus were finally in power. They couldn't believe their luck. All they had hoped for their entire lives was now theirs. This was the fulfillment of the expression that says "a loss for some can be a gain for others." This situation was about to generate another disaster throughout the whole region—one that would greatly impact Tutsis living in the Congo.

Hutus in Burundi believed that, after the election, Tutsis deserved nothing. They had a slogan called "Susurutsa," which means, "Get Tutsis away," or "remove them from any position they are occupying." This sentiment was based on the political propaganda that was used by President-elect Ndadaye. He vowed to his people (Hutus) that once in power, he would make sure that no Tutsi would be left in any high political position.

I lived a few kilometers away from Bujumbura, the capitol city of Burundi, and I watched everything that was happening from the beginning. I also visited Bujumbura on a regular basis.

On October 21st, 1993, four months after the election, president-elect Melchior Ndadaye was assassinated by a group of Tutsi military. This was a disastrous event in the region—but I had no idea that this had transpired.

On that day, as I was coming home from school, I looked over at Lake Tanganyika towards Burundi, and noticed that it was seriously raining. The mountains surrounding Bujumbura had grown darker, and within a few minutes, the whole valley of Bujumbura was completely covered with heavy, dark clouds. For months, Burundians had been talking on the radio and TV about the drought in their country, and complaining that the whole country was so dry, crops were dying due to lack of rain. So, when I first saw the rain over Burundi, I initially thought that God had remembered the Burundians, and sent rain to help them.

But, as I watched the constant strikes of lightning, and listened to the heavy thunder, I was filled with a very bad feeling, and I knew that I was wrong. I have always had a strong sense telling me when things are not right.

In the afternoon, my cousin and I were busy practicing music in the choir at church, and in the evening, as usual, we hung out with friends until 8:00 p.m. We had no idea what had transpired that day. We came home, and as we walked through the door, we were surprised by the great silence we found in the house.

Normally, at that time of evening, the TV would be on, and everyone would be watching the Burundian station—the only station we were able to watch in Uvira. This particular night was different. My uncle was not watching TV. He had just finished eating, and was sitting in the dining room. All the dishes were still sitting on the dining table.

Nobody in the house was talking—neither my uncle nor my Aunt. The whole house was quiet. My cousin and I wondered what had happened, and why such an atmosphere was present in the house.

My uncle looked at us with a twisted eye.

My cousin and I looked each other, assuming we must have done something wrong in order for my uncle to be looking at us with such unhappiness.

"Is the TV broken?" my cousin asked.

My uncle responded with a question of his own. "Are you still walking on the streets at this hour? Don't you know what happened?"

In my mind, I thought we must have lost a family member from the village. Our hearts started pounding harder. In unison, my cousin and I asked him what happened.

He responded in a low voice, saying, "Ndadaye has been killed."

My cousin and I exclaimed in my dialect, "Mana yajye!" ("Oh, my God!") Most of the time, we spoke Swahili in the house, but, in times of trouble, all thoughts naturally come out in your inner language.

We immediately understood that this new development was going to be a disaster—first for Burundians, and ultimately for all Tutsis in the Congo. And I knew that I had been totally wrong about the rain I had seen earlier in the day. It was not a blessing. Instead, Heaven had covered up its face, so as not to see the disastrous actions of Burundians killing each other.

Thousands of young and mostly educated Banyamulenge were scattered in the remote areas of Burundi, where they had found teaching jobs. Several of my cousins and uncles were among them. They were in the far villages inhabited by Hutus. It was obvious that they were going to be targeted.

We kept turning the Burundian radio station on and off. No details were broadcast about the death of Ndadaye. All they said was, "This is an emergency situation." We also heard typical funeral music being played in the background.

In the days that followed, we heard constant announcements on the radio, giving instructions to follow during that chaotic period. A curfew was put into place, as follows: "It is strictly prohibited to see more than two individuals, or a group of people, standing on the street. All residents are asked to remain safely in their houses at night from 6:00 p.m. until 7:00 a.m. Anyone seen on the roads after 8:00 p.m. will be severely punished."

Listening to this, we knew that things had gone very badly in Burundi. The beautiful city of Bujumbura was completely darkened, and fear mastered the atmosphere. People could not move in the usual ways, or engage in their typical activities.

We came to learn from the news that, as soon as the Hutu population heard that their president had been killed, they immediately took their machetes and every weapon they possessed, and started to kill every Tutsi they encountered. Their first reaction was to cut down the biggest trees on the street, and block the main roads, so that the military from the cities would not intervene, and prevent them from killing their innocent neighbors. The Hutus in the cities were finding it difficult to kill, because the Tutsi military had control over the cities.

We also learned that, along with President Ndadaye, many other Hutu leaders in the government had been killed.

That night, we prayed for the safe return of several of my cousins and uncles who were teachers in villages far from the cities of Burundi.

All the Banyamulenge in Uvira were so frightened by the whole situation, we were afraid of stepping out of our houses. Things had changed tremendously. It was difficult to know what the other tribes would do to us. We knew that an attack was coming.

My uncle warned us to stay in the house, and not to go to school, or anywhere else, for a couple of days. We waited to see how the situation on the street was going to unfold. We were certain that there was going to be some retaliation against us. It had always been that way. They would come after us for any reason.

Kids in our neighborhood started throwing rocks on our houses, screaming loudly, "Tutsis, kabila muchafu," meaning, "Tutsis are a dirty tribe." All the houses had metal roofing, and the rocks sounded like rockets as they landed.

They knew that we were innocent; there was no Munyamulenge in the Burundian army who would have planned the killing of president Ndadaye. They knew this very well, just as we did, but they amused themselves with mistreating us in many ways.

Every single day following that first terrible night, we heard news of people dying in Burundi. Although some Hutu civilians were actually helping the Tutsis, the majority of Hutu civilians were killing Tutsis in the villages, and the Tutsi military were retaliating against Hutu civilians. This was the beginning of the ongoing civil war in Burundi. Everywhere we went, they were angry and hateful towards Tutsis, and threatening to kill us.

On the other hand, the military—which consisted mostly of Tutsis—intervened, and tried to stop the killings. In most cases, it was too late to save people. Hutus confronted the army, and the number of casualties grew on both the Hutu and Tutsi sides. Several sources estimated that one hundred thousand died in that conflict of October 1993.

There were many people to be blamed for the whole situation. President Buyoya was the first one. People said that he was naïve in handing over the country to the immature, primitive tribe of Hutus, who were driven by emotion ever since the elections, and thought that it was time to take revenge against Tutsis.

Others blamed the military, for they were the ones who killed the president, without ever thinking about the consequences of their actions. In any case, killing is not acceptable.

It was very hard for us to know who had survived among the thousands of Banyamulenge who were in Burundi.

After a week, we started seeing thousands of Hutu refugees fleeing into the Congo from cities around Bujumbura. The presence of these refugees worsened our situation in the Congo, and particularly Uvira, where I lived. We knew their presence would be used against us as proof that we were driving them out of Burundi.

We also came to learn that hundreds of Banyamulenge died in Burundi, just as we had feared would happen. During that period, I lost my uncle from my mother's side, along with five cousins. We learned that they had been thrown into the septic (sewer) system, and died in the most disastrous conditions. This news broke my family's heart, and we grieved for a long time. I still miss my uncle. He looked like me, and people always thought that I was his younger brother.

My picture in 2013, a few months prior to publication of the first edition of the book.

My beautiful bride Lise Karara is ready for the dowry celebration.

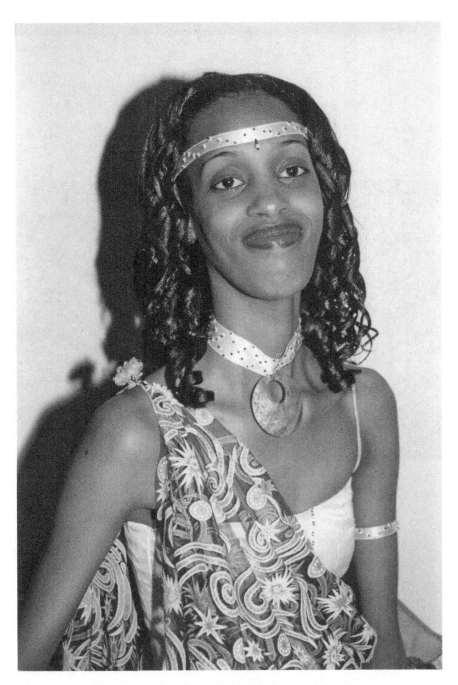

Lise with a half-smile before the dowry ceremony in Rwanda.

*Lise and I proposing a toast at the dowry ceremony,
one year prior to the official wedding.*

My best friend Alex Tung joining the toast.
We were all happy for this big day.

Lise and I quietly exiting the dowry celebration area.

*We relaxed in my sister-in-law Livine's house
in Kigali, Rwanda after the ceremony.*

*With our three-month-old son Ael Shimirwa, a
very joyful moment of our life together.*

My son and me. Holding him felt so joyous and natural.

My family with a new addition, our daughter Ais Shimirwa Budagu.

Another family picture

Another family picture

The beautiful girls

The handsome boys

My son Ael with his amazing and beautiful smile.

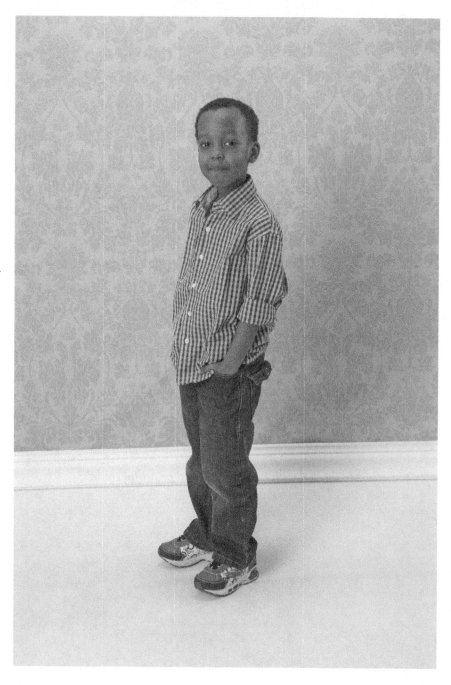

Ael with a more serious look.

Another family picture

In this family picture, we felt so close and in love.

My beloved mother Sifa and my sister-in-law Dorikasi.

*My mother with (left to right) my younger sister
who passed, my two nephews, and my niece.*

Businessmen with merchandise on their heads, hiking
3,000 feet above sea level. Life can be tough

~ TWENTY-SIX ~

There are many stories of the mistreatment that my tribe and I went through, some humiliating, and some life threatening. I cannot tell them all. Suffice it to say, they were beyond what I could explain in the few pages of this memoir. But, there are some that will always stay with me.

This is one of the many...

One day on a Sunday, my church was invited by a church of the Babembe tribe to an evening service. We knew very well that this invitation was coming from one of the tribes that didn't like us. But, as Christians, we had to transcend the barriers of hate, and love even our enemies, as the Bible teaches us. Many churches in the area, including ours, had been invited to participate in a big crusade. There would be a concert and preaching.

When that night came, we were all blessed in amazing ways. All during the services, we felt the Holy Spirit touching us and moving among us. At the end of the service, we all went home as a group, very happy, with the laughter and joy that dominated that special evening. Nobody from my tribe owned a vehicle, so we all had to walk.

The church was located near Lake Tanganyika, a little bit distant from the main roads that were always busy with people. There was a small hill that we needed to ascend before emerging onto the main street. As we exited through houses set very close together, we walked through a very narrow pathway. Suddenly, we faced a huge crowd of people coming from a soccer game at the stadium.

Only God knows why such a bad coincidence would take away the entire spiritual meal we had been fed, and replace it with a lot of pain and anger. When the crowd saw us, they were like hunters who had found a deer they had long been searching for. They had no respect for us, and plenty of time to waste.

They immediately started yelling at us, and throwing rocks. As we ran in opposite directions, we fell all over each other, trying to squeeze into the narrow pathways. They chased us all—men and women alike. Under normal circumstances, women were supposed to be respected by everyone. No one was supposed to fight with them. But, on this night, they were shown no mercy.

Those who were aging and could not run easily started falling down, and as they did, their garments tore apart, leaving them half naked. This was one of the most humiliating, embarrassing situations I had ever seen. It was especially humiliating to see elders and pastors that we highly respected treated with no respect whatsoever.

There was no real police force, only military, and they tended to be abusive. We knew better than to mess with them. That night, we had many injuries, and we felt completely helpless. This whole situation was beyond what any normal person could tolerate.

I went home crying out for God, saying, "Why? Why have you created us this way? Why are we hated this much? God, you know everything, and we have nothing to do with the Burundian President's murder!"

I was angry and rebellious, wondering why the tribes that we lived near cared so much about the situation in Burundi. I wondered why they didn't just go into Burundi, and avenge themselves against Burundian Tutsis. Nothing made sense in my life. This was the only day of my life when I felt I would rather die than continue to live such a humiliating life. The war was happening in one country after another, and civilians were the most victimized. Once again, only God knew what the end was going to be.

There is a saying in my language: "Aho impfizi zagwaniye ibyatsi birahashirira," meaning, "In the area where the bulls have fought, the grasses become the most victimized." This means that, when bulls or elephants are fighting, they step on grasses and brush, and break everything underfoot. In the same way, innocent civilians were being trampled underfoot during this conflict.

Meanwhile, as Hutus and Tutsis were busy killing each other in Burundi, there was a ceasefire in Rwanda. The negotiations process had started between the government and the Tutsi rebel movement, but peace in the region was not yet a reality.

Six months after the assassination of the Burundian president, a horrible event occurred in Rwanda. This event would prove to be the apocalypse—the end of everything in Rwanda.

It happened on April 6th. I woke up early in the morning, and started getting ready to go to school. As I routinely did, I went outside behind our house, where the water pipe was located, to get water for a shower. Many people were still sleeping, and it was very quiet. It felt like a normal day, like any other.

I always awakened before anybody else in our house, except my uncle, who was a businessman. On certain mornings, he had to wake up early to go to the morning market called Karyamabenge. There he sold cows that would be killed early in the morning, and the meat dispatched to the different marketplaces around the city.

On that particular day, April 6th, 1994, I was ready to leave when suddenly I saw my uncle coming back home. It was unusual for him to be coming back at that hour. His brown face had turned red, and he was walking very fast. When I saw him coming toward me, my mind started spinning with many thoughts. It is unbelievable the way our minds can run hundreds of thoughts simultaneously within a second.

First, I thought that he was sick—but he was walking too fast to be sick. So, I thought that maybe he forgot his money at home. I wasn't concerned over anything at that time; I was just wondering what had happened to bring him home at that time of day.

I was heading to the house of my friend, Alex, with whom I walked to school every day. We grew up together, and became like brothers. We switched off—some days, I would go up to his house, and we would leave for school from there, and other days, he would come down to my house. That day, he was supposed to come and pick me up, but he didn't.

I didn't understand why he hadn't shown up, and I decided I would go to his house and get him. It was right when I was about to cross behind our neighbor's house on my way to get Alex that I saw my uncle walking towards me.

He called to me in a very low voice, saying, "Yorogo!" That was a nickname he had always called me. "Yorogo!" he called a second time. "Garuka subira muzu," meaning "Go back in the house!"

I immediately knew that something big had happened. My heart started pounding harder; I could not imagine exactly what had happened, or where. I thought, *Oh, my God! Who died in my family?*

Millions of other thoughts came to my mind. When I looked around, things seemed normal to me—until I realized that I didn't see the usual Banyamulenge students heading to school. *That doesn't mean anything,* I thought. *It is just too early for them to leave for school.*

I went back home quickly, my heart pounding hard. I was very anxious to find out what had happened. I hurried into the house, and met my uncle there. He told me that president Habyarimana of Rwanda and Cyprien Ntaryamira, the new president of Burundi, had been killed the night before. Their airplane was shot down.

"Oh, my God!" I exclaimed in my dialect.

Immediately, my aunt heard us talking. She had been in the other room, unaware of the news. When she heard us exclaiming, she came and found us in the living room. We stood together, not knowing what to do. She was terrified to hear this news too, and stood there, trembling.

Within a few minutes, all my cousins heard us talking, and came out of their rooms. We closed the door and all the windows, and sat in the house. We knew what was going to happen. Two presidents—both of them Hutus—being killed on the same day created a terrible situation throughout the whole region.

We turned on the radio, and started searching for news on Radio BBC. The news bulletin stated that the aircraft carrying the presidents had been shot down in the night, as they were returning from Arusha Ntanzania, where they had been signing the peace agreement with the Tutsi rebel movement, R.P.F. The negotiations were being mediated by Tanzania, and all the presidents of the region were there at the official ceremony.

President Ntaryamira of Burundi was the victim of a ride in the Habyarimana airplane. He had his own airplane, but for some unknown reason, he had decided to ride with Habyarimana. From there, he was going to go home.

The news broadcast did not state exactly who was responsible for the assassinations. There were many speculations as to who may have been responsible for Habyarimana's death. One news source stated the assassination was carried out by Tutsi rebels, who knew that President Habyarimana would never follow through with the negotiations between the R.P.F. and the Rwandan government.

Another news source stated that President Habyarimana was killed by his commanders, who were unhappy because Habyarimana had given away their country. No one was sure what the truth really was—and to this date, the truth remains hidden. But, in the Congo, it was believed that both presidents were killed by Tutsis.

The following morning, only a few people in the surrounding tribes had heard the news, but as the day grew up, the whole city came to find out about the death of the two presidents.

Once everybody heard the news, the persecution of the Banyamulenge and other Tutsis started all over again. The sounds of rocks and stones thrown over our houses were signs that we should not leave the house that day. It was not safe for any of the Banyamulenge—or any Tutsi, for that matter—to walk on the streets. The throwing of rocks became so constant, we became very afraid that the next step would be to break into our houses, and slaughter us all. Every moment, we prayed, asking God to extend his mighty hand over us all.

After four hours of having rocks thrown on our house, it became quiet. We were surprised to see that the trouble had subsided so quickly; we had expected worse. We did not know what made them stop. As I've said, there was no police force we could have called to report the emergency.

We knew that God had heard our prayers, and we thanked him that, as night fell, nobody in our house had lost their life. We wondered what had happened for other Banyamulenge in the city, but we were trapped inside our house, with no way of communicating with each other. There was no telephone; our only means of communication was word of mouth. In the nighttime, under the cover of darkness, people from my tribe were able to start moving secretly, asking each other if everyone was safe.

That night, I sneaked over to the home of my friend, Alex, who lived a few meters up from me. I knocked on the door and nobody responded. I knew that they couldn't just open the door to anybody. I whispered my name, and they opened the door for me.

They too had stayed in the house all day long, frightened by the rocks and stones thrown on their house. We sat in his house, discussing the whole situation. We both had been involved in the R.P.F. club, and had a lot of information regarding the politics in Rwanda, and the process behind the negotiations. We predicted that there would be the apocalypse of Tutsis in Rwanda following the death of Habyarimana.

As word of mouth spread, we came to learn that there had been injuries in the city that day; anyone who had left their house was beaten to death. They were captured, and brutally beaten on the streets. The military finally intervened, and stopped all the violence against Tutsis in the city.

The military had never intervened on our behalf previously, and we didn't understand why they had done so this time—and then we found out their reason. Among the injured was a Tutsi from Northern Kivu who was a judge at the Uvira Court House. He had left his house and started on his way to work, figuring that as a judge, he had nothing to fear. Sadly, he was mistaken. Being a judge did not protect him. He was stoned and seriously injured.

The report went to the mayor of the city, and the military were sent to rescue him. He also reported that there were many abuses against Tutsis around the city, and these needed to be stopped. Thank God, this attack on the judge caused the rock strikes to settle down. If not for this judge's influence, the situation could have been even worse.

In Rwanda, genocide started the same night President Habyarimana died. A new government was put into place immediately. It was comprised of extremist Hutus who wanted nothing else but to shed the blood of Tutsis. It had been planned, and Hutu knew exactly what to do. They were ready to feed on Tutsi blood, with their machetes, knives, dogs, and guns.

As we watched the news on TV, we saw horrible images of houses being burned to the ground, and people being slaughtered and thrown in the rivers and sewer system.

There was also a radio station in Rwanda called RTRM, whose mission was to incite Hutus to get out and kill their Tutsi neighbors. All Hutu civilians were asked to "take care of" their neighbor Tutsis. Everyone knew what "take care of them" meant. They were being instructed to kill them.

There were thirty-five-hundred peacekeepers in Rwanda. But, the first night of genocide, ten Belgian soldiers were killed, so the UN decided to withdraw the whole group. This was an astonishing decision. Thousands of people were slaughtered with machetes, and yet, suddenly, peacekeepers were asked to leave. What a controversial decision by the UN!

All it would have taken was a word from the right people— and the genocide would have stopped. But, the whole world was silent during the genocide in Rwanda.

The UN soldiers were called peacekeepers, they talked about peace in Rwanda, they were sent into Rwanda to keep the peace, but they ran away from protecting and providing peace when it was most needed. Women ran up to them with kids on their backs, begging for peace and protection, but the peacekeepers turned their backs on them.

The horrible sounds of men, women, and children being crushed by the Hutus echoed in the ears of the peacekeepers. The earth swallowed innocent people, who sank into the earth to decay, with no hope of justice.

As people were dying all around them, the peacekeepers were called back home. It was very depressing to think of them carrying their loaded—and unused—sophisticated weaponry home with them, as the atrocities continued in the region.

~TWENTY-SEVEN ~

As the genocide progressed, we kept watching and hearing about the fighting between the R.P.F. and the Rwandan military, and Interahamwe militia groups, which grew to become very contentious and destructive.

Every weapon that you can think of was used in the fight. The combination of bombs exploding, machine guns firing, and bushes, houses, and forest burning had all of Rwanda up in smoke. Whatever was hiding in the bushes—birds, animals, and human beings—either had to stay in the bushes and burn, or get out, and be slaughtered by Interahamwe.

Birds soared high above the scorched surfaces, wondering what had happened to their human neighbors. Why had they turned so cruel, and burned the birds' niches, causing their young babies who could not yet fly to perish? The birds had no place to rest, as they looked down upon the bloody ground, and saw rivers flowing with thousands of human bodies. As they saw this, they decided to cross to the nearest border. For them, Rwanda was no longer a safe place to dwell.

Wild animals that had heard the violent sounds of bombs exploding, and the cries of people dying, rushed to the nearest border. Things were no longer the same in Rwanda. The entire world was watching their TVs, where they could see innocent blood as it dropped onto the ground, and dried.

The R.P.F. movement continued to fight tirelessly for the forgotten people, and by the middle of June, they were progressing with the speed of the wind, winning every piece of Rwandan territory. They were taking over the whole country. They were the only hope left in Rwanda for Tutsis—and moderate Hutus, who were dying every second at the hands of extremist Hutus who didn't like anybody who opposed them in the killing.

It was one-way fighting, with no turning back. Winning was the only choice. Retreat was not an option. It was a fight to the death. It became obvious that they were going to overthrow the new Hutu government, which was busy coordinating hundreds of battles at the same time.

The government was calling for Hutu civilians to kill Tutsi civilians. The Interahamwe militias and Hutu civilians were also fighting the R.P.F. army.

The world remained silent about what was happening in Rwanda—until the R.P.F. started winning the war. Then, suddenly, we heard about new developments: The UN Security Council was debating over allowing the French government to intervene in Rwanda.

The mission was called Operation Turquoise. Their mandate was to create a peace zone for the refugees who were fleeing the country. These refugees were Hutu civilians and militia, and the army, who was running away, as they were being defeated by the R.P.F. army. It was believed that in this mission, the French Government wanted to save the Rwandan Government, but it was almost too late.

Breaking news came on July 4th, 1994: The entire country of Rwanda was under the control of the R.P.F.! What a memorable day for all Tutsis!

Finally, the light brightened the dark days that had overshadowed Rwanda. Victory was upon Rwanda and Tutsis around the region wanted to believe they had finally found a peaceful home after many years of suffering.

Meanwhile, in the villages of Mulenge, people were shouting for victory. In Burundi, shouts of joy could be heard coming from the avenues where Rwandan Tutsis lived. In many other parts of the region, like Uganda, Tanzania and Kenya, you could feel the winds of hope beginning to blow. Both men and women were shouting, "Hallelujah! God has remembered us!"

In Uvira, where I lived, and in many other cities neighboring Rwanda, it was the opposite. We had to stay inside our houses, and celebrate the victory in hiding. We could not openly express our feelings, for fear of serious retaliation from the Congolese people, and Hutu refugees—who were already overcrowding the whole region, as they ran away from Rwanda.

On TV, we watched millions of Hutu refugees pouring into the Congo, especially, in the north of Kivu, in the city of Goma, and in the south of Kivu, in the city of Bukavu.

Mothers were carrying their kids on their backs, and over-loading their heads with tons of belongings. Soldiers were carrying machines guns, grenades, and explosives on their shoulders.

This was a scene such as I had never witnessed in my life. It truly did seem like the apocalypse—as the Hutu government had called it, when they were bragging about exterminating the Tutsi race.

In Rwanda, silence resumed as the sounds that had prevailed for months faded away—sounds of guns, machine guns, and bombs.

Virtually the entire population of Rwanda had emptied into the Congo.

During the month of July, in 1994, I was in the middle of a busy schedule, preparing for the national examination, so I could graduate from high school. In the midst of all the turmoil, my friends and I had found a quiet place where we could stay as we prepared for the exam. It was very difficult to focus and concentrate with everything that was going on.

My friends and I lived in constant fear of being targeted by the Congolese, as well as thousands of Hutu refugees who had moved into the city. We stayed in our houses most of the time. We were careful not to walk around in the late hours.

Sometimes, I looked at the trees, houses, rocks, and birds that surrounded us, and feared that they too could turn against us. I no longer trusted anything in that place. I had become suspicious of everything and everyone around us. I wasn't the only one—my friends felt the same way. If someone was particularly nice to us, we wondered why. The situation in the region had completely robbed us of our trust.

Whenever we heard people outside, shouting with joy about something, it made us curious, and we wanted to get out and take part in the moment. Then, we would remember that it was not safe for us—we had to stay inside the house.

And whenever there was terrible screaming, or we heard loud sounds outside, we sat in the house, and carefully peered out the windows, wondering who the victim might be, and imagining that it could be one of us, caught on the streets of hatred. I really despised that period of my life.

As I finished my examination, my friends and I made a decision to cross the border into Rwanda. The Congo had become a very cruel place to live for us Tutsis.

On October 1st, 1994, a group of twenty of us students who had just finished the national examination were about to leave for Rwanda. The movement of Tutsis heading into Rwanda had started on July 4th, and since then, Tutsis never stopped moving from the Congo to Rwanda. There was cross-movement, as Hutus were fleeing Rwanda, and moving into the Congo, and Tutsis were fleeing the Congo, and moving into Rwanda.

We started planning the safest way of crossing the border. The Congolese army had been alerted by the enormous number of armed Interahamwe militias, and soldiers from the ex-Rwandan army, who were in the camps all the way around the border of Rwanda. They had placed roadblocks at many points along the road leading to Rwanda.

Corruption was widespread, and some of the roadblocks had been set up as a means of looting civilians. In fact, the Congo had become so corrupt, every disorderly situation was now a special occasion for the military to rob citizens. Tutsis, in particular, were hunted by three lions in the Congo: the Congolese army, Hutu civilians (who never ceased threatening them), and the Interahamwe militia, who were very dangerous.

As we made preparations to leave, we learned of an officer in the military who had been using his influence to transport Tutsis from Uvira to the Rwandan border. He made a fortune, overcharging for the protection he offered against aggression on the road to

Rwanda. In a normal situation, the charge for a ticket from Uvira to the Rwandan border would have been no more than five dollars per person—but he charged us one hundred dollars each!

He had formed his own army, comprised of young people. He gave them military uniforms, and enlisted them to accompany and safeguard his vehicle as it passed through roadblocks.

The vehicle was scheduled to leave at four o'clock in the morning, to avoid being attacked by Interahamwe during the day. The night before crossing the border, we were all praying for a safe trip. We asked God to protect us as we went through "the valley of the shadow of death," to quote the Holy Bible. We were very aware that we could be caught by Interahamwe and never be seen again.

Every person who was supposed to leave the following morning had to stay in the same house that night—which was an additional charge. All twenty of us passengers had to sleep on the mat in one small room.

At four o'clock in the morning, we heard a rolling voice calling us in Lingala—the official language of the Congolese military. He was saying, "Ale, Bolamuka to kende!"—"Hey guys! Wake up!" He was very intimidating. We all startled awake, and stumbled as we tried to stand. Each of us began searching for his shoes. It was so dark, and I was so sleepy, I could barely stand on my feet.

He stood in the doorway, moving his flashlight from one person to another. We looked like goats about to be sold in the market. We were all overwhelmed with anxiety, and the fear in that room was heavy. Our hearts pounded hard as we left the house. Nothing serious had happened yet. It was just the beginning, yet our minds were burdened with the pressure of the whole situation.

We went outside and immediately loaded into his vehicle—which was designed to hold no more than six passengers. In order to accommodate the twenty of us, he had removed the back seats, so we all had to sit in a flat space. It was obvious the soldier transporting us cared more for money than the condition or comfort of his passengers.

As we loaded into the car, we could barely breathe. It was hot and uncomfortable, and we were squeezed to the bone. We were all sweating profusely, due to the heat and the fact that there were so many of us crammed together in such a small space.

The driver started the engine, and we emerged onto the main road. The whole city was quieter than quietness itself. There was nobody at all on the road at that time. I had never before experienced that kind of silence in Uvira. I looked around, as we passed all the beautiful places where I had walked as I went to school, and where my friends and I had walked as we moved around in the evenings, enjoying the beauty of the city.

Sorrow filled my heart and I cried. I missed the city already and wondered if I would ever see Uvira again. But, the area had become very unpredictable. I knew that the situation was deteriorating every day and nothing was going to change any time soon.

It was very hard for me to integrate my mind and body. My body was moving toward Rwanda, but my mind lingered in the place where I had been living for quite some time.

The driver moved very quickly, determined to reach the border before the sun rose. Our goal was to avoid being seen by Interahamwe, who had resettled in the refugee camps all the way along the road that we traveled. Thirty minutes from the time we left, we met the first roadblock. Luckily, we passed through it. We would encounter another very dangerous roadblock before we reached the border.

We traveled about thirty minutes more. The driver warned us that we were close to the last roadblock of "Beret vert"—the military in their green caps.

We all started trembling. My legs had gone numb from fear and the fact that I had been unable to move my legs for hours. There was just no room to stretch our legs.

As the vehicle pulled over to stop, I prayed in my heart, saying, "Lord, help us here!"

Before I'd finished my prayer, the first soldier approached the car with a flashlight, pointing it into the car through the window. He was speaking in Lingala, saying in a loud voice, "Wapi uzo mema bamukotanyi oyo?" He was asking the driver where he was taking us, and calling us Mukotanyi—the name of the R.P.F. movement.

His voice reverberated with great violence in my heart. He sounded like a lion, roaring into a deep forest, and causing the small animals in the trees to fall down. We couldn't look into his face.

He kept walking around the vehicle, asking what we had on us—did we have any guns or anything illegal? Then he started asking if we had money or anything valuable he could take from us. He asked us to get out of the vehicle. We had no idea what his intentions were. Our hearts were heavy and we were traumatized by fear—the same fear that consumed the whole region. We could hardly think. Our minds had gone blank, and it was hard to coordinate our thoughts. People said things that made no sense at all. We were totally confused.

By this time, five soldiers with guns had surrounded us, ordering us out of the vehicle. As we climbed down, they checked us, kicked us, and insulted us. They were full of hatred and contempt for Tutsis, and kept telling us to never again return to the Congo.

We all wanted to save our lives, so we were willing to accept everything they did to us, as long as they didn't kill us. We did nothing to defend ourselves, and remained as quiet as lambs on their way to the slaughter.

After the inspection, we all got back in the car, empty handed. All the money we had was gone. We had believed that once we had paid our transport fees to the man transporting us, he would protect us against being looted. We were wrong.

~ TWENTY-EIGHT ~

We were unable to send a message to the others who were about to take the same route. So, no one else knew what was happening to us.

At about 7:00 a.m., the sun rose eastward. Within a few minutes, we were at the border. The officials who were guarding the Congolese side of the border started interrogating us. Rwanda was five hundred meters on the other side of where we had stopped. We could see it!

The R.P.F. army, standing at the entrance to Rwanda, watched how we were being mistreated by the Congolese officials. They had been alerted to the fact that the Congolese army was torturing Tutsis who were coming into Rwanda, but they could not help us. It was a nightmare.

Immigration officers at the border checked us, trying to get the last penny left over, but unfortunately, we had nothing left. They were so angry that nothing was left for them, they started taking from us everything that had any value—clothes, watches, and necklaces. As they robbed us, they were calling us every bad name they could think of.

The vehicle that brought us could not cross the border, so we had to cross on foot. At last, we walked across the bridge towards Rwanda. As we crossed the bridge over the Ruzizi River, and reached Rwanda, I could not believe my eyes. We had just emerged out of a tunnel of darkness, and found ourselves in an area considerably brighter. I looked back with great dismay. I did not believe I would ever return to the Congo in my lifetime.

I lifted my eyes, and looked at the mountains obscuring the view of my village. Sadness filled my heart and I cried again. I had no idea if I would ever again see my family who remained behind in Mulenge.

The R.P.F. soldiers, who had been watching the whole scene since we started crossing the bridge, expressed their sympathy to us. They expressed to us that they had seen us being mistreated and were saddened that they could not help. They really cared about us. Never before in my life had I engaged in conversation with the military in a friendly way. I had learned to run away whenever I saw them in the Congo.

They took us to the location of the High Commission for Refugees, which was also the base for the United Nations Mission in Rwanda (UNMR) forces. We were taken through the process of registration.

The city was surrounded by hills, and the tents of the R.P.F. army were spread throughout the hills overlooking the city. UN forces patrolled in huge tanks. Military vehicles circulated through the area. It was quiet and safe, but it still looked like a war zone. The city had been completely trashed during the genocide, and few people had resettled there (in Bugarama). The traces of war were everywhere.

Being in Rwanda felt very foreign to us. As we walked around the city, we were puzzled by the scene. The city seemed nearly empty, but the people we did encounter were very welcoming and happy to see us. It was so strange to see soldiers coming up to us, and asking if we needed anything. In the Congo, they always asked us if we *had* anything—and then they helped themselves to whatever we had. Things had changed. After years of being discriminated against, we finally felt secure.

As darkness started falling, we went to the rooms where they were lodging us. Our rooms were former classrooms in an old schoolhouse. We found a place to build a fire, and cooked the food that they had given to us. They also gave us blankets and mats to sleep on. That night, I slept like a baby. After all the exhaustion and fear I had felt on the trip, I was finally able to rest. It was so peaceful there.

In the morning, we woke up, and went to enroll as passengers on the trucks that were leaving for Kigali. We traveled for many hours. As we traveled, we could see how the entire country had been destroyed. Above our heads, the flags of victory were hanging from the trees. But, at ground level, we saw very few people walking on the streets. The war had been severely damaging.

Even though we were now safely inside the border of Rwanda, we encountered many roadblocks, and had to stop for each one of them. The roadblocks had been placed to prevent criminals from entering—or re-entering!—the country. The trip should have only taken eight hours, but including the time consumed by stopping at roadblocks, it took us ten hours to get to Kigali, the capital city of Rwanda.

When we finally reached Kigali, we discovered more activity than in any of the other cities we had come across on our journey. Perhaps this was because most people wanted to live in the capital city.

I have a cousin, in fact, who had left for Rwanda long before us, and he had already resettled in Kigali. He had been a teacher in Burundi, but the minute he heard that Kigali was now in the hands of the R.P.F., he decided to move there—and did so immediately. He had found a beautiful house in Kigali, because all the houses were empty, and whoever arrived first and found an empty house could live in it. (There was no rent payment; houses were free until the owner returned. If the owner returned and needed to occupy his own house, he would ask you to leave—or else, he would ask you to pay him rent.)

I was so happy to see my cousin again! I had gone a long time without seeing him or his family.

That night, I went to bed fatigued by the journey from Uvira. As I tried to sleep, I could hear dogs crying all night long. It was so strange to hear dogs whimpering and crying loudly through the entire night. I had never heard such a thing before in my life, and I couldn't understand it. It was very disturbing.

In the morning, when I woke up, my first question was, "Why do the dogs here cry this way?"

My cousin told me that he had asked the same question when he first arrived. He explained to me, "The dogs are traumatized by the whole war situation. Their owners have abandoned them, and they have no place to live now. Since the genocide started, they have been wandering the streets, feeding on human corpses. The military shoots them whenever they catch them."

In the days that followed, I walked into the city, looking around. Unbelievable marks of the war were all over the place. I was so overwhelmed by the fact that the same Kigali that was a precious piece of history in my mind—the place I had heard about on the radio, and seen on TV, was actually going to be my new home. At the same time, many of the images I was seeing were very disappointing and disturbing.

I did not see the millions of bodies killed in the genocide; they had already been buried in mass graves around the country. But, the bullet casings were as numerous as sands on the shores of a river.

Big buildings had been leveled to the ground by bombs attached to bricks that were thrown through windows, spraying debris all over the area. Bridges and roads had collapsed, sinking into deep ditches. Banks had been robbed. The government reserves were now sitting in the wallets and safe boxes carried on the backs of various individuals who were fleeing the country.

Even statues of Mary—the holy mother portrayed in cathedrals across the country—were smashed on the ground, simply because Mary looked like a Tutsi in the statues. This shows the kind of hatred that drove the extremist Hutus.

The ground was covered with landmines—planted there to kill any leftover Tutsis. Thousands of landmines erupted every day, killing those who walked the streets, trying to find their way after leaving the places where they had been hiding for months. There were thousands of casualties still occurring in the country every day.

People were warned to use extreme caution as they walked around, and to remember that the ground was full of landmines. Kids could not play safely without being hit. The survivors of genocide tripped on the bones of their loved ones.

Rwanda was the country where death came during genocide and sat down—but instead of rebuking it, Hutus had welcomed, comforted, and entertained it. Death wasn't a one-time strike, as we normally see it. It had taken control of the whole country, and its stench filled every corner. Death's shadow frightened whoever entered the gates of Rwanda.

Years ago in the time of kings, when Rwanda was a monarchy, there was a belief among Rwandans that "God sleeps in Rwanda." Back then, Rwandans were so confident in their strong culture, their trust of one another, and the beauty of the land, they made a statement so bold, I had never heard it anywhere else before: "God rests peacefully in Rwanda every night."

They believed that God went around in the daytime, visiting other places, but in the nighttime, he always found his way back home to Rwanda, and there he rested. Normally where someone sleeps is his home. This statement proved the decency of Rwanda in an earlier age.

God had made a peaceful covenant with Rwandans, and vowed to dwell among them, to the point that he made Rwanda his place to rest. When Rwandans broke the covenant with God, deciding to invite evil and hatred among themselves and start killing each other, the God of peace had no more place to sleep. He turned away from Rwanda, and ran into the places of peace. He could not stand to watch the deeds of Rwandans who had become evil. Now everything was left in the hands of the God of power and judgment.

Many Rwandans wondered where the God of peace had moved to, and why things had turned out so badly. People longed to see justice in Rwanda. They longed to see God come and punish whoever had served the hatred and shed the blood of millions of Rwandans.

When I got to Rwanda, there was a new united government. Both Hutus and Tutsis were represented. (There were almost no educated Abatwa who could participate in any political system. They were mostly hunters, lived a primitive lifestyle, and rarely had the opportunity to become educated.)

The president was a Hutu named Pasteur Bizimungu. The vice president was General Paul Kagame, and the premier minister was a Hutu named Faustin Twagiramungu. General Paul Kagame was like Joshua in the Bible. He took over the R.P.F. movement after the death of General Fred Rwigema—whom I will call Moses. He never reached the Promised Land. He saw it, but died on the battlefield.

People in Rwanda adored General Paul Kagame, especially Tutsis. He was known to be a great leader, with charismatic power. People talked about how he was a hard worker—and strict.

I will never forget the first time I saw General Paul Kagame. I was in Nyamirambo stadium when the first house of representatives was sworn in. It was a big event where thousands of people were gathered. We knew that General Paul Kagame was going to be there, and I was desperate to see him.

Sometimes in life, we have individuals that we admire and respect because of their works and heroism. These individuals can be people we live with, or have lived with—or, they can be individuals we have never seen, and never *will* see in our entire lives. If you are lucky enough to see someone that you have longed to see, it gives you a great sense of satisfaction and happiness.

I first heard about General Kagame and his works when I was in the Congo. I heard that he was a great leader of the Tutsi movement. Ever since then, I was filled with great admiration and respect for him. As soon as I moved to Rwanda, I started wishing I could see him. Now, here I was, in the stadium, knowing he would be arriving within a few minutes! I was very excited over the whole celebration, but seeing Kagame was most important to me.

The ceremony started at 10:00 in the morning. It was very pleasing to participate in this type of event, after the many years I'd been deprived of public places in the Congo. Everyone inside the stadium was awaiting the arrival of Paul Kagame. We were trying to get closer to the gate he would be using to enter the stadium.

Since my earliest years, I was very serious in everything I did. Whenever I didn't get what I wanted, I felt defeated and believed I was a loser. Most of the mistakes I have made in my life were due to this belief of mine. My brother has warned me about this many times, advising me to be realistic in everything I do. He always told me that, if I didn't get what I wanted, it didn't mean it was the end of the world. I needed to understand and realize I can't get everything I want.

I understood what he was saying—but I was determined that this would not be one of those times when I was defeated. So, I stood right on the front line, the closest I could get to the gate. I knew there was no way I was going to be able to touch him because of all the security, but I edged as close to the gate as I could, hoping to at least see him up close. I was probably no more than ten meters away.

Suddenly, I heard the sound of the military vehicles escorting dignitaries from outside the stadium. They were speeding, blowing up dust and covering the whole stadium with it. I knew right away that it was Kagame's convoy arriving, because his entrance had a different quality to it than the ones that came before it.

It was announced over the loudspeaker, "Please stand, and give a warm welcome to His Excellency, Vice President and General Paul Kagame!" As this announcement was coming over the loudspeaker, his convoy was swinging around the track with great speed. Then, they stopped right in front of the stairway he was going to use.

He exited the vehicle, stood up, and waved to the crowd. He was quite tall, wore his military uniform, and looked very elegant. Seeing someone I admired brought me great satisfaction.

The whole stadium stood up, and endless loud cheering erupted. People shouted, and some became so emotional that they fell onto the ground and cried, unable to stop. There was a popular song of victory that had been played on the radio since the R.P.F. took power. At that time, the same song sounded throughout the whole place. "Itsinzi Bana Burwanda…" meaning, "Victory, children of Rwanda!"

As they heard the song, people started to go crazy, dancing everywhere.

At this time, I remembered all the horrible situations in the Congo, and I thought, *God has used this man to rescue our lives from death.* I prayed for him to live a long and honest life.

I strongly believed in victory. Tutsis were moving in the city freely, with no one insulting or bullying them. I felt like I had reached the place where I belonged—the land of justice and equality, and I thought, *I am going to spend the rest of my life here!* But, my whole family was still in the Congo, and I cried for them and prayed for their safety.

After the celebration, we went home, and my friends and I went to take a drink in the bar. People in the bar spoke about the history of the war, and I heard many heroic and brave stories.

I had several cousins and a lot of best childhood friends who had belonged to the R.P.F. movement since 1990. I helped many of them cross from Uvira into Burundi. We sat with many of them and talked, and it was very good to see them. Many others died.

I felt so sad, remembering the last night that we all sang, "Wherever you go, remember me, and whatever you do, remember me…" I wondered, *Where are they now? If they are watching from above, what do they think about this country they fought for and died for?* I felt so sad that they never survived to live in the Rwanda they had fought for.

We all cried. Since we were drunk, we could not control ourselves.

~ TWENTY-NINE ~

After the storm of genocide tore apart Rwanda in 1994 and claimed millions of lives, any hope of better days was still far away like the sky. The new government was frightened by thousands of armed forces of Interahamwe and the former Rwandan army that was camped in the Congo (Zaire), right near the Rwandan border.

There was a substantial threat of being attacked. When the lions and tigers that devoured your children are still camping around your village, you can't go to sleep. And, if you do, one eye has to sleep while the other stays awake, watching out, because you know that unless you are ready to stand and engage them, and push them away far into the forest where they belong, they will surely harm you.

In 1995, several attacks against Rwanda were launched from refugee camps in the Congo (Zaire). Survivors of genocide were slaughtered. Villages were burned to the ground, and buses en route from one place to another were overtaken and burned. The souls of Rwandans grieved again, and it hurt to face this reality after the few months of peace they had enjoyed since the genocide had stopped. This is called in Kinyamulenge "Gukinira kumubyimba," meaning, "hurting someone who has already been greatly hurt."

In the Congo, the Banyamulenge were facing a serious threat of extermination by Interahamwe, and thousands of them started fleeing into Rwanda. Others endured the threats and never gave up their land. The Congo was the only place they had known to be their home. They were born there and lived there. Where else would they have gone?

Conflict was pervasive and total confusion reigned. We had entered the days of evil, and fear became the air that we breathed. People went home earlier than usual, before night fell on them. They were like chickens afraid of nighttime—except, they were strong men! Only those who possessed the strength of lions and could face horrifying nights were able to get out.

The Interahamwe did the same things they had always done against Tutsis around the region, with no fear of punishment. To put an end to consecutives attacks from the Congo, Rwanda had only one option: to destroy the refugee camps around the borders, which had become a military base of Interahamwe. This was the cause of the war that broke out in the Congo in September of 1996.

The war started as rumors, and the first time I heard the news, I had difficulty believing it. A picture of Rwanda invading the Congo was hard to even *envision,* much less believe. It seemed suicidal for a country like Rwanda to partake in such an adventurous mission as fighting against the giant Congo.

I was a student at the National University of Rwanda when rumors grew bigger among the students on campus. As the situation started to unfold, the Banyamulenge were about to be placed in the center of the whole movement. The fear of a heavy sky about to fall shadowed the Banyamulenge. We believed that the Congo had a mighty army, ready to destroy Rwanda in one second.

Rwanda had to face the devil right at his gates—but they needed a reason to present to the entire world to explain why they were invading another country. Rwanda actually had two legitimate reasons: defeating the Interahamwe, who never stopped attacking Rwanda, and preventing another genocide against Tutsis—and Banyamulenge—in the Congo.

There was substantial fear of genocide being prepared against the Banyamulenge and Tutsis around the Congo. The security for the Banyamulenge in the Congo had deteriorated so rapidly that a military action was urgently needed.

Thousands of young Banyamulenge were trained in Rwanda to take on the greatest mission in their history. During this time, school activities were no longer our preoccupation. We knew that we were going to take the front line in the battle to rescue our families in the Congo.

It felt so bad knowing that our activities as Banyamulenge students were coming to a screeching halt, whereas other students on campus lived a normal life. When a particular animal is targeted by hunters in the forest, other animals don't ask the victim what is happening. They are intent upon escaping the scene, and leaving the victims to follow the path of death, alone.

We were ready and waiting.

One night, there was a meeting that brought together Rwandan high-ranking military and the Banyamulenge community around Rwanda, and a few students were invited to participate. As the meeting progressed that night, we waited, desperate to find out what had been discussed. This was a defining moment for us, and we could not sleep.

The following day, all Banyamulenge students on campus were called to assemble in the auditorium's basement. We were going to be informed about the outcome of the meeting which had taken place the previous evening and lasted late into the night.

We were squeezed into the basement until it became so overcrowded, we could hardly breathe. The message was straightforward: we had to attack the Congo, and rescue our families that were facing imminent danger of being exterminated by Interahamwe and the Congolese government.

The message resonated among us, because we knew exactly what our families were going through. But, we also feared Mobutu and his mighty army. Since my earlier age, I had believed that Mobutu, the president of the Congo (Zaire) was an unshakable person. Congolese people worshipped him like their God. No one imagined that he could ever be removed.

Only God knew how things were going to turn out.

As we left the basement of the campus auditorium in Butare, nothing else but the war in the Congo was discussed among the

Banyamulenge students. We had all been alerted that the Rwandan army would be coming to take us into military training, and we were instructed to stand by until they came for us.

Everything about the war was planned and orchestrated by the Rwandan army. The strategy developed by the Rwandan Army was to provide military training for thousands of young Banyamulenge who had fled into Rwanda since 1994.

After training, they were going to be sent secretly into the Congo to infiltrate, and fight against, the Congolese government that was targeting thousands of Banyamulenge citizens still living on the high plateau of Mulenge. The plan was to form a strong army, capable of engaging negative forces against Tutsis in the region. This mission was a huge undertaking for Rwanda—a small country still recovering from a horrible genocide, and without the means to oppose an army as strong as the Congolese Army.

As I mentioned previously, ever since the Hutu moved into the Congo—especially in the southern and northern Kivu region—they had been plotting with the Congolese government to exterminate Banyamulenge and other Tutsis in the region. They wanted revenge against Tutsis after the Hutus had lost their war in Rwanda.

At this time, there was insecurity surging throughout the whole region and war was inevitable. For the Banyamulenge, war was the only way of surviving. Everyone was ready to lend a hand to this noble cause, to rescue innocent people in danger of being exterminated, and to fight for their own rights and dignity.

In a few months, while we were still waiting on campus, the war started prematurely in the Congo. This event completely destroyed the whole initial strategy, because the plan of invading the Congo was intended to be carried out *methodically* over a long period of time.

This complete reversal would cause the Rwandan military to pragmatically develop a new and immediate strategy to salvage the urgent situation and prevent thousands of innocent Tutsis in the Congo from being wiped out.

The way this incident occurred was very unfortunate for all Tutsis in the region, especially the Banyamulenge. It all started with young Banyamulenge being trained in different groups in Rwanda. As I mentioned above, after the training, they were then secretly sent into the Congo. Each group was to cross the southern Kivu border, enter the Ruzizi plain, and go up to the high plateau of Mulenge, where they would mix with other Banyamulenge civilians. Two groups of at least forty soldiers each had already crossed the border and reached Mulenge safely. These two groups were consecutively led by Lieutenant Nicholas Kibinda and Gakunzi Sendoda.

The infiltration process was very risky and dangerous. The distance was one night or one day walking, from the Rwandan border to the high plateau of Mulenge. It was imperative that they avoid being seen by anybody from the villages of the Bafulero tribe along the way. The two groups had developed the same strategy— crossing the border at night, walking all night long, and reaching the high plateau of Mulenge before daylight.

The third group, led by Lieutenant Mathias Bigiritsibo, did not succeed in its mission. They failed on their way up to the mountains. While maneuvering to secretly cross the Congolese border before daybreak, the soldiers lost their way. Unfortunately, the sun rose before they could reach the mountains of Mulenge. It is said that a bird that is about to die never knows how to fly.

In order to salvage its mission, this group had to find an immediate alternative. Worrying that they would be seen, they decided to hide in the bushes near a village called Mugatoki. There was no forest in this area to provide cover for them, so they had to hide in small bushes. Their hope was to wait in the bushes, unseen, until the following night when they could continue their journey. Exhausted from their long night of walking and carrying heavy military equipment, the soldiers suddenly fell into a deep sleep where they were hiding.

Women from the Bafulero tribe were going to cultivate the fields and happened upon the sleeping soldiers. Shocked, they immediately went to alert the nearby Congolese military camps, which rushed to the scene and found the Banyamulenge soldiers still deeply sleeping. They ambushed the area, and started shooting at them. Twenty Banyamulenge soldiers were killed and six captured. The rest escaped miraculously to the mountains.

This event was a fatal blow, and the beginning of a disastrous time in the Congo for the Banyamulenge and other Tutsis. It also prematurely provoked the so-called Banyamulenge War in the Congo—a war started in 1996 in the Congo. (Later, the name of the movement would be changed.)

You would think that an incident like this could have been handled locally and carefully, because it occurred in a remote and completely unknown area, and was caused by the smallest and most unknown tribe in the Congo—the Banyamulenge. But, this was not a typical situation. When the news broke in the media, the incident sent shock waves that spread throughout the region like wildfire. Everyone in the Congo was outraged, and it was obvious what would happen next.

The media talked about a rebel Banyamulenge Tutsi movement from Rwanda attacking the Congo. This media chatter doomed thousands of Banyamulenge lives, and plugged the entire Banyamulenge tribe around the region into chaos. Everyone lived with the fear of what was coming.

Putting this situation into perspective, the Banyamulenge is one of the smallest tribes among the two-hundred-fifty ethnic groups in the Congo. As I described in the first chapters, they have been living in a remote and completely inaccessible area on the high plateau of Mulenge—a location which has made them lesser known than other tribes in the Congo.

In fact, few people knew the Banyamulenge before the war. The only tribes that knew them were their neighbors—the Bafulero, Babembe, Bashi and Banyindu tribes. For the most part, the rest of the tribes in the Congo knew little or nothing about the Banyamulenge prior to the incident and the broadcasting on Congolese TV stations of video of captured Banyamulenge.

Another important factor in the conflict is this: the politicians from the Bafulero, Babembe, Bashi, and Banyindu tribes of southern Kivu, who occupied high positions in the Congolese leadership, took the incident very seriously and found it to be a great opportunity to tarnish the history and credibility of the Banyamulenge in the Congo. Aided by the media, these politicians turned the rest of the tribes in the Congo against the Banyamulenge.

The hatred and discrimination against the Banyamulenge that I described in the previous chapters was mostly confined to the southern Kivu region, and was perpetrated by tribes that were neighbors to the Banyamulenge. In other regions, they had no idea who the Banyamulenge were—until this incident, after which these politicians promoted a flow of false information about the Banyamulenge. These lies were spread wildly around the Congo, with the intention of inciting people to hate, and even viciously kill, the Banyamulenge. They were seen as snakes to be crushed.

~ THIRTY ~

The Banyamulenge were placed in the gravitational center of a very complex geopolitical conflict, and they started experiencing a systematic series of horrifying events following the Mugatoki incident.

Never before had the Banyamulenge lived in such a vulnerable situation. They were scattered all over the region without any protection, and surrounded by thousands of Interahamwe, former Rwandan Army, and Congolese forces that were complotting to exterminate them. The biggest question was how people were going to be rescued, and by whom.

There were thousands of Banyamulenge living on the high plateau of Mulenge—those who had never fled into Rwanda after the Interahamwe moved into the Congo. Now, they found themselves under threat of extermination. They were targeted even more heavily after the incident, because the Congolese government had reason to believe that there were infiltration forces from Rwanda that had turned the area into military camps that intended to attack the Congo.

The truth was that, so far, *only eighty soldiers* from Rwanda had made it to the high plateau of Mulenge, and these were nothing compared to the well-equipped coalition of Interahamwe, former Rwandan Army, and Congolese forces.

Vyura was the second area where a large number of Banyamulenge were living. It was located in the southern region of the Congo called Shaba, in the zone of Moba. In the 1980s, thousands of Banyamulenge had immigrated to Vyura from southern Kivu. They were in the middle of nowhere, in an area occupied by other tribes, and they were completely unprotected. Thousands of kilometers away from southern Kivu, they were far from any kind of help.

The third area was the villages of Bibogobogo. These very remote villages neighbored the Babembe tribe and were members of the same religious community. Even though they were neighbors, and brothers in the same religion, this did not stop the Babembe tribe from later betraying and killing them.

There were many other cities populated by a good number of Banyamulenge, including Uvira and Bukavu (both in southern Kivu), Kinshasa (the capital), and Lubumbashi (in Shaba). There were also many students and businessmen dispersed throughout the Congo at the time of the incident, and they were potential victims, as well.

Meanwhile, in Rwanda, where the whole idea of attacking the Congo had been started by the Rwandan army, the Banyamulenge were also afraid and confused. They feared the danger faced by the thousands of Banyamulenge families scattered throughout the Congo.

As I have said, it was difficult to believe that the Rwandan Army was going to fight with the Congo and expect to win, considering that the Congo is eighty-nine times bigger than Rwanda, with a population approximately seven times greater than the Rwandan population. The idea of Rwanda winning the war against the Congo was just a dream. The fact that they would even consider going to war against the Congo made us wonder if maybe Rwanda had the blessing and support of superpowers (like America) behind them.

As the media reported on the invasion of the Congo, sometimes they blamed it on Rwanda and sometimes they blamed it on the Banyamulenge rebels. This was very confusing to the Congolese people.

The propaganda spread by the Congolese government encouraged people to fight against the Tutsi empire and kill every Tutsi across the country. Everyone who looked like a Tutsi in the Congo was targeted.

There were many Banyamulenge spread all over the Congo who had no information about the incident, and no awareness of the preparations for war being made in Rwanda. In southern Kivu—especially in the cities near the Mugatoki village where the incident had occurred—all the Banyamulenge were suddenly captured and put into jail. Men were separated from their families and placed into prison, where they were seriously tortured. Some were even put to death, including Bishop Bugunzu, pastor Muzuzi, and many others.

Women and kids were placed into a compound, left without food, and subjected to starvation. All the Banyamulenge houses in these cities were looted, leaving them void of light and sound.

When the eighty soldiers who had successfully reached the high plateau of Mulenge from Rwanda heard about the Mugatoki incident, they decided to attack the few Congolese military camps that were in the area. Congolese soldiers were chased out of Mulenge and into the cities.

The whole situation became terrifying, for the Congolese government never ceased calling upon civilians to rise up against the Banyamulenge and other Tutsis. This was exactly the same message of hatred against Tutsis spoken in 1993 in Burundi and in 1994 in Rwanda during the genocide—a message of incitement, calling upon civilians to kill their innocent neighbors.

There came a time when a seven-day ultimatum was given to the Banyamulenge to leave the Congo and go to Rwanda; otherwise, the ground was going to be flipped over them. This was a message given through Radio Bukavu, by Rwabanji, the governor of southern Kivu. I was in the campus of Butare in Rwanda when I heard about the Mugatoki incident, and also when I heard about the process of expelling to the Rwandan border all the Banyamulenge captured from different cities.

Hundreds of Banyamulenge from different cities in Rwanda rushed to the border, waiting to see their family members who had survived. We expected mostly women and kids because men and young boys were targeted and killed. Banyamulenge students in the campus of Butare had gathered money and clothing, because they knew that those who had survived had been looted of every piece of their property and clothing.

My friend Alex from Butare and I went to the Rwandan border in the city of Bugarama. I was expecting to see my uncle's family, whom I lived with in Uvira, and Alex was also waiting for his uncle's family. There were many more students waiting for their families and relatives. It was a horrible journey. In the bus, we could not speak—we were too fearful. I had a strong feeling of emptiness that came with not knowing who had died or survived. We were all afraid to face the unthinkable reality of loss.

As we reached the city of Bugarama and approached the border, we found hundreds of Banyamulenge from different cities in Rwanda standing right at the border, along with a few Rwandan border guards. Our eyes focused on the bridge over the Ruzizi River, just a few meters away from the Congolese border.

We saw women and kids crossing the border with no man among them—and we had to face the terrifying reality that no man did survive. Although it was very hot (35 degrees Celsius or about 95 degrees Fahrenheit), deep in our stomachs, it was much colder than that, and everyone was shivering.

At this time, we were told that hundreds of men were placed into one house right at the Congolese border. It was very saddening to know that they had come that far, only to die right at the border.

The area was consumed by the agonizing cries of kids, and wives who had left behind their husbands, knowing that they would never see them again. The scene of women and kids being mistreated and beaten at the Congolese border tortured our minds. They were also being searched and looted of anything of value before being allowed to cross the bridge. This was an unbearable scene.

After the survivors crossed the bridge, the cries of kids, women, and people who were desperately waiting to see the survivors, shadowed the whole Ruzizi Valley. There were mixed feelings—a little bit of relief over meeting with family members who had survived, combined with sadness and mourning over people who did not make it. This was truly "the valley of the shadow of death."

A few minutes after the women and kids had crossed the border, it started raining. We all ran into nearby houses, and while we waited for the storm to pass, we discussed various places where we might host the families who had survived. In the midst of the rain, a miracle happened at the Congolese border. The group of men who were placed into the house, and expected to be killed later on in the night, miraculously survived! A Good Samaritan—a Congolese official and friend of the Banyamulenge—saved them.

When the Good Samaritan realized that the people around him were distracted by looting the piled belongings of Banyamulenge families crossing the border, he immediately rushed to the house where the men had been locked up. He kicked in the door, screaming loudly to the Banyamulenge men: "Get out quickly and run toward the Rwandan border!"

All the Banyamulenge men happened to be naked, as they had been stripped of their clothes. But, once the Good Samaritan broke down the locked door, the men rushed out of the house and started running towards Rwanda. Two soldiers standing guard were shocked to see hundreds of naked men running towards them. Luckily, the guards did not shoot them.

Many of the men survived the swords that had been sharpened to draw their blood, and only two individuals died at that time, including Rukenurwa Ntayobrwa and Kange Sebugorore. They were unable to run because they had been severely beaten and injured.

Throughout the whole period following the incident that provoked the war, we prayed for our people to survive the killings. We saw in this miracle—the men being freed from the locked house—the hand of God. We had already mourned over these men, but God brought some of them back. We were also aware, however, that this was only the beginning. It was very hard to contemplate what fate might await the thousands of other Banyamulenge still left unprotected in different cities.

The Mugatoki incident occurred on September 27th, 1996, and every day that followed cost the Banyamulenge their lives. There were Banyamulenge, as well as many other Tutsis, killed in different cities and villages throughout the Congo. Some areas were more seriously affected than others. In the four villages comprising Bibogobogo, for instance, more than three hundred families were first arrested and then expelled to the Rwandan border.

Once there, the men were separated from their families, killed, and thrown into the Ruzizi River.

I remember my friend, Freddy, for example, who lost his father and three of his younger brothers. There were also more than three hundred young girls and boys who were taken into captivity.

Here is the reason why they were killing them at the border: Many human rights organizations were accusing the Congolese government of killing innocent people. In the end, the Congolese government said that they were expelling all Tutsis to Rwanda, but once Tutsis arrived at the borders, the Congolese government selected men and boys (who were seen as potential soldiers) and killed them.

Within one month of the Mugatoki incident, things had become uncontrollable. The killing of Tutsis was happening everywhere. The Rwandan Army could no longer bear the agonized cries of women and kids crossing the border day after day after losing their loved ones. (Unlike the former Rwandan Army, which was comprised primarily of Hutus, and was part of the coalition attempting to exterminate Tutsis, the new Rwandan Army was highly sympathetic to Tutsis.)

It was traumatizing to see Tutsis being hunted on the streets of Congolese cities, and to witness the border killings and the throwing of bodies into the Ruzizi River. This was a disastrous crime against humanity—and specifically against the Tutsis, who still carried the memory of the 1994 genocide. The Rwandan Army had to take serious action and this was the beginning of a military operation that started in October.

We were all scared, picturing the so-called Banyamulenge rebels supported by the Rwandan Army fighting against the Congo. And, as I said above, we couldn't help but wonder if there was another force (a superpower) backing Rwanda. Otherwise, fighting against the Congo would be like trying to move a mountain. There were rumors that Uganda was behind the movement of attacking the Congo, but it was still hard to believe that this would be enough support for Rwanda to take on the Congolese army, which we saw as a giant.

The war started on two fronts—southern and northern Kivu, both of which border Rwanda. I was in Bugarama, not far from the Congolese border, when the fire was set off between the so-called Banyamulenge rebels and the Congolese government. The explosion of heavy machine guns and rockets echoed throughout the entire plain of Ruzizi. A heavy, dark smoke from the firearms and the burning of the bushes colored the whole sky.

At this time, there were practically no civilian Munyamulenge left in cities around the border. Some had gone up onto the high plateau of Mulenge, where thousands of Banyamulenge were managing to resist the Congolese forces that had launched attacks against them—thanks to the eighty soldiers who had made it to Mulenge and the fact that the terrain was inaccessible by vehicle.

In northern Kivu, on the other side of the Rwandan border, near the city of Goma, was the largest refugee Hutu camp of all—Mugunga. It was home to hundreds of thousands of refugees, thousands of Interahamwe, and former members of the Rwandan Army. This camp was the first target of the rebel movement backed by the Rwandan military when they launched their attack. Rwanda had longed to destroy this camp for ages because of different attacks constantly coming from the camp since 1995.

One morning, the camp awoke under fire. The rebel movement backed by the Rwandan Army had encircled the entire camp, but they left a corridor heading to Rwanda. As the fighting continued, it looked like the refugees had only one option—going through the open corridor towards Rwanda. But, thousands of others escaped through the corridor and went into the forest.

At this time, millions of Rwandan refugees who had been living in camps in the Congo for more than two years came back into Rwanda. This scene—where millions of refuges were forced to come back into Rwanda—was apocalyptic. The whole region was under a chaotic situation.

As the war progressed, the so-called Banyamulenge rebels were making significant progress. Day after day, the Congolese Army was losing. Every day of the fighting caused the Congolese Army to lose a city. Exhausted civilians were on the run, traveling thousands of miles from one city to another, as the war progressed to the capital city of Kinshasa.

It was a miraculous situation. No one had ever expected that the Rwanda-supported rebel forces would overpower the coalition of Congolese Army, thousands of Interahamwe, and ex-Rwandan Army.

The success of the Rwanda-supported rebel forces was due in part to the weakness of the Congolese military. The Congolese soldiers never got paid, which is why they were looting everyone. They were now demoralized and had little interest in fighting for a government that had failed them. Ruined by corruption, the Congolese Army was now like a dead lion, which scares people even though it has already died.

The same Congolese population whose cheers and shouts had been heard on the streets as they hunted Tutsis started running away to save their own lives. The fear of death shadowed the entire Congo. The war became very frightening for them, way beyond anything they had expected. They never thought that a small country like Rwanda would overpower a giant country like the Congo.

At this time, there was controversial information coming from different sources. In the Congo, they talked about the Rwandan invasion. The international media talked about "the Banyamulenge rebel movement" which was later changed to a revolutionary movement named AFDL (Alliance of Democratic Forces for the Liberation of Congo). This change came after many people from other tribes in the Congo joined the movement to overthrow the Mobutu regime that had reigned for more than thirty years.

There were Congolese who had opposed Mobutu's regime for many years, including Laurent Desire Kabila—a senior politician and opponent of Mobutu since the 1960s, who went on to become the leader of the movement. His arrival changed the dynamic, and altered the Congolese view that the war had been a Rwandan invasion from the beginning.

~ THIRTY-ONE ~

One year after the beginning of the war, the Mobutu regime ended and Kabila became president. The war concluded much more quickly than anybody could have predicted.

During this time, the new Congolese government was fostered by Rwanda. There were thousands of Rwandan and Banyamulenge soldiers in the new Congolese Army, but also for the first time in the Congo, the Banyamulenge occupied higher positions in politics. The Minister of Foreign Affaires, Karaha Bizima, was a Munyamulenge, and many others occupied different key positions.

No one ever believed that the Banyamulenge would be given such rights and honor in the Congo. It was like Heaven had come down to support a tribe that had once suffered horrible hatred and discrimination.

In 1997, I was curious to visit the Congo. I went to Uvira, where I had lived for years while attending high school, and I also went to Bukavu, the capital city of southern Kivu. It had been two and a half years since I had moved to Rwanda. During my visit, I could not believe my eyes. Things had completely changed for the Banyamulenge and all Tutsis in the Congo; it was totally different from how things used to be before the war.

As I've said, before the war, it was almost impossible for the Banyamulenge to walk on the streets of Uvira or Bukavu without being bullied, mocked, or humiliated. But, at this time, things had completely changed. Life in the Congo had never been easier for the Banyamulenge.

The Banyamulenge started believing that evil was finally behind them, and they started to dream again about a bright and prosperous future in the Congo. But, they were completely wrong. This was false hope, and the worst was yet to come.

About a year later, a new disastrous situation started to unfold against the Banyamulenge and other Tutsis in the Congo. Another war broke out suddenly in the Congo.

Somewhere in the leadership of both the Congo and Rwanda was a misunderstanding. The new Congolese President, Laurent Desire Kabila, along with Rwandan leaders that had helped him to access power, did not properly cooperate, and a sudden split occurred in their relationship. As a consequence, President Kabila ordered an immediate withdrawal from the Congo of all Rwandan military.

People in both Rwanda and the Congo were shocked to hear this news. It was very hard to understand such a sudden breakup of what was believed to be a strong alliance. The speculations were that President Desire Kabila never trusted Rwandans during the course of the movement of liberating the Congo. It was speculated further that Kabila's plan had been to wait until Rwanda helped him get into power, and thereafter avoid them.

Kabila was brought into the Congolese liberation movement by the Rwandan Army, which took him from Tanzania where he had lived in exile for many years. The Banyamulenge had warned Rwanda not to integrate Kabila into the movement because Kabila was among the leaders of a rebel movement back in the 1960s that killed thousands of Banyamulenge in the Congo. This was believed to be the origin of the hatred between the Banyamulenge tribe and the other neighboring tribes. In the eyes of the Banyamulenge, Rwanda was very naïve to trust Kabila.

During the process of removing Rwandan forces from the Congolese territories, President Kabila humiliated Rwanda on the radio. His slogan was that "Rwanda is a very tiny and poor country. Rwandans have found honey and milk in the Congo, and now they are saddened by being asked to go back to their poor country."

He also spread a very incendiary and controversial rumor about "the Tutsi Empire Movement." He repeatedly said that the

Congolese people should be aware that Tutsis were on a mission to take over the great Lakes Region. He called this mission the Tutsi Empire Movement. In this way, Kabila was very smart, because he knew exactly how to get the support of the entire Congolese population. He spread rumors into Congolese communities, scaring them into believing that Tutsis had a mission to take over the whole region and turn it into a Tutsi empire.

This rumor resonated. It got the attention of millions of Congolese people who then believed that Kabila's position was advantageous to them. They immediately embraced their same old spirit of hatred and mockery against Tutsis in the Congo.

There was another critical aspect of the conflict in the Congo that Kabila emphasized in his incendiary message: the idea that all Tutsis were foreigners and enemies of the Congo. He never mentioned anything about Congolese Tutsis, including the Banyamulenge and Tutsis of northern Kivu often referred to as Banyejomba and Banyaruchuru.

At this time, all Congolese Tutsis—including the Banyamulenge—were confused as to what position to take in the new war. They did not know where to go. They vacillated between staying in the Congo, and moving to Rwanda. They had relied heavily upon the support of Rwandans, and trusted them for the help they had received in changing the regime that hated them. And, they had always been mistrustful of the Congolese people, especially Kabila. Because of Kabila's reputation for hating Tutsis, they felt they could trust anybody but Kabila.

When I was a kid in my village, every hateful person in the village was nicknamed Kabila. I was told many stories of how Kabila led multiples attacks that wiped out hundreds of villages. In fact, Kirumba—one of the villages of my close relatives—was burned by Kabila's movement. Dozens of people were killed.

The lack of understanding between Kabila's regime and Rwanda was the direct cause of the second war in the Congo in 1998. This was the time that a new movement supported by Rwanda named Rally for Congolese Democracy (RCD) started in southern and northern Kivu, with the mission of overthrowing

Kabila's regime. During this new war, the cycle of killing civilian Banyamulenge and many other Tutsis started all over again in every city in the Congo.

This was the most deadly war for the Banyamulenge in the Congo. The new war turned out to be very divisive. Many countries in Africa, including Rwanda, Uganda, and Burundi, became involved in the fight against President Kabila, who was supported by Zimbabwe, Angola, and Namibia.

I know of no other tribe who has undergone suffering as great as the Banyamulenge. We are a tribe that lives for, and seeks, peace—yet peace has always slipped out of our hands. Whenever we thought that we are about to hold peace, we suddenly lost it. I have never understood, and still don't understand, why we are so hated among other tribes in the Congo.

In this book, I have been able to tell you about a few of the events I have lived through, but hundreds of more horrifying events have happened since I moved away from the region over a decade ago. I have decided to tell this story, because the story that is not told dies in someone's mind, and the truth goes along with it. Evil flourishes whenever it is not pointed out.

The Banyamulenge—along with millions of other innocents from all backgrounds in the Congo—have died every imaginable death. No matter how hard our heroes have tried to stop the killing, it hasn't stopped yet. The sacrifice of soldiers who have shed their blood in the process of saving innocent people on the mountains of Mulenge, and throughout the region hasn't yet paid off, and the struggles have continued.

I remember hundreds of young soldiers who became the shield that protected people from the plot intended to exterminate the Banyamulenge.

First, I think of the late Honorable Gisaro Muhoza. For many years until his death, he vigorously fought for the rights of the Banyamulenge.

Then, there was the late Lieutenant Nicholas Kibinda, the first Munyamulenge officer who died on the battlefield in 1996. His zeal for saving his people exceeded his ability.

There were hundreds of other brave Banyamulenge soldiers and officers, including Gakunzi Sedoda, Rumenge, Budurege Bitebetebe, Twabwe Ntumbira , Nkumbuyika, just to name few. They were with the first group who crossed the border. In the midst of the rampant fear that had swept through the whole region, they never held their feet, but rose on the mountains, becoming the shield for thousands of families who were about to be exterminated. When the enemy rose furiously against them, and splashed bullets like rain on every hill of Mulenge, they cut them off, preventing the enemy from succeeding in piercing through the mountains of Mulenge.

I will never forget the hundreds of officers who were training in the Camp of Kamina, in the southern region of the Congo (Shaba). In 1998, they were captured by fellow military—their colleagues; the very people who were training them!—and hanged from trees, humiliated. Their bones decayed, but we have lived to tell their story and pay tribute to their heroic sacrifice.

There were also soldiers who were left in Kinshasa, and got isolated in the Camp. Because of their heroism, they never surrender to the will of their enemies. They resisted the Congolese Army for days, until the army launched bombs and rockets at them with the intent of flipping over the ground to bury them. Instead, the soldiers found their way through and crossed the Congo River into the neighboring country of Congo Brazzaville.

I will never forget the victims of the Gatumba massacre of August 13th, 2004, which took away one-hundred-sixty-six innocent people in one night. These were Banyamulenge who had fled the killings in the Congo, but were followed by the killers into the land of refugees in Burundi. They got slaughtered and burned.

The perpetrators were a coalition comprised of a militia group called Mai Mai, and a Burundian militia group named FNL, led by Agato Rwasa and Pasteur Habimana. These groups claimed responsibility for the massacre, but to date, they have never been brought to justice. They are still moving freely in the Congo, committing more crimes, because they know that no judgment will ever be brought to them.

I could go on and on, talking about isolated cases of individuals—innocent Banyamulenge who were targeted and killed in the Congo—as well as thousands of Banyamulenge livestock consecutively looted by Mai Mai, a group that always aims to kill and destroy Banyamulenge.

There is no one from the Banyamulenge tribe who hasn't lost a family member between 1996 and the present day. I have lived in the U.S. for over ten years now, and during that time, rarely has a month passed without someone from the Banyamulenge community being killed in the Congo. The list of people that we have lost in the Congo since 1996 is endless. We have lost our hope, our strength, our love, and our wisdom.

Thousands of young Banyamulenge that perished on the front lines of the battlefield trying to save us from killings were our hope and strength. Elders brutally murdered in different villages and cities were our wisdom. Hundreds of women and young girls raped and killed on the streets of the Congo were our love.

Many others were taken into captivity, never to be seen again. Some were brainwashed and are now lost, living in total ignorance of their true Banyamulenge identity. I heard of one woman who returned to Uganda from Tanzania in 2007, and was told, "You are not who you think you are! You are Munyamulenge!"

There were Banyamulenge who had married into other tribes, and were betrayed by their in-laws. Some were beheaded, and their heads hanged on trees. Their sons and daughters watched the drops of their fathers' blood falling and drying on the ground in terrible humiliation.

It is very hard to understand how, during this war, the Congolese were entertained and amused by the way they killed and hunted the Banyamulenge on the streets.

Since 1993, as a consequence of the war in the region, the Banyamulenge have spread throughout the world. There are thousands of them who moved to Rwanda after genocide, and are living there still. Most of them are suspended in the ambiguity of not knowing what to call themselves—Rwandans or Congolese. It is hard for them to predict what the future will bring for them in Rwanda.

In Burundi, there are thousands of Banyamulenge living as refugees in the camps and also in different cities. They hope for peace in the Congo, so that they can go back home.

In Tanzania, Kenya, and Ethiopia, there are thousands of refugee Banyamulenge placed in camps full of Rwandan Interahamwe, who hate them and threaten to kill them every day.

In Europe, America, Canada, Australia, and New Zealand, there are thousands of refugee Banyamulenge who have resettled, and are wrestling with the process of integrating into a new world, totally different from that which they were born into. And, there are many who are still in Mulenge, who never gave up their land.

~ THIRTY-TWO ~

There are three categories of people in Africa. The first category consists of those known as "low people." These poor, uneducated people comprise the majority of the population. The sad thing is that they are victims of everything—killings, diseases, you name it. They have been placed in the center of misery, and they die every death imaginable.

The low people in Africa constantly pray for peace—and for food. Many of them never live to see peace or many other things they pray for. They can't understand what they have done to deserve such great punishment—and they have no idea what to do to stop what has been going on for generations.

The Congo is full of natural resources like diamonds, gold, and copper, to name a few. But, all these resources have been exploited by the leaders, leaving the rest of the population to eat dust (called in Swahili, "Kukula vumbi").

The second category of the population in Africa is the middle class. They are more or less educated and informed about the state of their country. They know how the government functions and have some understanding of its politics. They know very well what the stakes are once someone is in a position of leadership, and they strive to go higher into the privileged category of leaders.

They constantly seek to connect with people in power, and whenever they try to break through the barriers and enter into the privileged class, they present themselves with humility and a submissive spirit—rather than with their ethical and skillful ability to perform good work.

Africa is different than America in this regard. In the U.S., if you are smart and skilled, employers will select you on that basis. In Africa, you must submit yourself humbly, and you will be selected based on your ability to be obedient.

People in the middle class who do not have access to power are lonesome and isolated. They live without any hope for their future. This creates a tremendous amount of frustration, and leads to them creating their own power groups—rebel movements or militia that oppose and fight the existing power.

There is a saying in Swahili: "Dawa ya moto ni moto," which translates to, "The cure for the fire is another fire," or, "You fight fire with another fire." This is the ideology that has prevailed in Africa for decades.

Another ideology that is often seen in Africa can be clearly illustrated by a children's game. We used to play this game a lot as kids. You would ask your friend (in our language, Kinyamulenge) to be unselfish and share with you something that he has. You would say, "Uture tugabane niwanga bimeneke," asking him to share kindly, otherwise you will both lose it. You can both lose it as you struggle over it—or it can be lost as you take it from him and throw it on the ground.

Every time someone requests something of you in this manner, you have two options—you share it or you lose it. This is exactly how politics is played in Africa. When people in power cannot share their power, they fight against whoever wanted to share in their power.

The third group in Africa is comprised of the privileged family of the leaders. They are a small minority of the population. One of the strategies many African presidents have used for years to secure their power involves constructing a strong royalist group around them, mostly presidential relatives and relatives of the president's wife. This is known as "Akazu" in Rwanda or "Kindeko" in the Congo.

The privileged group rules over the whole country, and the resources necessary for the entire country belong to them. Members of this particular group serve as connectors or discriminators. They decide to bring into power—or push out of power—whoever they want. In this way, many people have been victimized.

One of the primary motives for seeking power in Africa is wealth. Power is very lucrative, and when someone gains access to power in Africa, the next thing you know, they become millionaires.

Their sources of enrichment are twofold: exploitation of their country's resources, and misuse of foreign aid. It is a shameful fact that billions of dollars are transferred every year as aid or loans into African countries—and yet, for generations, nothing has changed, in terms of poverty and the country's development. All these billions fall into the hands of leaders, who claim the money as their personal wealth, and yet the poor people continue to die of poverty.

The superpower leaders have knowledge of the situation in Africa, but they have ignored it for generations. As a consequence, millions of innocent people die every year. This is a serious betrayal by the international community. The silence of superpowers in the face of the injustice and corruption of African leaders toward their citizens is the killer of peace in the African continent.

The African presidents are among the richest people of the country, and the international community knows this. Former Congolese president Mobutu, for instance, was among the richest people in the world, whereas millions of his people were suffering from extreme poverty. This never seemed to bother the international community, for Mobutu continued to reign for over thirty years. The current Congolese president, Joseph Kabila, rose to the presidency in 2001, and he has already become a millionaire. I could go on and on, down the list of African presidents.

There is something unique to the African political system: There is not opposition, but enemies! This is in stark contrast to the situation in western countries. Here in America, politicians strongly believe in the concept of disagreeing—but without being disagreeable. The freedom to engage someone's ideas without fear of becoming enemies is deeply rooted in American society.

In Africa, whenever politicians disagree on some idea or issue, it results in an ugly and hateful enmity between them. In many African nations, there is no room for classic opposition, no political platform where constructive opinions, ideas, and truths are balanced for the benefit of the nation. There are, instead, enemies who harbor deep hatred for one another and constantly fight. As a consequence, they destroy everything.

This is, in my opinion, the fundamental problem of many African nations, and unless this is changed, there will never be peace. African people, who are aware of the dirty politics being played around them, have limited possibilities for survival. They can be quiet and suffer the consequences of alienation, never raising their voice against their leaders. They can flee the country, going far from the scene of injustice, corruption, and killings. Or, they can develop a plan to fight against the people in power. This scenario has given rise to the dozens of militia groups created in Africa, and it is rooted in the fact that there is no true democracy.

Ever since I was a young boy, I have heard politicians emphasize the French saying, "Qui veut la paix prepare la guerre," meaning, "If you want peace you have to prepare for war." This cycle of civil war and conflict is exactly what has been happening in the Congo, Rwanda, and Burundi for generations.

Just as there are political parties in western countries, you will find dozens of militias in one country that are constantly fighting each other. The sad thing is that innocent people are always used and become victims of the conflict. It is in this area where the international community has to develop a plan to prevent war—and this can be accomplished by simply promoting true democracy and supporting the entire democratic system rather than individuals in power.

But, it is not elections in and of themselves that signify democracy. It is the respect of rules and laws, and the presence of a system that allows the people who give power to the leaders to take it back whenever the leaders do not serve the interests of the people.

Leaders in America, and elsewhere in developed countries, are elected to assume key positions of power, and they take the opportunity to serve their nation—the people. In Africa, whenever leaders take over key positions, they see the occasion as an opportunity to loot all the resources of the country and oppress their citizens. This reality may not bother the international community, but it bothers me and many people like me who have fled the African continent because of conflict.

In the land of poverty, poor people suffer the misery of not meeting their basic daily needs. Poverty breaks people's hearts. It hunts them down, and it's almost impossible to break through the ceiling of misery. Some parents wake up early in the morning and wander around the city, begging friends or relatives for anything they can take home to feed their kids who have gone hungry for days.

Kids long to see their parents back home, and they can only hope to eat in the nighttime. Many times, parents come home empty-handed, regardless of their exhausting efforts. They suffer failure and shame once they cannot find food to bring home. Some parents, unable to find food to bring home, wait outside until their kids have gone to bed, ashamed to face the reality of a silent and desperate household that goes hungry every night. The look of hungry kids tortures their parents, who wonder why they have brought their children to the earth.

Not being able to provide for your loved ones creates a terrible feeling deep in your soul. The smells of meals cooking from the houses around—the ones that are lucky enough to get their daily meal—torture the ones that went to bed hungry.

Thousands of kids run away from their hungry families when their parents are not capable of providing food for them. The kids wander around the city, feeding from the garbage, stealing, using drugs, or prostituting for food. These are beautiful and smart kids, except that they have been torn down by their circumstances and the reality of this world that we live in.

Many people in Africa rest on their beds whenever they get sick, and wait for a miraculous healing. Beds don't heal sick people, medicine does, but where to find money to buy medicine? Poverty is like a terrible itch you can't cure—it stays there until you don't know what to do with yourself. Evil thoughts find their way inside people's souls, and it is hard for some to keep their inner nature.

Millions have become subordinate to the devils, not because they are bad people but because it is the only way for them to survive. Under the yoke of poverty, human nature is lost; people become who they never wanted to be.

Some people believe that they have been made to be miserable forever, and so they decide to serve evil because they think nothing good can come out of them. They become angry and nothing pleases them.

Whenever people see someone around them who has been successful in breaking through poverty, they marvel over him. Rich people in Africa don't make it easy on the poor. There are not many rich people in Africa, but the few who are rich have a lot of money—and they step on the feet of the poor. They are arrogant and they look at poor people with great contempt.

It hurts to be poor in Africa. It is different from Western life, where you can hardly tell who is poor and who is rich. In Africa, you can tell the poor based on what they eat, how they dress, how they walk, and how other people talk to them. If you are poor, you lose your human dignity, and it hurts to live this type of life.

In my case, my financial circumstances fluctuated as I went from one place to another. In my village, I never considered myself poor. In fact, I always thought that we were rich. I had almost everything I needed. When I moved to the city of Uvira in the Congo, I came to understand what it means to be poor. I saw people who were miserable and could not find anything to eat because they had no money. Money in the city is like a God from whom we expect everything. This was not the case in my village.

Seeing this awakened my consciousness. I realized how much we had been blessed in my village, where I never went hungry. This is how all the Banyamulenge had grown up. They lived in a land that was free of hunger. When I moved to Rwanda, my life changed completely. There were more poor people than I had ever seen before.

I was frightened by the life in Rwanda. I believed in having a family, a wife, and kids. But, I was horrified by the thought that one day, if life became tough and I could not provide for my kids, they could end up on the street. After all, each of the kids on the street was born from their parents.

I started fighting my way into the new lifestyle that I found in Rwanda. I was no stranger to hard work, and I had grown accustomed to moving around. I was ready to face new challenges. I followed in the footsteps of those who had gone before me, emulating them. And, I vowed never to get distracted from what I wanted to achieve.

~ THIRTY-THREE ~

In 2000, I was completing my last year at university, majoring in business and administration. Ever since I'd started, I had been focused on finishing school. My program was five years of study, and it was different from many other programs that required only fours years for a bachelor's degree. By that time, some of my friends who had begun their four-year program at the same time I'd started my five-year program had already graduated and found decent jobs.

Since my earliest age, I had always been a competitive person, so watching my friends tapping into higher positions in the government made me feel like I was behind the game. I felt tremendous pressure to try and rise above. My feeling was, *I am just as capable! If they can do it, I can, too!* I could think of nothing else but success. I wanted to find something I could do that would be perceived as exceptional—something noticeable that would cause others to call me successful.

I looked everywhere I could, trying to find a good opportunity to get a decent job or start my own business. I was horrified at the thought of becoming poor in Rwanda. I woke up very early in the morning and went around the city, looking for information about opportunities, hoping to find one thing that would instantly change my whole life. In the evening, I came back home with nothing, and lay on the bed, worrying and wondering if I would ever succeed in Rwanda.

I had never in my life been a lazy person, and I never got tired of searching for opportunities. As the days progressed, the pressure kept building inside me. Things changed so quickly in Rwanda, and every day, new friends found decent jobs and good opportunities to travel around the world.

Like I've said, my life has always been up and down. This was another time in my life where I felt like nothing would ever work. I was physically exhausted, and no matter how hard I tried, nothing worked as I anticipated. I knew that things were not working, but I felt deep in my heart that this situation would one day come to an end.

Then, in November of 2000, around noontime on a hot day, I grew hungry. In Rwanda, people went to work at 8:30 in the morning and then at noontime, everyone took a two-hour break. All services—like banks, for example—closed at noon and opened again at 2:00 p.m. Restaurants stayed open to serve the lunch crowd.

Although I was hungry, I didn't have the bus fare to go home to eat lunch. So, I didn't have lunch that day. Instead, I went downtown and was sitting with my friend in a public library which did not close for the lunch break. I was waiting for the government offices and other services to reopen for the afternoon, so I could continue looking for information on jobs and opportunities.

My friend, Seth, had a brochure in front of him, and on the cover page was a beautiful picture of girls and boys holding hands. The brochure was for the International Student Festival in Trondheim, Norway.

I grabbed the brochure, gave it my full attention, and tried to read it. Sadly, it was in English, and I could hardly understand it. I asked my friend, "What is this that you have here?"

He explained that he was going to apply, and see if he would be selected to participate in the festival in March of 2001 in Norway.

Traveling to Norway? What a dream! I thought to myself. I was very interested, and asked him if he knew anybody from Rwanda who had ever gotten the chance to participate in this festival.

He said, "Oh, yes!"

The application deadline was one week from that day. I made a copy of all the information, and took it home with me. Since it was in English, I needed to be able to take my time deciphering it. I found out that a student association in Trondheim, Norway organizes a festival every two years, and looks for participants from universities around the world. For every conference, they get more than four thousand international applications. From the four thousand applications, only four hundred students are selected. Knowing the selection process was very competitive, I tried my best to make sure that I had everything they requested.

Amazingly, in January of 2001, I received a confirmation letter saying that I had been selected! Food and accommodations were going to be provided to every participant, but few students were going to get the support of an airline ticket. I told myself that I would do whatever it took to make this adventure possible. I felt more energized than I had felt in years.

Since the day I received the confirmation letter, I worked very hard to get the funds for the airline ticket. I went to almost every embassy and international organization that was known in Kigali, but couldn't find any support. At the last minute—as always—a friend of mine who worked at the Youth Ministry told me that I should go and see if they could assist me.

The way I got the money from this ministry was totally unexpected—and miraculous! No one could believe that a student like me would make this kind of official trip, and receive money from the government for travel expenses.

In order to obtain a visa for the trip, I was required to travel to Uganda, because Norway had no embassy in Rwanda. The actual check for my airline ticket had to be issued through the Finance Ministry. The whole process was a nightmare. I was completely exhausted. I almost went crazy thanks to the bureaucracy that took me from one office to another for signatures.

Everything I needed to accomplish before I traveled seemed to be scheduled during the same week before my trip, and I could be in only one place at a time. When I went to Uganda for the visa, I returned to Rwanda to find that the process had stagnated, because it required me to be there and keep pushing.

Finally, all the arrangements were in place. I would be traveling with Ethiopian Airlines, and had to be at the airport at 3:00 a.m., two hours before the flight. The fact that I was about to take this journey was remarkable. It was going to be the greatest adventure of my life so far. It would also be a breakthrough that opened up many opportunities for me in life, beyond what I had dreamed possible.

My friends and relatives marveled over how lucky I was. They could not understand it. In disbelief, they watched me boarding the aircraft, and watched the airplane take off and soar through the sky, way above the hills and mountains of Rwanda, as we headed to the airport at Bujumbura, the capital of Burundi.

I had a window seat over the right wing, and I could see down as the darkness started to break and surrender to the daylight. Within a half hour, I was struck by the morning view of Lake Tanganyika, the lake I had grown up around in Uvira. The sight from the hills above as the airplane maneuvered to land broke my heart until I cried.

I turned around and saw the whole city of Uvira in the Congo. I saw the mountains of Mulenge—there was the one I used to climb as I went back to my village on vacation! Standing on top of the highest mountain of Mulenge, I used to look from a far distance upon the Bujumbura Airport, as airplanes landed and others flew over me. Millions of times, I had hoped so deeply that I could be flying. I never knew that in my lifetime, I would actually fly, but I always believed that everything was possible, and I had faith.

I looked down and saw fishing boats that were approaching the shore after a long night of fishing. I knew their customs, as someone who had lived near the lake. I started crying, but I hid myself so I wouldn't be seen by the passenger beside me. I was so nostalgic, filled with old memories of Uvira, and the knowledge of what had happened. Thousands of people had died on that ground since the war first started.

We landed and picked up other passengers from Burundi, and in a few minutes, the aircraft took off again. Not knowing the direction that we were about to take, I prayed that we might fly over the high plateau of Mulenge so that I could see my villages again. Unfortunately, we were heading eastward, and my villages were in the west. We were heading to Addis Abba, where the sun rose.

We faced the sun as its rays grew stronger and warmed the airplane. When I looked down, I had a view of river basins I learned about in geography class in high school—basins where many streams flowed downhill, and drained into the rivers that looked like bathtubs radiating from the central areas as we flew over the highlands of Ethiopia.

I could not believe my eyes! I thought I was dreaming. We landed at Addis Abba Airport for a few hours and then took off again. I was tired, but my curiosity kept me from finding sleep. I did not want to miss anything on my way to the new world.

Within a few hours, we landed in Cairo, Egypt. Everywhere I landed, I thought of what I knew about the place from my geography classes in high school. We took off from Cairo, headed for our next destination—Frankfurt, Germany. We flew at a high altitude, way above the sky where even eagles cannot make it, and the scene on the ground became less visible.

The sound of the airplane had become tiring and overwhelming. I had been sitting for a long time, and my legs were getting tired. My mind had almost run out of thoughts, after going back and forth, thinking of anything you could ever imagine. Up in the airplane, I had nothing else to do but think—and I thought about my entire life, from my village where I was born to the present day.

At some point, the airplane dipped down, and it scared me to death. I started thinking about what would happen if the airplane crashed down. I imagined what my mom would think of my death in an airplane. I could picture her asking herself where I was going. (My mother still lived in the Congo and I had no communication with her.)

As we flew above the Alps, the mountains were covered with snow, and the view was astonishing. Finally we were about to land in Frankfurt. It was nighttime, and I was struck by the brightness of the city. As we touched down, and disembarked, I was surprised by how everyone was rushing at the airport. It was the busiest place that I had ever seen! For the most part, nobody talked to anybody else.

I had been traveling with a friend that I'd come with from Kigali, and who was going to Bangkok, Thailand. (This was not my friend, Seth, who had the magazine containing the information on the Norway festival. Sadly, he was not selected to attend the festival.) Before we separated in Addis Abba, my friend warned me to be careful that I didn't miss my connection to Oslo, the capital of Norway.

I had no idea that it was going to be that busy and confusing at the airport. I struggled to find my gate, fighting off exhaustion. Everything on the scene had turned white—the floor was white, the ceiling was bright with rays of lights, and the people were white. I was the only black one at the gate.

I thought I had landed on the moon! I had never in my life experienced a greater feeling of being lost. I was not enjoying anything at this time. I was just tired, and wanted to sleep. This was the culmination of weeks without getting enough sleep, ever since I'd realized that my journey was coming together.

Finally, after hours of sitting, I boarded the airplane to Oslo. I sat down in my seat and immediately fell into a deep sleep. I have no idea how long it took us to fly from Frankfurt to Oslo. It wasn't until we landed that someone touched me and said, "We have reached our destination."

As I disembarked from the airplane, I asked how I could get to Trondheim, the city where the festival was taking place. I was told I had to travel two more hours to get there in the airplane—but there was no flight going there until the next morning. I slept in the airport, waiting to catch the first flight in the morning. I was so tired that night, and slept so deeply, that when I woke up in the morning, I did not know where I was. I was a little bit refreshed and was able to start thinking again, but my English was so horrible, I could not explain to anyone where I was going or what I wanted.

I managed to explain myself well enough to get someone to help me call the festival office. I gave them my airplane schedule so that they could come and pick me up. So, when we touched down in Trondheim, I found a young fellow waiting for me. I arrived there on Monday, and the festival had been going on since Friday.

As we went out of the airport toward his vehicle, I was shocked by the snow and cold that I felt. It was beyond anything

I'd ever imagined. My hands froze in two seconds, my lips went numb, and my forehead ached terribly.

We were divided into different groups with team leaders who walked us around. I went through the process of registration, and then I was dropped off in my classroom where my classmates were following a lesson.

The topic of the whole festival that year was "Global Responsibility" and my workshop was "Conflict and Disaster." As someone from the Congo and Rwanda, I had a lot to share with my classmates about the conflict. As I worked in the classroom full of students from different countries and background, I was horrified by the attention that I got. I looked horrible. I hadn't taken a shower in the two days since I'd left home.

My classmates were so kind and they wanted to talk to me, but I avoided them because I could not talk to them in English. When we took a break at the end of the session, they all came up to me, introducing themselves and shaking hands, but I was too shy to speak to anybody in English.

Then, I found two students who spoke French—Olivier Gilbert from France, and his girlfriend at the time, Henny Rahardja from Australia. We are still in touch to this day. I became tied to them and went with them everywhere they went. I wanted to make sure that any time someone wanted to talk to me, they would interpret for me.

The festival was so moving. Everywhere we walked in the hallways, there were students from different backgrounds, playing a variety of music. I was told that, later in the evening of my first day there, we would be going up to the mountain to the students' cabin and spending the night there—dancing, interacting with colleagues, and having fun.

That evening, we boarded the bus heading up the mountain, away from the city. On the bus, I sat with my French-speaking friends. It was extremely cold on the mountain and the trees were covered in snow. As we rode to the cabin, I saw people across the mountain skiing and really delighting in the weather. I had difficulty believing that people could live in such conditions and still find ways of enjoying it.

That night, I did not stay as long as the rest of the group did, dancing and chatting with friends. I was completely exhausted and ready to sleep. There were dormitories for boys and girls. There was no heat in the room upstairs. The only heat came from the wood fire that was set in the middle section of the house. I was cold and I wrapped myself in my clothes and sleeping bag.

While I was sleeping, something surprising happened. I went to bed with only one sleeping bag on me—the one that I brought from Rwanda, which was not warm enough. That was the reason I decided to sleep with all my clothes on. When I woke up, I found a warm sleeping bag on me.

What angel knew that I was cold, and covered me with a warm sleeping bag? I did not know who it was, and I never asked. I was afraid of engaging in conversation with anybody because of my difficulty speaking in English.

When I'd walked into the classroom for the first time, I noticed something right away. There was a special looking, young Norwegian girl, who was constantly looking at me as I sat down in the classroom, and thereafter when I went out. I could tell that she was curious and wanted to talk to me, but I avoided her because I could not talk in English and she did not know French. She was one of the team leaders. Her name was Linda Henriksen, a very beautiful and friendly girl, who cared for the whole group.

Since the very first time she introduced herself to me, she was smiling, and her laughter was sincere whenever she talked to me. It was not the kind of forced smile that many people wear to show kindness and courtesy. I could tell that she was deep and trusting.

At that time, there was no way that I would have guessed that she was interested in connecting with me particularly, because she was just as nice with the whole group. But, since my second day at the festival, we became very close friends, and we were together all the time. I very much enjoyed her companionship, and I was grateful that she always made sure I got home safely, without getting lost.

Something naturally made us belong to each other, and she became more than a friend. She really relaxed me to a smooth level of comfort—and then she told me that she was the one who had covered me on my first cold night in Norway. We could not talk much, but we laughed all the time. The souls that fit together have their own language. They smoothly belong and relate to each other, regardless of the language barriers. I was afraid to see the end of the conference which was going to separate us.

It felt so bizarre to know that my soul had found comfort in the warm arms of a strange white girl. Deep in my mind, I wrestled with the understanding of my beliefs, and what I grew up knowing to be moral behavior. But, I trusted her more than I had ever trusted any girl in my life. With her angelic beauty, she had stolen my reasoning, and her smile had struck down all my nerves, and eased the fear and discomfort that could have come with being in an unfamiliar environment.

I rested even more in her incredible laughter. I never thought of engaging in any thought that would compromise what I felt at that moment, and I slid into the rhythms of real love. It was the very first time that I understood what it means to be in true love, and once we fell in love, we continued to speak the language of love and laughter.

After the festival, I stayed one more week, and went with her to southern Norway to visit her family in Sandnes. I had no idea what it meant for her, taking me to meet her family—whether she considered us boyfriend and girlfriend, or was just taking me out of kindness. But, I did not care where she was taking me or why. I already trusted her and was no longer afraid of anything except losing her.

~ THIRTY-FOUR ~

We boarded the airplane and flew to the south. As we got to the airport, her father, Paul, was there waiting for us. We spoke to each other in our language and she explained to her family what we were saying.

Her mother, Bjoerg, was so nice and caring, but I could see that she was frightened by the fact that her daughter had brought someone from Rwanda. She had already Googled articles about Rwanda and the Congo, and all she could see were pictures of dead people, and news about the high prevalence of HIV and AIDS.

Linda's younger sister, Lena, was also very beautiful. I didn't talk to her much, but she was also very nice, smiling a lot. Her father was a cool guy. He probably understood that men can face any situation when it comes to love. I wondered what they were thinking about me, but I could not tell. All I knew was that, whenever Linda was around me, I felt like I could live there, no matter what her family thought of me.

In her family, I saw a new and different kind of life, unlike anything I had ever seen before. They were very demonstrative in the way they loved each other. Before going to bed, Linda would go and hug and kiss her father and mother, wishing them goodnight. I was perplexed by their culture and their way of life.

The following day, Linda and I took her father's vehicle and went on a tour of the area. We drove on the flat, beautiful roads. She was driving very fast, heading towards the ocean. Nobody else was around the shore because it was in the deep winter. As we got to the ocean, we started looking around, and playing in the cold sand. In that moment, I wondered why I was born so far away from my love.

I had only one day remaining before I would return back home. I did not know if I would ever see her again, and I couldn't imagine how I would survive her absence in my life. The idea of leaving her felt like a bad dream.

It was late in the day and time to head back home. We stopped at the mall where she bought a gift for me to take home. I felt like having to go back to her home and into the whole family environment, with the eating and talking we would have to do there, was stealing our time.

The next day, Friday, March 23rd, I had to return home. I woke up feeling like my stomach had flooded with water, and I had difficulty eating. We flew from Stavanger Airport to Oslo. She had to go back to Trondheim, where we had met, because she was attending school there.

My flight was at night, and we sat down and spent our last minutes together laughing. But, the toxic feeling of separation was already injected into our hearts, like an insect sting in our bodies. Our happiness was declining every minute that brought us closer to separation. We knew that soon we would be separated, and sadness and loneliness would swallow us.

Finally, it was time to face the reality—I had to leave. She walked with me towards the gate. We were holding hands, and kissed goodbye. At that point, we were so filled with emotion, we could not talk, and she was crying. All I managed to say to her was, "Will you ever come and visit me in Rwanda?"

She said, "Yes, I will!"

I said again, "Do you promise that you will?"

She said, "Yes!"

My heart desperately wanted to believe that I would see her again. I knew it wouldn't be easy for me to get back to Norway, so I hoped she would come see me in Rwanda. Believing that she would visit gave me the courage to walk away from her and prepare to board the plane. At first, when I turned away from her, I did not want to look behind me, thinking that would help me deal with leaving her. I made a few steps, but I looked back, and she was soberly crying.

I went running back, and hugged her again. And, then I rushed to the gate, so I wouldn't be late. When I turned to look for her again, I could not see her. She had disappeared into the crowd. I kept looking for her long, red hair, but she was gone. I went home in total emptiness. Nothing excited me on my way home. I was in complete despair.

My friends back home were very excited about my trip, and had been writing me emails, letting me know that they were looking forward to hearing my story. But, the idea of telling the story felt so bitter. As I got to Kigali, my friends came to ask me what I have seen in Europe, but my thoughts were mostly focused on how to get internet service so I could see if Linda had written to me. Sure enough, she had written to me, once again promising to come and visit.

In July of that same year, four months after I left her in Oslo, Linda kept her promise and came to visit me in Rwanda. I welcomed her with mixed feelings. On the one hand, I was excited. On the other hand, I was nervous because, in my culture, it was viewed as immoral and unacceptable to live in an open relationship before the wedding.

In her culture, everything was open. People held hands, and kissed in the street and on airplanes and buses. In Rwanda, everything was done in private. Not until night had fallen would people hide in the corners of streets, deeply kissing. These things never took place during daylight.

I didn't know what to do. There was no way I could hide her and decline to take her to meet my family. I wanted to show her the same kindness and love she extended to me when I stayed with her and her family. At the same time, I was terrified of what people would say about me.

From the very first day that I took her to downtown Kigali, we drew the attention of everyone who passed us. Every time we encountered someone on the street or on the street corner, we were greeted with stares and questions. People wondered who we were and made no secret of the fact that they were talking about us.

Linda had no idea what was going on in my mind and heart, and I did not share with her the realities of my culture and the ways in which it differed from hers. On several occasions, she wanted to hold me and play, but I spontaneously rejected her, leaving her wondering why.

During her stay in Rwanda, Linda visited almost all the memorial sites of genocide. She was shocked by the poverty she saw, and realized how lucky she was to have been born Norwegian. I had never met anyone as pure-hearted as Linda. She was a loving person that cared very much about other people's lives.

She was so excited, laughing all the time, and people liked her very much. Kids on the street were constantly running after her, asking her for money. She loved them, and cried over these beautiful kids with no place to stay. I remember one day in particular, she refused to eat in the restaurant where we would have spent about five thousand Rwandan franks, because she knew that there were thousands of kids who would go to bed hungry.

I had to beg her to stay and eat, explaining that she had done nothing wrong. Life is not easy for everyone. Certain people suffer while others don't. I told her that if the world was so perfect, and all the people were perfect, then the world would no longer be called the world. It would be the paradise where we expect to one day live a perfect life, free of misery. That time has yet to come.

One particular story broke her heart. We were visiting the memorial site in Gikongoro, where we met a tour guide who watched over the bones of his entire family. He showed us the bones of his kids and brothers. We soberly cried that day, and went home with little hope that the world would ever get better. Justice didn't seem sufficient to appease the souls who have suffered the loss of everything. That night we dreamed of everything that would bring peace to Rwanda and the rest of the world.

The time came when she had to go home and leave me again. The same feelings that I had when leaving Norway returned, but this time, I had the hope that I was going to visit her soon.

In April of 2002, I went back to Norway and stayed there for two months, until June 19th, when I had to travel to the United States for a conference on conflict resolution at Georgetown University in Virginia. From there, I planned to attend a conference in Australia, and then return to Rwanda to start a nonprofit organization in conflict resolution.

While I was in the U.S. for the Georgetown conference, I discovered that tensions back home were escalating, and it was unsafe to return to Rwanda. This completely changed my plans. There was no point in going to Australia for the other conference, since all my conflict resolution projects ultimately related to Rwanda. It was my plan to learn conflict resolution as a way of helping to solve the conflict in the Great Lakes region of Africa.

I was in America for five months on a visa. During that five-month period, I decided to seek political asylum. I found an immigration lawyer, who submitted the application for me. It would take one year for approval to be granted, but during the period in which I was waiting to find out whether I would ultimately be approved, no steps would be taken to deport me.

One year after submitting my application for asylum, my paperwork was approved. I decided to settle in Portland, Maine because I personally knew two Banyamulenge who were living there, and there were others from my tribe who were living there, as well.

As for Linda, I always believed I would see her again. But, in January of 2007, I got horrible news from Norway—Linda had died in an unimaginable accident.

Following are messages I received from Linda's sister, Kristin, and my friend Kirsten from Norway:

> *Dear Georges,*
>
> *I am sorry to say that we have very sad news for you. Linda died in an accident last night. She was hit by bricks falling down from a roof [while] walking in Oslo. You can read about it in the news. If you feel like talking to us, you can call us. God bless you. We are very happy for*

the dimension you brought into Linda's and our lives, and I know she admired you a lot. She will be buried in Sandnes, but we still don't know when. Yours sincerely, Kristin Henriksen, with family

* * *

Dear Georges,

It is with deep sorrow that I have to tell you that Linda Henriksen died in an accident in the centre of Oslo two days ago, as a house fell down on the walkway where Linda was walking, and caused grave head injuries. Linda had just come back from 18 months in Dadaab in Kenya working with Somali refugees.

Best regards from Kirsten.

I was sitting in my office when I read these messages. When I finished reading, I felt like my chair was sinking with me into the ground. I felt so completely lost in my mind, I could not think straight. I could not conceive of how a house in Oslo could possibly fall on someone. I went home and stayed there, not knowing what to do. I called her home and talked to her sister, who confirmed that Linda was gone.

I could not grasp it. I was terrified. What came to my mind was our last moment together. She drove me to Stavanger Airport in Norway, where I would board a plane for the U.S. We sat down, while waiting for a KLM flight—a Dutch airline that was going to take me to Amsterdam, and then the U.S. We waited for half an hour. Suddenly, we could see through the gate that the aircraft was landing. A few minutes later, we heard the pager calling the passengers for boarding.

I stood up and picked up my luggage. We looked at each other with deep love and a sense of longing. We said, "We shall see each other again, and very soon."

I was so certain that I would see her. We'd had many separations before and we had met again—but this time was different. I never saw her again after that day.

There is so much we don't know about the future, and yet we are so hopeful when we say things about the future, never knowing what will rise ahead of us. I learned a great lesson from this experience in my life: Love as if you will never love again, and do something as if it is your last time to do it.

We can only talk about the past and the present. The future is not for us to know.

~ THIRTY-FIVE ~

We never know where life is taking us. Sometimes life takes us far away like sheep to be slaughtered in the market, and we have little control over our own liberty and happiness. We must learn to live with whatever situation we are facing.

My first job here in the U.S. started at 5:00 a.m. and I worked until 2:30 p.m. Since I had no vehicle, I walked to work, about three miles round-trip every day. The alarm that woke me up every morning traumatized me. I could hear it everywhere I went, even when I was busy shopping in the mall. It took many years, until long after I'd left my first American job, for my ears to clear out the sound that hunted me down.

I was working in a company that produced different types of fast-food chicken. I raced with machines that ran nonstop at every corner of the building. It was very cold and loud inside. Because we had to wear a helmet, protective glasses, gloves, and waterproof boots, it was hard to recognize each other as we walked by.

When my machine would break down, I found great relief and tried to rest while it was being fixed. Sometimes I was completely exhausted, and I went behind piled boxes of frozen chicken and fell asleep. At such times, I had to urge my friend to watch over me so that my supervisor would not find me sleeping and send me home for good. I knew what I was doing was risky, but I was tired. I slept very easily and never minded cold or freezing temperatures.

For one year, I worked for this company. In that job, my intellectual capacity and education were unnecessary. What mattered was my physical strength. I began to miss every piece of my life back home—even the parts of my life I never used to like! I suddenly realized that my new world had turned rough. My work environment destroyed my hope, along with the expectations of a better life that I'd held onto since I'd left Rwanda and started traveling around the world, believing that things could only go from good to great.

I have realized that sometimes life can be so misleading, as we become deeply absorbed in our present emotions and feelings. Whenever we have what we need, and are striving for a bigger future, we rarely think that we can lose what we already have. And, when we have lost everything that we had once held onto, we can completely forget that we ever had them in the first place.

On July 12th, 2004, I was fortunate to finally get free from my first job. I was hired by Avesta Housing Corporation. This was a dream coming true, and a blessing I had prayed for—but I had no idea what a heavy burden it would be, or how weary I would become trying to carry it. The system was totally different than any workplace I'd ever seen back home.

It was a demanding and detailed job, with many deadlines and regulations that I had to pay attention to. It required a lot of effort. I found everything puzzling, from day one when I walked into the company and was introduced to my future colleagues, whose names I could hardly retain. People were very nice, smiling, and shaking hands, but my heart was troubled. I wondered, *How am I going to survive this whole new world in front of me?*

When they brought me a brand new computer I thought, *They have wasted their money.* I thought that I could do everything manually. I had no idea that nothing is done in America without a computer. I had no way of knowing what lay before me. It frightened me, wondering how I was going to do everything with a computer, but what frightened me most was not being fluent in English.

I needed more English than I had, because understanding is the beginning of knowledge. I knew deep in my mind that I needed to grow professionally, and Avesta Housing was the best place for me to be, but I went through such tremendous pressure that I almost quit.

Every day I went to work thinking, *This may be my last day before I resign.* The whole situation was very stressful for me. Some days, I felt so stupid and discouraged, I went home thinking that it was over. But, the following day, I found myself taking a shower and going to work again. It is so difficult to contemplate losing something you had once desperately wished to have.

Quitting would have been a horrible mistake—one I would have carried for the rest of my life. There is a saying in my language that says, "Utewe nigwe arayirinda," meaning, "If you are attacked by a leopard, you have to resist it, and never give up, until it kills you or you kill it."

I was lucky to have a very patient and understanding supervisor. She had told me from the first day that she wasn't expecting me to learn everything at once. But, she had no idea what type of person she was dealing with—where I was born, how I had grown up, or what I was going through at that moment. If I had explained everything to her in detail, I probably would have lost my job.

She didn't realize I had never sent a fax before; I had never made a copy, or used the many other complex pieces of office equipment which were around me, and which stressed me to death as I learned to use them. I could not talk clearly on the phone, and listening to voicemails was a nightmare; I spent minutes and minutes trying to make out the meaning of the voicemails. When my phone rang, it scared me to half to death. I was terrified of how I sounded on the phone with my broken English, knowing that my colleagues were around me, overhearing how I stumbled over my words.

At that time, I wished I had been born here; it would have been much easier for me. My hands sweated and trembled whenever I tried to type anything on my computer. And, whenever my supervisor or a colleague was standing by me, I was very slow.

When I overheard my colleagues speaking eloquently on the phone, smoothly interchanging their words at will, it generated an endless feeling of stupidity inside of me. I walked around the office embarrassed, thinking that my eagerness and willingness to engage in this unfamiliar situation had brought me shame. I wondered if I would ever recover the confidence that had always defined my personality.

The only way I could do my work correctly was to be bold and ask questions. Even though asking questions during every step of my work seemed like too much, I had no choice—I had to ask. Occasionally, a colleague would seem to be bothered by my questions and this added to my frustration.

The progress that I was making was overshadowed by the poor impression that I thought I had made on everyone. I started getting better at many things, but my belief that I was making a bad impression began to erode my confidence, and I became discouraged. I reacted to every circumstance, and my mind and body were plagued with endless fear and anxiety.

I was constantly seeking peace and happiness, but I was in fear more than I was happy. I wondered why it seemed so natural for my mind to stay down, rather than rising up and living a life free of fear. I could not grasp what was behind the mysterious misery that I was accepting as my dwelling place. I knew that the worst thing that could ever happen to me in life was death, and that the things I feared in my daily life were unlikely to kill me. Yet, I ruined my life with anxiety and worries, every minute of my day. Living in constant fear is to face death every day.

I was afraid to share personal things with people in the workplace, and so I was slow in making new friends. This was mostly due to the language barrier, but also the cultural differences.

Although I experienced all kinds of emotions while becoming acclimated, I remained resilient and never quit. I am happy that I stayed on course because the work that we do at Avesta Housing is fulfilling and inspiring. We have helped thousands of people find a home that they can afford. Many residents appreciate what we do for them, and there are others who never appreciate anything. This never bothered me because some people just don't know how to appreciate what is given to them.

With the different people I have met and lived with throughout my life, I have always had a sense of inner connection or disconnection that made me feel comfortable or uncomfortable in our interactions. With some people, trusting them and being friends comes so naturally. With others, I have had to dig deeper—and sometimes it simply doesn't work. I know it's not wise to press too hard, for it only causes emotional and physical pain.

God has been faithful and gracious to me, and he has given me, through many experiences, an exceptional understanding of other people. I have always managed to control my emotions, and tell the difference between the eyes that looked at me with compassion, and the ones that underestimated me. In everything, I have been able to refrain from taking the steps that lead me to hate.

I have lived the story of a man who was once thrown into the ocean without knowing how to swim. He got lucky—he hit a piece of wood and immediately grabbed hold of it. He did not sink, but managed to tread water, moving to the rhythm of winds that took him back and forth. He didn't die—but the winds and waves never pushed him far enough to reach the shore, either.

There were times when the waves pushed him *near* the shore, and he hoped that he was about to survive, but suddenly, a strong wave would hit, and bring him back to where he started. His life was an endless series of struggles, until a kind soul came along to help rescue him. In my case, I believe it was God who rescued me. As it is written in Psalms 34:4: "I sought the Lord and he heard me, and delivered me from all my fears."

I have found myself in situations that marked my life here in the U.S. and became the motivation for writing this book. For one thing, I have worked two jobs since arriving here in "busy land." I was in Rome, so to speak, and so I did as the Romans did. For many years, I mastered the art of dressing up in the morning before going to one job, and then quickly dressing down as I got ready to dirty my hands. My second job was totally different from my first one, but I somehow managed to survive both.

After having these two jobs for quite a long time, and saving a fair amount of money, I felt that it was time for me to embark on a quest for the so-called American Dream—buying a house. I had no experience in how to get a mortgage, but I was very encouraged by the money I had in my bank account, and the boundless energy that convinced me I could work as many jobs as I wanted to, for as long as I wanted to.

~ THIRTY-SIX ~

By this time, I had already met my fiancé, and I thought that a beautiful house would be a wonderful gift for her. On September 15th, 2007, seven months after I purchased my house, we got married.

Every day of my life, I had prayed and wished for good things to happen to me, but not every day that I prayed was I able to get what I prayed for and wanted. I had asked God a long time ago to give me a beautiful wife, a perfect soul mate suitable for me. And, God heard my prayers and gave me Lise.

I met Lise while I was in Rwanda. My best friend and room-mate, Fidele, happened to be dating her sister. At this time, I was doing my internship in the Rwanda Parliament, and my friend, Fidèle, worked for the Ministry of Justice. These two institutions were very close to each other, and most of the time, we took our break lunch together. He had a vehicle and I didn't. So, I would ride with him to lunch, and after work, he would take me home.

One particular day, he had to stop to pick up a date before lunch. I had never met his date before, so I decided to stay in the parked vehicle while he went inside the house. I waited for half an hour, and fell asleep. Suddenly, I heard someone knocking on the car window. I woke up to see a very beautiful girl, asking me to come into the house. I could not say no. I walked with her to the house, where I was introduced to the members of her household— including Lise, who was still very young, but beautiful.

I became very good friends with her entire family.

A few years later, in 2001, Lise and her two older sisters, Liliane and Livine, along with her older brother, Dodo, moved to Canada. As you may recall, I came to the U.S. in 2002, and settled in Portland, Maine, which is only three hours from the U.S. border with Canada.

I became reacquainted with Lise. We started calling each other as friends, and stayed in touch. Things never did last between my friend, Fidele, and Lise's sister. But, God intended that Lise and I would become one, years after our first meeting, here in the U.S.

During our talks over the phone, we fell in love and officially decided that we could spend the rest of our lives together. I am one of the luckiest people that God has ever given a beautiful and loving wife, a true helper, the greatest gift of all from God.

We were married on September 15th, 2007, and our wedding day was unique. We had a blast—singing, joking, and crying. The following year, on August 31st, we had our firstborn—a baby boy we named Ael Shimirwa. The nine months that we had to wait for him felt more like a decade. The feelings I experienced while expecting my son were incomparable.

My wife had a very smooth pregnancy, but there were days that scared us, due to our lack of experience and a tragedy suffered by my best friend Alex and his wife, Esther. They regrettably lost their first son, who died in the very same week that he was expected to be born. Only God knows why he took him before we could meet him. We all loved him and longed to see him, but he never made it out into the world alive.

One day, Ael did not kick or move as he normally did. For the whole day, we wondered what had happened, and we rushed to the hospital, scared to death. But our doctor told us that everything was fine, and sent us home. As we returned home, still worried, we sat in the living room, and finally Lise felt the baby kick. We were greatly relieved to have the baby talk to us in that way.

On the day he was born, he came as a surprise. We expected him one week later, but he suddenly decided to begin making his entrance on Saturday, August 30th, 2008, while I was working at my second job, forty-five minutes from home.

My wife called me, and urged me to come home quickly. I did not ask why; I immediately knew the reason. Ael was pushing his way out of the cage that had held him for months. I was anxious over the realization that our son, whose arrival we had anticipated for nine months, was finally here. I could not think of anything but the logistics of the situation. I did not know how to organize my thoughts. I was seriously anxious to get home and rush Lise to the hospital.

On my way home, I could not feel my vehicle's pedals and I felt that my car wasn't running fast enough. When I got home, I found Lise sitting there, very calm and not in a hurry at all. Her composure kind of irritated me, because I was on edge, feeling that the world was about to end. How could my thoughts be rushing through my mind while Lise sat at home, moving slowly, perfectly calm?

For some reason, she was holding CDs in her hands. This triggered my temper and I raised my voice. I demanded to know what the CDs had to do with her being in labor!

When Lise heard me raising my voice, she became very upset. I had never before heard her talk to me that way. I immediately calmed down, realizing that maybe I was overreacting. I really didn't know what she was thinking at that particular moment in time, but I sat down and impatiently waited for her. We finally left for the hospital, and on our way there, we did not talk much.

I have never in my life been the type of person who waits until the unknown smacks me in the face. I have always wanted to have a little bit of insurance that things are safe. So, after we were admitted, I annoyed nurses by asking the same question over and over: "How long is it going to take before we will meet Ael?" It was a stupid question, but I kept asking it. It was the only thing on my mind.

I tried to read a book or watch TV, but it didn't work. I couldn't force my mind to think of anything but the birth of my son. The pain had not yet hit Lise, who was calm and patient. A dozen times, I asked her how she felt, and each time, I got same answer: "Fine."

I wondered why she wasn't feeling any pain after we had been there for almost five hours. I wondered if childbirth in America was really going to be that easy. In Africa, I had heard that there is nothing as painful as going through labor. Of course, I had no direct experience with childbirth, and no way of knowing what to expect. In our culture, back in my village, men were never around their wives when they were having babies; only women were around.

Lise didn't ask for an epidural, and I couldn't understand why she wasn't feeling any pain yet. It's not that I wanted her to suffer, but the absence of pain concerned me. Little did I know, the time had simply not yet come. She went into a room with a hot tub to help relax her while we were waiting.

Her hospital room had a beautiful view of the street, facing the cathedral. It was Saturday, and there was a wedding taking place at the cathedral. I looked at the people dressed up and taking pictures. They were smiling and enjoying their day, and I thought, *Next year at this time, you may end up here in the maternity room, having a baby!* The previous year when we got married, having a baby was just a dream.

I was very impatient all during that day. I just wanted to be done with the anxiety that I had carried during the nine months of waiting. At midnight, Lise finally started experiencing a tremendous amount of pain. Her face changed, her mouth was completely dry, and her lips started cracking.

I thought, "This is it!" A few hours after Lise started feeling the pain, a nurse came in and checked on her. She was surprised to realize that Lise was completely dilated. The nurse panicked, and her face turned red—it was time for Ael to get out! Lise's doctor was not yet present because everything had gone much faster than they had predicted.

In a few seconds, the whole room was full of nurses, who warned Lise not to do anything until her doctor was there. Watching all the nurses panic, and waiting for the doctor, caused me to panic, too.

Within a few seconds, Lise's doctor came rushing in. As he struggled to put on his scrubs, I wondered, *Where has he been? Was he sleeping?* But, he had just arrived at the hospital, and was changing from his regular clothes into his hospital clothes.

The scene was terrifying—nurses were rushing around the room, performing every detail necessary, while the doctor coordinated their every move. I stood at the top of the bed, holding Lise's hands, and prompting her to do what the doctor was telling her. Lise's hospital bed had turned to a war zone, full of blood. It hurt me to see her in such agony, and I wished I could share some of her pain.

Finally, at 3:45 a.m. on August 31st, 2008, Ael arrived.

As soon as he came out, he cried loudly, and his sound struck my heart. I immediately rushed to hold him. The doctor, who was holding him, was startled by my reaction. He didn't realize that I'd reacted that way because I thought my son was hurt.

The umbilical cord was still attached, and the doctor handed me the scissors to cut it. The way it felt to cut the cord was terrifying. My hands were shaking, and I was afraid I would harm him. But a man's got to do what a man's got to do, and both Ael and I survived the cutting of the cord.

I felt an unbelievable sense of relief with the arrival of Ael, my firstborn, and my first strength. He was the sweetest baby I had ever seen. Never before had I felt a feeling so exceptional. This milestone eased my mind into believing once again that God is good. I held the greatest gift of my life in my arms. He was the cutest baby I had ever seen, and a sense of joy and love filled my whole heart.

After one day, we went home and started adjusting to parenthood. I never wanted to leave home. In my culture, once someone has baby, people call him or her after the name of their firstborn son or daughter. It felt so good to be called Papa Ael.

~ THIRTY-SEVEN ~

Each event in my life has held its own measure of emotional impact. Some of them struck me with great pain and sadness, and caused me to doubt my ability to survive. Others brought me a great amount of stress and pressure before they turned out to be a blast of joy and true happiness, almost beyond my capacity to describe.

The birth of my son stressed me deeply, but afterwards, I felt happiness so great, it completely changed my way of thinking. As Ael grew bigger and got to know me, he always wanted to be with me, to spend time together and play. I never had enough time with my wife and son.

The immigration process unfolds slowly, and I've had to be patient while I wait for the time when I can bring my wife and son to live with me full-time in Maine. Until then, they can never spend more than a few months with me in Maine (due to visa restrictions), and when I visit them in Canada, I can never spend more than a couple of weeks with them (due to work obligations).

On many occasions when Lise and Ael were visiting me in Maine, I came home after a day without seeing them and Ael was so happy to see me, he went crazy. When I wanted to leave again, he would hold my leg tightly and cry. This hurt me deeply, and I started wondering, *Why do I have to live this life of missing my family?*

In 2010, two years after Ael was born, we were expecting another child. We were so excited, and nothing concerned us or made us worry—until Saturday, August 14th, when Lise called me at work and asked me to come home quickly and take her to the hospital. I quickly left work, rushed home, and took her to the hospital. After taking a blood test and ultrasound, the doctor came to us and said that Lise was going through a miscarriage. I will never forget the rhetoric used by the doctor: "Unfortunately, this child is not going to be among the ones that you will carry or hold."

The doctor's words foretold the burial of our son or daughter. There was nothing more the doctors could do for us; we would have to wait at home until the miscarriage ran its course. We left the hospital holding hands tightly, and I could feel the sadness connecting one hand to the other. We could not have prepared ourselves for the horror of the loss. There is nothing you can do when the life of someone that you hoped to see and to love is wasted.

Every time Ael came to me, it made me feel worse, because it reminded me of how Ael's lost sister or brother would have been cute and happy like Ael. The loss of our second child was the loss of a joy we will never recapture until we go to Heaven. We lost a part of ourselves, and from the beginning to the end, it hurt so badly. We still haven't recovered from the pain of the loss.

Then, another horrible event struck us down—the loss of my mother. For eighteen years, she had been sick. There were many times when we thought she was going to die, but she always survived. Finally, the day I had always been afraid to face came to pass.

It was on the night of August 17th around 11:00 p.m. We were sitting in the living room, and I had left my cell phone in my room upstairs. When I went upstairs to put my son to bed, I looked at my cell phone and saw dozens of missed calls from Rwanda, Burundi, and Europe. I immediately knew that my mother had finally gone home.

As I stumbled around the house, feeling completely lost, looking for my landline phone to call home, my cell phone rang in my hands. It was my brother calling from Rwanda. As I responded "Yes?" and heard his voice, he went silent, and we both started crying. Through the phone, I could hear the cries from the house in Rwanda, which was full of people mourning the deep love and comfort that we had lost. My hands and legs were shaking so badly, I couldn't move them, so we just sat in the living room until the next day.

In the morning, my son woke up happy and energized and wanting to play with me. He had no idea what had happened. I looked at him and saw how playful and peaceful he was, and I wished to be like him. He went into his game room, and grabbed a soccer ball and started kicking it toward me, urging me to play. I was completely incapable of lifting up my leg, which felt so heavy that I just wanted to rest it. I forced myself to kick the ball while I was sitting, but I couldn't stand up to kick it.

I did not go home for my mom's funeral. My wife was still in physical and emotional pain from the miscarriage, and I had to be there for her. On Wednesday, August 25th, 2010, I followed my mom's funeral by phone, from the time she was taken out of the morgue, around 1:00 a.m. local time here in the Eastern U.S., until 3: 45 p.m., when I finally heard the coffin of my mother striking the bottom of the tomb where she would rest the flesh that had suffered a great deal of pain.

I spent nearly fifteen hours on the phone, listening to every step of the funeral ceremony, and every word that was spoken. At the end, my bed was completely wet with tears, and I felt a total emptiness in my heart such as I had never felt before. I missed my mother horribly. There is a saying in my language: "Akaburantikaboneke ni nyina wumuntu," meaning, "Something that is never found once lost is a mother."

My friends tried to offer me comfort for this tremendous loss, but no words spoken touched me in the depths where my emotional pain and sorrow were felt. My thoughts about the whole situation tortured me, and I could not sleep or think of any way to distract myself from the heaviness in my mind and heart. The pain stayed deep in my heart, until it absorbed within.

Two weeks after my mother passed away, I lost my second job. I had spent all my savings on my mother's funeral, and I was seriously troubled. Being at home on the weekend seemed like bad luck and I did not enjoy it at all. I was frightened of losing my house, and I desperately looked for a second job. I could not survive with just one job, because of huge financial responsibilities, here and back home.

Fear hunted me down, until I heard the voice of a lady named Madeline, calling me for a job interview. This voice rescued my mind, which was about to stray into fears over what might happen tomorrow. This was good news—but hopefulness was still beyond my grasp.

Mama Immaculate from Burundi, whom I met here in Maine at our church, passed away. There have been some wonderful people in my life, to whom I gave a big space in my heart—but after a short period of time, they left me in total emptiness. Mama Immaculate is one of them.

She was connected to us through my wife's family, and she had been suffering with terminal colon cancer. Lise and I decided to host her in our home while she underwent treatment. She stayed with us for six months, until the last days of her life. We had an amazing experience during her stay with us, and she became like a second mother to both my wife and me. My son called her Tate, which means grandmother in Swahili.

When she passed away, I asked myself a millions questions. It was very painful to see her leaving, and I asked God why he would let me get to know such a wonderful person only to take her away within such a short period of time. Then, I remembered Romans 8:28, a verse in the Bible that says, "And we know that in all things, God works for the good of those who love him, who have been called according to his purpose." I am glad that I got to know Mama Immaculate during my lifetime. I wish things could have gone differently, but it was time for her to cross the river towards eternity.

Her incredible faith—a faith stronger than I had ever witnessed with anyone else—had made me believe beyond a shadow of a doubt that she was going to be healed miraculously. We prayed, fasted, and hoped to see her healed.

In the end, everything happened so quickly. She was taken into hospice in Scarborough, on her way onto the road of no return, where death dwells. I had thought that even in that place, God could bring her back. We were in her room, praying without ceasing. Hundreds of people from the community visited her—so many that there was not even enough room to sit down.

Every night that I visited Mama Immaculate, she seemed to lose her vivacity more and more. I was frightened that the outcome would be the same as it was just one year before, when I lost my friend in the very same building—Benjamin Serukiza, former Vice Governor of southern Kivu in the Congo.

On the night of Mama Immaculate's passing, while she was still wrestling with her last breaths, the room grew quiet and hopeless. We did not talk, and the only sound in the room was her labored breathing, which had turned to a loud rattle. We watched every minute of her beautiful face fading away. Her eyes had already glazed over. She could no longer talk.

Her faith that she would be healed slowly drifted away. As she was facing an unknown reality, I wondered if she could hear the words and prayers spoken around her. That night before I went home, I prayed for God's will to be done. I was certain that I was not going to see her still breathing following day.

My wife and son were in Canada, so I returned home alone. When I got home, I could feel the shadow of death—a heaviness in the house. I prayed and asked God for more strength to face the next day.

On November 20th, she made her transition.

Her husband had been in Burundi until the last two weeks of her life. Then he came to America to be with her in the hospice. He called me and I met him at the hospice. Mama Immaculate was lying on the bed, very peaceful. All the pain that she had struggled with for years was gone, and she was resting very peacefully. The support that we received from the community surpasses my imagination. People were at my house for a week, mourning, while we made arrangements to send her remains to Burundi.

From the very first moment Mama Immaculate arrived here, until the day she went home dead, we experienced incredible generosity from many people. I will never forget them, and their inspirational charitable work. I think of Pastor Mike's family of First Baptist Church in Portland, Maine; Doctor Kurt Ebrahim,

Barbara Appleby, Pastor Ruben Ruganza, Maman Laurence, Francine Rutiririza, Maman Ali Kabiligi, and of course, my wife, who was there for Mama Immaculate during her horrifying nights.

They were there for her the entire time, until the last minute when her coffin was closed and sent back home for burial. May God bless their souls and their hearts with love, the gift from God.

~ THIRTY-EIGHT ~

Thereafter, I was so afraid of everything. I needed to rest and recover from months of tragedy and trauma, but I couldn't rest—I had to work. Because of the things that had happened to me here in the U.S., I started questioning every step of my life. My mind was lost in trying to understand why bad things had happened to us, even when we prayed very hard. In the midst of all the turmoil, I lost my balance, neglected my physical needs, and suffered the consequences.

I again went deep into contemplation of the world in which I now found myself, and I suddenly realized that I was serving an evil master, a true oppressor who controls me and has no intention of allowing me to be free. He fills my mind with tremendous fear and makes me believe that unless I serve him, I cannot survive. I am no longer a free man, but a slave of my master.

This oppressor? My bills!

I have learned to wake up, and go to work at an hour when I don't share the road with anybody else. I welcome the day to come at an hour when most people haven't yet thought of getting out of the house. I go to work when my eyes are still so heavy with the unfinished sleep of many nights, I can hardly open them—and when my body is so exhausted, it feels like it weighs twice my regular weight.

I am always rushing, every minute of my way to work, and I have never been late. The road is so familiar, I know the next speed bump and stop sign, and the next railways to cross. Sometimes I am confused as to whether I am living in today or yesterday. My shift is very long on certain days, and I count every minute as it passes, knowing it is bringing me that much closer to home. There are times when I watch the sun rising and setting through the window—and, even though morning is about to come, I still have not gone home.

I have seen thousands of sunrises and sunsets while going to and from work. I am the man on the road when the world is so quiet that I can hear every single sound around me; when the trees are still sleeping because the morning wind hasn't yet shaken them awake from their deep sleep.

Dozens of times, I have nearly hit deer, coyote, foxes, and raccoons that were dragging their feet around, at an hour when the sun had not yet risen, and vehicles had not yet begun pouring onto the road and scaring them into the bushes. At this hour before the day grows busy, they are certain that they are still alone—but they are wrong. I am there also. I have always wondered if they are asking themselves where this man is going at this time!

The rocky road that I have traveled towards a normalized life in the U.S. holds millions of immigrants around the United States. Complete integration into American society is very elusive, and many immigrants have fainted, weary, and never make it through. Many people get lost and take years to find their way back.

In America, there are numerous aircraft soaring through the sky and landing on the flattened land. There are millions of engines running nonstop on freeways. There is high technology in every single field, and skyscrapers that rise high above every city. People from outside marvel over these things and believe that whoever lands in the U.S. gets everything they ever dreamed about. But, the reality is very different.

The American life seen in movies and on TV steals the minds and hearts of millions of people around the world, and they perceive the U.S. as a celestial city where life starts all over again and new pages of life are written. So, whenever someone falls short of the grace of entering this land of dreams, it feels like they have missed out on the happiness of life on earth.

The reality here in the U.S. has proven to me that this country belongs to a few of the rich. But, I never knew this until my feet stepped through the gates. Thereafter, I was left alone to search for the hidden treasure which is found by only a few, who thereafter put the rest of us to work.

Poor people are the transitional point for money that moves from the rich to the rich. Poor people's efforts, courage, and tireless work hardly pays off. Most of the time, money melts in their hands. This leaves them with the shame of their daily failure to acquire the freedom and happiness they hoped would become a long-term dream come true.

Proverbs 22:7 says, "The rich rule over the poor, the borrower is servant to the lender." The poor here in the U.S. pay their rent—but never get enough time to sleep in their house. They get married and love their beautiful bride—but rarely get enough time to see her. They have kids—but rarely get to spend time with them. This is a picture of life as an immigrant here in the U.S. There are millions of native-born Americans who live busy lives, too, but for immigrants, things are even harder, due to barriers that always rise up before them.

I wish I never had to write this paragraph, but after finishing the writing of this entire book, the unthinkable happened—the loss of my brother, Eraste. On October 5th, 2011, while spending some wonderful time with a friend celebrating my birthday, back home a disaster was occurring. It was as if my soul knew what was happening because, for two days, I had been wrestling with the spirit of fear.

It was 3:00 in the morning when my phone rang. I was told that Eraste and six others in his vehicle had been slaughtered on their way to Minebwe. Dying is one thing—we are all going to die one day. But, being killed and cut into pieces and burned is the humiliation of humanity, and the destruction of our family's souls.

As I write this, my hands are shaking, and my heart is heavy as a rock and full of immeasurable sadness. The arrows of sorrow are stinging every muscle. The cries of my nephews and nieces, left without the love of their father, will never fade from my ears. To select and slaughter Banyamulenge people simply because of their tribal origins is a tragedy for Banyamulenge everywhere.

At the burial, my nephews and nieces were not able to see for the last time the face of their father, because of the brutal way in which he had been killed. (I was unable to attend the burial because it was not safe to travel to the Congo, and because of my work obligations.)

The killing in the Congo has got to stop! If there is any shred of justice left in the world, it must be used to save millions of innocents who are dying in the Congo. Despite the death and tribulation that has risen against my people, I have to say that there is hope for the Banyamulenge—but the killing has to stop immediately.

We, the Banyamulenge who are still alive, are here for a reason. We have lived to save our people and defend our cause. In the Bible verse of Job 14:7-9, it says, "For there is hope of a tree, if it be cut down, that it will sprout again, and that the tender branch thereof will not cease. Though the root thereof wax old in the earth, and the stock thereof die in the ground, yet through the scent of water it will bud, and put forth boughs like a plant."

The hatred against the Banyamulenge in the Congo has been rooted so deeply in Congolese society that it will require the efforts of people who advocate for justice and peace. In addition to the Banyamulenge, who are hated and targeted because of who they are, there are also millions of other Congolese who have died the victims of corrupt government.

During the regime of Mobutu, corruption was perfected until it became mainstream in the Congo. No soul has been left clean. During Kabila's regime, corruption has been dressed up in the robes of death and slaughter.

There are more than sixteen militia groups that operate in the Congo, and all they do is kill, rape, and loot civilians. Kabila's practice of placing such militiamen into the ranks of the National Army, and then rewarding them with remuneration, has been the ruination of justice. There has to be a better way of serving justice!

The world must stand for justice and truth, and bring to an end decades of agonizing death in the Congo. Five million people dying in the Congo since 1996 is enough! Those who stand for good must rise up and stop those who serve evil. Global responsibility must be established to save millions of victims in the Congo.

Parents around the world who love having their kids live in safety must realize that there are millions of orphans in the Congo who have lost their parents and grieve for justice. There are millions of widows in the Congo who are victims of injustice and corruption, and they cry out every day and night for justice.

As Martin Luther King, Jr. once said, "Injustice everywhere is threat of justice everywhere."

Writing this memoir has been a long journey of retracing my steps, retrieving my memories, and healing things that I have never before shared with anybody. While this book is full of sad stories and challenges, I do not celebrate the misery and sadness that I have gone through. Rather, I celebrate resiliency, hard work, and the hope of better days ahead. I have not praised injustice and persecution, but advocated for justice, freedom and liberty wherever it is needed most.

AFTERWORD

On November 18th, 2011, I sat in the Federal District courtroom in Portland, Maine, and waited to take the last step in a very long journey—being sworn in for my U.S. citizenship. The night before the ceremony was long and tiring. I had to work an overnight shift, covering for one of my colleagues at my second job, and I was filled with anxious anticipation.

I was looking forward to seeing how the special day was going to unfold, and, in my excitement, I could not rest my mind. I spent the entire night thinking about the ceremony. I had difficulty believing that, after nearly ten years, I was finally going to be an American citizen.

In the morning around 7:00 a.m., I finished work, went home, and started getting ready. It was early still, but I could not hold myself at home to wait until 9:30, which was the arrival time for the ceremony. I took a long shower, and refreshed my mind from my long night of work. Then, I put on my suit and drove out to the courthouse building. I arrived around 8:30 a.m., and had to wait in my vehicle for a little while. I was very anxious and just wanted to get into the building, and wait there.

At 9:30 a.m., I finally walked into the building and stood at the check-in station, where two gentlemen welcomed me with warm congratulations before allowing me inside. This time was different from previous experiences. When I first started my immigration process ten years ago, it was very intimidating and confusing.

There were many of us going through the check-in point at the same time, and thereafter heading upstairs into the courtroom. The footsteps of new citizens, followed by their family members who had come to celebrate with them, echoed throughout the hallways. You could see the excitement on the face of every individual who walked into the building, and it felt like a graduation ceremony.

After check-in, I went upstairs to the second floor and presented my document. I then had to complete a questionnaire. Finally, they handed to me a folder with a bunch of documents that I had to take with me into the courtroom. In exchange, I gave away the green card that I had been carrying in my wallet for five years. At last, I walked inside the courtroom and sat down comfortably, while waiting for the ceremony to start.

The courtroom was beautiful and inspiring, and as I looked around, I was carried into deep thoughts. My reflection took me way back to my tiny village in the Congo where I was born. I began to weep, as I realized what a long road I had traveled alone, and what terrifying and erroneous steps I had made since leaving my village in the Congo. I contemplated how this long journey brought me to the U.S., far from the region where I was raised, and where I imagined I would grow up and eventually decline in age.

I kept looking at the high and beautiful ceiling, ornamented with amazing architectural and decorative details that enhanced its structural beauty. There were so many paintings and pictures hanging on the walls of great men and women of American history. This made me marvel over the greatness of the United States of America.

At the same time, a snapshot of millions of people—black, brown, and white—from around the world who had become U.S. citizens kept running on the screen, and I was suddenly filled with a great joy that I hadn't had for many months. I felt so proud of my new country, and the pain and hardship of the process that took me up to that conclusion were gone.

I felt like I had been born again and given a new name. I remembered a saying in Kinyamulenge that translates to: "Something is sweet…like a new name!" I never clearly grasped the meaning of this saying until that very moment. A new name means a new identity, a renaissance, a change of season from difficulty to ease. At this time, I felt that the seasons had changed.

I remembered the year 2002, when I landed here in Maine after realizing that I would not be going back home because of the ongoing conflict in the region. A friend of mine approached me and tried to encourage me, because she knew that I was going through a very intense and unexpectedly confusing immigration process.

She told me that the U.S. was an appropriate home for someone from the Banyamulenge—a tribe that has historically suffered denials and mistreatments. She explained that the U.S. is among the few nations that embrace the great idea that *everyone has come from somewhere, at some time.* This idea is in stark contrast to the belief held by some people—that they have sprouted out of the ground that they are living on, right then and there. As I was waiting in the courtroom, the comforting words of my friend rang very true to me.

My mind continued to contemplate this momentous occasion as the room started getting full to capacity in anticipation of the start of the ceremony. I kept thinking of how I'd survived many situations to reach this moment, and joyous tears flowed constantly from my eyes.

After half an hour of waiting in the courtroom, the ceremony began. I had never been to this type of ceremony before, and did not know what to expect. All the new citizens were given the seats of honor, and the rest of the participants were seated behind us.

The introduction was given, and outlined the program to follow. They gave us an overview of what it means to be a U.S. citizen—our rights and responsibilities—and thereafter, we stood to sing the national anthem, "The Star Spangled Banner." As we sang, I really paid attention for the first time to the meaning of the song, and also its melody, which vibrated in my heart, making me very emotional. The song felt so deep and inspiring.

After singing, we pledged allegiance to the flag, and recited the Oath of Allegiance. Thereafter, the word from President Obama congratulating us was on the screen. They started calling each applicant's name. Whoever was called went up front and picked up their Certificate of Citizenship.

The entire room was filled with joy and the feeling of honor and dignity given to us as new citizens. This was something that I had never experienced in my entire life. As joyful and emotional as this was to me, and to every person in the room, my heart suddenly dropped, and I was consumed with troubling thoughts of home. I thought about millions of people—friends and relatives who would probably never live to see liberty and dignity offered by their nation.

As we left the courtroom, everyone was happy and laughing, but I told my friend, Alex, who had also been sworn in as a citizen, that I was filled with great sadness. He was shocked that I would say such a thing on such a momentous day, but once he heard my explanation, he understood. I started talking to him about missing my family, and about how badly I felt over the fact that my people were not being treated with respect and dignity.

For one thing, I knew it would be some time before the immigration paperwork could be processed that would allow me to bring my wife and son to the United States so we can be together full-time. Every second spent apart from my family I count as a great loss of time. I was made to be with my family. Every night that I spend away from them brings me tremendous discomfort.

I have fought the circumstances that rose like mountains to keep us away from each other. I have waited patiently for the moment that we are brought together, never again to live the days of separation, as long as we shall live.

I have always prayed the serenity prayer, and I know in my heart that there is time enough for everything. Our Lord is gracious, and just as he has helped us through many situations, he will help us now, for this situation is neither different nor greater than the ones that we have already survived. If life were such that, after a certain amount of pain and suffering, someone becomes exempt from all future challenges, I would be now exempt—but life is never easy.

Just as I was thinking about my wife and son and how much I missed them, I was also remembering people back home, and thinking about how they had inherited from their nation unbelievable misery.

I reflected on the fact that African leaders are to be blamed for the misery of their people, because they have failed millions of people around the African continent. Their selfishness has caused them to hold tightly to the entirety of the resources and power of their country, so that nothing is left to their citizens but misery. They have ruined their countries by embracing politics based on divisiveness, discrimination, terror, and killings.

As I returned to my home in Maine following the ceremony, I continued thinking about my home in the Congo. I started remembering some of the "low people"—those households with many kids where the children have to take turns eating. Let's say a family has ten kids, five will eat one night and the other five the following day. This way, the children at least get to eat and feel full, whereas if the ten children shared the limited food available at each meal, there would be so little food that none of the children would feel full.

It is hard to have confidence that "the peace process" will bring justice and democracy to the Great Lakes region of central Africa. The conflict has been deeply rooted and its ramifications go beyond what people see around them. The generations that have sought—and fought—for peace and democracy have passed away. The new generations cannot talk about or promote peace because it is something they have never known. You can only give what you have.

The current violence, hatred, and mass killings have been going on for more than a century, and it deeply saddens me every time I think about it. Beginning in the days of colonialism and continuing through to the present, there has been little peace for the people in the Congo. A continuous series of exploitation of resources by foreign powers has culminated in the killing of millions of people.

This is a region where many people never grow to maturity. It is a land of graves, where millions of souls lay down without the hope of justice. It is unimaginable that over a period of seventeen years, more than seven million people have died as result of the civil war and genocide in the Great Lakes region of central Africa.

Since 1993, half a million people have been killed in Burundi.

In 1994, one million people were killed in Rwanda within only three months.

Since 1996, approximately six million people have been killed in the Congo.

This is like wiping out the entire population of Maine, New Hampshire, and Connecticut in a couple of decades. You would think that the whole world would know about a region where seven million people have died. This is more than a calamity—but, sadly, very few people know about this tragic situation.

Millions of people around the region have spent their lives hoping to see better days, but it hasn't happened yet. If death takes them first, and hell becomes their final destination, they will have already lived in one hell.

It saddens me whenever I think about this reality. Misery has a face—and I don't wish anybody to see it. I always say to my friend that the world is now serving the devil more than he had ever anticipated.

To the countries that I have come from, where millions of souls have been corrupted by an evil which feeds their hearts with hatred, and makes them dirty their hands with the blood of millions of innocents, I say this: There is always hope and better life ahead if global responsibility is promoted.

To the countries that have hosted millions of people who have lost their homes, and to the Americans who have given beyond what is perceived to be normal, I say this: In this world, there is always the fight between evil and good, light and darkness. Those who follow the light strive to save and build and make peace around them, and their love and sacrifice for the sake of peace will pay off.

Those who follow evil ways are full of hatred, and they cannot sleep without planning to destroy and harm many. They are entertained by the sight of people around them suffering and hanging on their last thread, about to collapse. They need to understand that truth and justice always prevail, and will ultimately conquer evil.

In the Congo, Rwanda, and Burundi, every time there are elections in the U.S, France, or Belgium, local people on the street discuss the candidates. Some even fast and pray that a good candidate wins the election, and frees them from the oppression of their local dictators.

So, when President Obama was elected in 2008, the least villages in Africa celebrated the victory. They rejoiced because they hoped that once president Obama was in power, he would change everything in the dark continents. But, nothing has changed so far—people are still dying.

All they have hoped for from the American president is to influence their leaders to help *the people,* not just themselves or their families. But, these leaders are chosen not based on their skills and ability to serve the people, but on their willingness to submit to the interests of the superpowers.

The biggest difference between dictatorships and so-called civilized countries has to do with the way people are treated by their leaders. African leaders abuse their power by controlling everything—resources and people. This has undermined the freedom of millions of people around the African continent.

After living here in the U.S. for over ten years, I have come to believe that African leaders have missed the opportunity to build nations of peace, based on justice and the rule of law. All they think about—and strive for—is becoming more powerful and imposing their thoughts and will (which are mostly corrupt) upon others. They have never allowed "a growing zone" for citizens in Africa—a free space where people can truthfully share their constructive ideas.

In Africa, whenever someone is bold and courageous enough to speak out and express his or her views on matters that are important to the people, he or she becomes the victim of their courage, and the consequences are unbearable. After living in the U.S., I have been sometimes shocked by the level of freedom here. People have so much freedom, sometimes they even abuse it.

For instance, I have heard common people saying publicly that their president's ideas are stupid. Such a thing could never happen anywhere that I have lived in Africa. If anyone were to say such a thing about the president, the same day, he or she would find a very restful place in the cemetery. We were told that walls have ears, too, and they can hear anything that comes out of your mouth.

There is a saying in the Congo: "If you are angry with the president or any authority, just insult him in your heart to ease your mind—because you can never express yourself out loud, and your heart is the safest and freest place to express yourself."

I have learned a great lesson about the exceptional blessing it is to live with an extreme abundance of freedom and liberty. Americans can never understand the blessings they have inherited, until they get to visit or live in different countries where nothing is allowed but silence. As the saying goes, "You never know how important something is until you have lost it."

When I remember the many years that have passed, I realize something: my old ways have gone, and everything around me now is different from what I knew growing up. I could have never foretold where the future was going to take me. I must remember that I have no control over the past, and I cannot know what God may bring tomorrow. All I have is the present.

Today, as I write this, it is very peaceful and beautiful outside. It feels like the country, but downtown is close by. Sometimes when I walk outside, I find the neighborhood dog in the driveway. When I look at him, I remember being told stories about my uncle, who was killed by a rabid dog before I was born.

There are also many cats around this neighborhood. One of my neighbors has ten cats. I have to be very careful when I am driving home from work at dusk. I have to make sure to keep my eyes open so I don't hit the cats with my car. They are not easy to see—not like the big cats that lived in the jungle near my childhood village, where we had no cars.

When I go to sleep at night, sometimes I remember the animals in my village. The sounds they made lulled me to sleep. In my Portland home, the sounds of birds singing in the morning are mixed with the sounds of vehicles passing by, so you can hardly hear the birds.

I am grateful for all the opportunities and safety that America has provided for me and many in the African community. I have made great memories, and my roots in the community are growing deeper all the time. To some extent, Maine has come to feel like home.

At the same time, I will always be homesick for my first home. It is far away from me now, an entire world away. My journey, from my tiny village in Africa, to my home in the U.S. has been like climbing a ladder to the moon.

EDITOR'S NOTE

As this book was being prepared for publication, the author received notice from U.S. Citizenship and Immigration Services that his petition to bring his wife and son to America had been approved.

The very same week that Georges received this good news, he was honored by the U.S. Department of Agricultural Rural Housing Service and Maine Rural Development with the 2012 Maine Multi-Family Housing Site Manager of the Year award.

Then, on the afternoon of September 28th, 2012, Georges and his wife, Lise, welcomed Ael's baby sister, Ais, into the world. He gave both children as one of their names his own nickname, "Shimirwa."

All in all, 2012 was a very good year for the author.

ACKNOWLEDGMENTS

To God, my provider and the source of my daily energy: Glory to you in the highest. You increase my strength every time I feel like I am at my weakest point. I will continue to praise and worship you.

To Lise Karara, my wife, my love and helper with whom I have vowed to share the rest of my life: I treasure the commitment that I have made to you. I consistently seek to cherish and love you more. I know that beauty is what gives deep satisfaction to millions of minds in this day and age—and you are so beautiful, honey. But, more than that, I believe in the greatness of your heart. Your love and tender care for our family and others has always astounded me. This is the fragrance that drew me close to you, and I have held onto you as a precious jewel ever since. I humbly relish the gift of our life together and I thank God for his plan that made us one.

To my children, Ael Shimirwa and Aïs Shimirwa: You are my joy and my inspiration. I pray daily that you may gain knowledge and wisdom to honestly serve your God and the world that you have come into. I love you more than I can express in words.

To my parents: Although you long ago departed the earth, the warmth of your love remains alive in me. I have learned from you a powerful lesson of resiliency, and used your experience as I held out against my own trials. I will never forget the extraordinary courage that you demonstrated to us, as your children, over the many years that you experienced rejection and suffering.

To my siblings, Nyanoro, Shoshi, Nyarukundo, Sabuwera, Nyamberwa, Nyandatwa, Rushimisha and Akiza, and all my relatives: I love you very much. We have no choice as to whom we will be born with or from, but if God would have asked me to choose, I would have chosen you as brothers, sisters, and family. Your love speaks loudly to me and makes me believe that the world can be a better place in which to live.

I would like to especially recognize a few individuals who have moved and touched my heart during the process of writing this book...

To Vivien Kooper, the developmental editor of this book: Our working relationship has become a true expression of faith. In the face of the skepticism of my mind and the stumbling of my reasoning, you continued to make it clear that this book was worthy of perseverance. You have helped me to rediscover myself, and to heal some of the long-festering wounds of my heart. You have shown me how to relive and enjoy again the suitable memories of my childhood. I have learned a lot from your skillful writing and your ability to straighten some of my twisted words. To me, no greater writer equals you, because you have taught me to write from my heart, and the words that I have scribed in this book are the songs and tears of my soul. You have brought me to a very positive dimension and helped to make sense of the words that I see around me every day. I strongly believe that this book is a cut path for my family and thousands of my people around the world. You have worked with me very patiently and generously and nothing excites me like holding this piece of work in my hands.

To my brother-in-law, Adolphe Karara: I cannot find the right words to express my sincere thoughts of gratitude to you. During all these years that my family has been travelling back and forth between the U.S. and Canada, you have sheltered us. Everything you have done has stayed deep in my heart. In the same way, Ange Munezero, Cesar Ndayiragije, and Mireille Ndayishimiye—you have been more than friends, and your support to my wife and children means a lot to me. You went beyond your means and my expectations. I pray that God gives you the desire of your hearts.

To Alex Tung: In our twenty-six years of friendship, I have never known what to call you—a friend or a brother; either of these words are too light compared to what I feel within. You know me better than anybody who has come to be my friend and I have always valued our honest friendship. Over the years, you have become like the mirror that sees me before I wash myself up and head out elegantly into the presence of others.

To Melinda, Olivia and John Whittaker: Your compassion and gracious love to me and my family have impressed my soul. I love you guys.

To all of my colleagues at Avesta Housing and Goodwill Industries of Northern New England: You have elevated me to a higher level of professionalism and service to others. You have helped me in different ways, and I have been inspired by the work that you do that changes people's lives. In particular, I would like to acknowledge my supervisors in both workplaces—Barbara Soloway, Crystal Chamberlain, Linda Poland, Madeline Groeger, and Kim Nisbet.

To Sharon Cleaves: Thank you for the work that you have done for me. It means a lot.

To Tracy McLeod: Ever since I started working at Goodwill, I have been impressed by your compassion, your kindness, and your caring heart. You have helped me in many ways. May God bless you.

To Leslie Merrill, from the office of Chellie Pingree, Maine congresswoman: Your help to my family and many people in the community has changed people's lives. I sincerely thank you for your heart of compassion for people that you serve.

To my brothers and sisters of Philadelphia Church: Your prayers have held me up when I was about to fall.

To all my spiritual friends, including Alexis Semuhoza, Pastor Ruben Ruganza, Pastor Amos Mukiza, Pastor Adrien Rutiririza, Fidele Masengo, and Theo and Lily Runuya: You have helped me a lot. Thank you for all your prayers.

To Richard Wilson, my friend with whom I shared the long road to peace and justice advocacy in the Great Lakes region of

Central Africa: I sincerely appreciated your time spent in reviewing my book, and your insightful input.

Beginning in my childhood, and throughout the years that encompassed primary school, high school, university, workplaces, and neighborhoods, I have had the help and support of many friends and family members. I am still in touch with some, with others, I have lost contact, and some have passed away. Although I have not named them all here, by no means have I forgotten the dimension that each brought into my life.

ABOUT THE AUTHOR

Georges Budagu Makoko is a member of the Banyamulenge—a Tutsi tribe. He was born in the southern Kivu province of Eastern DR Congo, spent his early years living among extended family in his villages, and later moved to the urban areas of the Congo to further his education.

He lived for many years in war-torn Congo and Rwanda. After barely surviving the atrocities in the region, Budagu sought—and was granted—asylum in the United States, taking up residency in Portland, Maine. In 2011, he was sworn in as a citizen of the United States.

The author is a devout Christian, who believes strongly in God the Father, the Son, and the Holy Spirit—the giver of eternal life. He is a devoted family man, who has built his life in America upon the same principles of mutual support he enjoyed as a child.

Budagu believes that justice, freedom, liberty, and the pursuit of happiness should be available to all people *equally,* and he is deeply wounded by the suffering and injustice he witnesses. He also believes that integrity, honesty, and hard work are the keys to a good life; that knowledge and wisdom are among our most powerful tools; and that without forgiveness, we will never conquer divisiveness or oppression.

Georges lives by the philosophy that, "The story that is not told dies in someone's mind—and the truth goes along with it. Evil flourishes whenever it is not pointed out."

Made in United States
North Haven, CT
05 January 2024